SAVING SOCIETY

Advancing the Sociological Imagination

A Series from Paradigm Publishers

Edited by Bernard Phillips and J. David Knottnerus

SAVING SOCIETY

BREAKING OUT OF OUR BUREAUCRATIC WAY OF LIFE

*Bernard Phillips and
David Christner*

Paradigm Publishers
Boulder • London

Copyright © 2011 Paradigm Publishers

Published in the United States by Paradigm Publishers,
2845 Wilderness Place, Suite 200, Boulder, CO 80301 USA.

Paradigm Publishers is the trade name of Birkenkamp & Company, LLC,
Dean Birkenkamp, President and Publisher.

Library of Congress Cataloging-in-Publication Data
Phillips, Bernard S.
 Saving society : breaking out of our bureaucratic way of
life / Bernard Phillips and David Christner.
    p. cm.—— (Advancing the sociological imagination)
 Includes bibliographical references and index.
 ISBN 978-1-59451-776-1 (hbk. : alk. paper)
 1. Bureaucracy. 2. Organizational sociology. 3. Social
problems. I. Christner, David. II. Title.
 HM806.P55 2010
 302.3'5—dc22

                                                      2009026875

Printed and bound in the United States of America on acid-free paper that meets the standards of the American National Standard for Permanence of Paper for Printed Library Materials.

Designed and Typeset by Straight Creek Bookmakers.

15 14 13 12 11   1 2 3 4 5

Contents

Preface

SAVING SOCIETY, WHICH BUILDS ON THE IDEAS within six books published since 2000, needs a short introduction to help the reader understand its significance. For it makes use of what we see as a fundamental breakthrough in the social sciences—sociology, psychology, anthropology, history, political science, and economics—to yield, in our view, an integrated understanding of modern problems and directions for solutions. This preface consists of two parts: an introductory section that puts forward the vision of the breakthrough promised by the book and an outline of the book's basic procedures for moving toward that vision, with both sections making references to specific material within *Saving Society.*

A Vision: "If You Don't Have a Dream, How You Gonna Have a Dream Come True?"

The Evolutionary Manifesto

An old proverb claims, "Where there is no vision, the people perish." More recently we have "Happy Talk" from the musical "South Pacific," revived on Broadway in 2008 and shown on PBS in 2010: "If you don't have a dream, how you gonna have a dream come true?" It was President Obama's message of hope—with the idea that we can indeed solve our problems—that was much of the basis for his victories in the primaries and in the election of 2008. We illustrated this optimistic view of human possibilities on the website of the Sociological Imagination Group, www.sociological-imagination.org, a group that we founded in 2000 with the help of others. Just as Martin Luther King had a dream "that one day on the red hills of Georgia the sons of former slaves and the sons of former slave owners will be able to sit down together at the table of brotherhood," we too have a dream, a dream that:

> there will be a future for our children, our grandchildren, our great-grandchildren, and their great-grandchildren;
>
> one day we will all learn to see ourselves as children who are only just beginning to understand ourselves and our world, and we will also learn to dream about our infinite possibilities and move toward those visions one step at a time;
>
> one day we will all learn to pay close attention to the accomplishments of all peoples throughout history as well as to our own personal accomplishments, and we will also learn to pay close attention to the failures of the human race and to our own personal failures;
>
> one day we will be able to bring to the surface and reduce our stratified emotions like fear, shame, guilt, hate, envy, and greed, and we will learn to express ever more our evolutionary emotions like confidence, enthusiasm, happiness, joy, love, and empathy;
>
> one day we will see peace on earth and fellowship among all humans;
>
> one day we will no longer look down on any other human being;
>
> one day we all will learn to be poets, philosophers and scientists.

It was Fred Polak, a Dutch sociologist, who saw one's image of the future as potentially the most powerful force for actually creating the future, as he wrote in his *The Image of the Future*. *Saving Society* ends with a quote from Polak's book in which he views images of the future as essential in order to "release the Western world from its too-long imprisonment in the present." We see that imprisonment as most dangerous, given our conviction that problems are increasing throughout the world. The above "evolutionary manifesto" might well appear to point toward a utopian book. Yet deep immersion within the discipline of sociology has taught the senior author that realism is essential to achieve any fundamental change in society.

Realistic Optimism: The Sociological Imagination

Along with Polak, we are not just interested in dreaming: we are equally interested in fulfilling our dreams. That is what *Saving Society* is about: both the dream and the fulfillment of the dream. The dream gives us the potential that its fulfillment is in fact possible, and our resulting confidence in that possibility helps us to face up to the forces that are working against the dream. In that way we become realistic as well as optimistic. It is when we combine our optimism with such realism that we can emerge with what we might call realistic optimism or realistic idealism. Indeed, the entire history of Western philosophy is a history of idealistic philosophies as well as realistic philosophies, although never do the twain meet.

Our confidence in the possibility that even these humongous problems can be solved stems from the potential of what we see as our breakthrough in the social sciences, which carries forward the optimism linked to the immense power of the scientific method into the area of human behavior. *Saving Society* builds on the work of the Sociological Imagination Group. We have held nine annual meetings since 2000, developing seven books that include the work of twenty sociologists and one philosopher.

We are attempting to follow in the footsteps of Francis Bacon, who claimed, "I have taken all knowledge to be my province." Given the enormous complexity of human behavior, it is exactly such breadth that is required. This contrasts with the specialization with limited communication to be found throughout the social sciences, as illustrated by the 46 Sections—and counting—of the American Sociological Association. Our development of the Sociological Imagination Group was inspired by C. Wright Mills, who wrote these widely quoted words in his *The Sociological Imagination* half a century ago: "For that imagination is the capacity to shift from one perspective to another—from the political to the psychological; from examination of a single family to comparative assessment of the national budgets of the world; from the theological school to the military establishment; from considerations of an oil industry to studies of contemporary poetry."

Yet it is one thing to put forward a vision of the breadth that social scientists should achieve, and it is quite another thing to come up with a direction for achieving that breadth. It is exactly here that our own focus on language has been basic to our direction for a broad scientific method for the social sciences.

Our Most Powerful Tool

It is our complex language, more than any other characteristic, that sharply distinguishes us humans from all other forms of life, and that has made us the most interactive creatures throughout the known universe. It is the centrality of language for understanding the nature of human behavior that is the most important discovery of the social sciences throughout the twentieth century. It is language that is the basis for the human being's capacity to continue to learn throughout his or her life. It is language that yields the basis for the capacity of the individual—by contrast with all other known species—to continue to evolve intellectually, emotionally, and in the effectiveness of his or her actions, with no limit to how far one might go. It is language that yields the basis for a scientific method that can penetrate the enormous complexity of human behavior along with the complexity of the world around us. And it is language that yields the most important tools that we humans who invented the scientific method require for confronting effectively the huge and increasing problems that we face.

Yet given this fantastic tool of language, how are we to explain our creation of the enormous problems that now threaten our very survival, let alone our failure to understand enough about their nature so that we can move toward solving them? What has prevented us from transforming the incredible capacities that language has given us into abilities to understand and solve our problems? Why have our Nobel Prize winners, our professors throughout our universities, our highest governmental officials, our captains of industry, our novelists, journalists, playwrights and filmmakers, and our leaders in all walks of life failed us in the very tasks that are most important for our survival? With the almost unbelievable power of language, how are we to understand the desperate situation of the human race at this time in history?

The research of the Sociological Imagination Group points clearly toward the incredible power of our tool of language coupled with our failure to make full use of its capacities. It is this very failure that has yielded the barriers to the communication of knowledge across specialized areas, illustrated in particular by the failures of social scientists to integrate their knowledge of human behavior so as to penetrate its enormous complexities and yield the basis for understanding and solving our threatening social problems. For it is social scientists more than any other group who are responsible for learning what is going wrong in today's world and determining how to correct it.

As for what is missing from our usage of this tool of language, we can distinguish among the languages of social science, biophysical science, and literature (Phillips 2001). They emphasize, respectively, three capacities of language: dichotomy, gradation or number, and figurative language or imagery. The emphasis on dichotomy of the social sciences reflects the fundamental nature of all languages: the phenomena denoted by a given word, on the one hand, and all other phenomena, on the other hand. The biophysical sciences, by contrast with the social sciences, emphasize the gradational component of language, as illustrated by their use of mathematics. Literature centers on images or metaphors, thus communicating sense experiences with their biological or perceptual background.

To illustrate the limited usage of language's potentials, social scientists along with biophysical scientists generally avoid imagery or metaphors because of their vagueness. As a result they lose deeper understanding of just what they have learned and how to communicate effectively, given the importance of perception or the senses. If we look to the table of contents, we may note an alternative: our usage of the metaphors or images of "head," "heart," and "hand." Those images have helped us to organize the book as well as to pay attention to the range of phenomena that make up human behavior.

From Bureaucracy Toward Interaction

This specialization among usages of language emphasizing dichotomy, gradation, and imagery or metaphor is fostered by our "bureaucratic" focus on the isolation of phenomena, which emphasizes not only patterns of specialization with limited communication but also patterns of hierarchy with limited communication. The subtitle of *Saving Society, Breaking Out of Our Bureaucratic Way of Life,* points away from our bureaucratic barriers to communication. Those barriers within society as well as within the individual are illustrated in Figures 1-2a and 1-2b.

One might wonder why social scientists, who should understand the importance of avoiding the barriers to communication depicted in Figures 1-2a and 1-2b, generally persist in erecting those barriers and thus violating the ideals of the scientific method. Yet social scientists, just like the rest of us, are products of their experiences in contemporary society. And they experience, along with the rest of us, our extremely powerful and comprehensive bureaucratic way of life that shapes those experiences. Those patterns of specialization and hierarchy are illustrated in almost every single one of the organizations and groups throughout societies in every part of the world. This failure of social scientists is particularly damaging for the rest of us, since it is they more than any other group who are responsible for uncovering the forces that stand in the way of our ability to understand and solve our threatening problems. And this is why a breakthrough in the social sciences that can enable us to eliminate those forces is so significant and so urgent.

Our vision of the result of such a breakthrough is illustrated in Figures 1-3a and 1-3b. Instead of the barriers to communication among specialists depicted in 1-2a as well as the barriers separating "head," "heart," and "hand" in 1-2b, what we have in 1-3a and 1-3b are two-way arrows depicting interaction that conveys the exchange of information as well as relationships among individuals. It is that interaction that makes it possible for groups and individuals to move toward ever more understanding of problems and ever greater ability to solve problems, following the ideals of the scientific method.

We might introduce another metaphor to help us understand how the scientific method works to yield increasing understanding and ability to solve problems: a pendulum that swings in ever-widening arcs. The pendulum's movement to the left suggests awareness of ("head") and commitment to ("heart") making progress on a given problem. That awareness is based on taking into account and building on the knowledge of that problem developed in the past. That movement of the pendulum to the left then provides the momentum or motivation for a swing to the right, making progress on the problem in question ("hand"), and that swing then yields the momentum for a swing of the pendulum further to the left, based on an awareness ("head") of our progress as well as our satisfaction ("heart") with what we have accomplished. In this way, our pendulum can come to swing in ever-widening arcs, granting that there will also be setbacks based on our limited understanding of how to apply the scientific method to human behavior.

This image of a pendulum—that interacts between awareness of and commitment to a problem, on the one hand, and progress on that problem, on the other hand—is so useful because its interactive nature parallels the interactive nature of the universe. Ours is an interactive universe, for no phenomenon can be completely isolated from any other phenomenon. And it is the interaction between organisms and their environments that is the very basis for biological evolution. Still further, it is the ability to achieve interaction among the findings of scientists as well as among scientists themselves that is the basis for a scientific method that knows no limit as to how far it can yield understanding and the ability to solve problems. And further still, it is we human beings who have invented the scientific method who are also not limited in our capacities to achieve awareness of ("head") and commitment to solving problems ("heart"), as well as to making progress toward solutions ("hand"). More generally, there are no limits to our capacities to understand phenomena ("head"), to express ourselves emotionally ("heart"), and to develop the ability to solve problems ("hand"), just as there are no limits to how far the scientific method can take us toward understanding and solving problems.

Yet given this general understanding of a broader approach to language and the scientific method that promises to yield a deeper understanding of human behavior and an improved ability to solve the complex problems of modern society, exactly how are we to proceed more specifically? How are we to cover the ground of "head," "heart," and "hand," and how are we to make full use of the dichotomous, gradational, and metaphorical potentials of language? We turn here to the next section of this preface for answers.

Working Toward Having the Dream Come True

Ordinary and Extraordinary Languages

Phillips was not only fortunate enough to have been a student of C. Wright Mills. He was also lucky enough to have been a colleague of Alvin W. Gouldner, who followed Mills by two decades and who was also committed to a very broad approach to the social sciences as well as to applying that knowledge to society's problems. Responding to a review of his *The Coming Crisis of Western Sociology* (1970), Gouldner commented on the role of the "extraordinary" language of the social sciences: "At decisive points the ordinary language and conventional understandings fail and must be transcended. It is essentially the task of the social sciences, more generally, to create new and 'extraordinary' languages, to help men learn to speak them.... To say social theorists are concept-creators means that ... they are from the beginning involved in creating a new culture."

Social science language, relative to ordinary language, is "extraordinary." For one thing, it is language that communicates the research within the social sciences, thus following the ideal of the scientific method requiring that we "stand on the shoulders of giants." For another thing, it is generally more abstract or general than our more concrete everyday language, as illustrated by the concept of "bureaucratic way of life," which includes our specific patterns of thinking, feeling, and acting. As a result, the extraordinary language of social science can work to integrate a great deal of our knowledge. By so doing, social science language can reach far down language's "ladder of abstraction" to relate to our everyday concepts like "thoughts" and "feelings." Yet it is by no means a replacement for ordinary language, which we may see as lower on language's ladder of abstraction. Rather, the social scientist shuttles up and down that linguistic ladder. This is the way language works in general, for we shuttle up and down between the relatively concrete concept of "love" and the more general concept of "emotions." Social science's extraordinary language can help us move both higher and lower. By shuttling up and down that ladder we gain both generality and concreteness.

We might note as well that Gouldner is not merely writing about the progress of social science within the academic world. He is centered on the business of social scientists proceeding to "help men learn to speak" the extraordinary language of social science. It is in that way that we can all learn to use the broad approach to the scientific method that this language embodies. In this way, Gouldner follows Mills's vision that we all can and should learn to develop a "sociological imagination" or, more accurately, a "social science imagination." In this way Gouldner and Mills point us away from the bureaucratic or hierarchical idea of a social science elite, on the one hand, and the rest of us, on the other hand. Instead, they are advancing a vision of a society where all of us can and should develop a social science imagination as a basis for understanding human behavior and solving personal and world problems. Granting that they were both sociologists, their focus is not only on society but also on the development or evolution of the individual.

The extraordinary language of the social sciences is, more specifically, the set of concepts together with their relationships that embody what social scientists have discovered about human behavior. It parallels the technical languages of the physical and biological sciences, with their concepts such as "atom," "element," and "organism." It is this extraordinary language of the social sciences that is fundamental to the way the scientific method works within these disciplines. If we return to the pendulum metaphor for the scientific method, it is that language that helps us to swing the pendulum far to the left, where we become aware of and committed to making progress on a problem. For that awareness and commitment require that we build on what scientists have learned about that problem in the past with the aid of the extraordinary or technical language of the social sciences. And that language is equally important for our swing to the right, where we make progress toward solving that problem. For it is the extraordinary language that can give us a vision of alternatives to patterns of behavior that yield problems, just as "interaction" is an alternative to specialization with little communication.

The importance of making good use of the extraordinary language of social science may be underlined by the fact that the fundamental problems of contemporary society appear to be increasing. That those problems are escalating was a major conclusion of *The Invisible Crisis of Contemporary Society,* which found "substantial evidence" for an increasing gap between what people generally want and what they are actually able to get. In other words, there is a general increase in people's "aspirations-fulfillment gap" or "values-fulfillment gap." It is that very gap which is the problem that has been the focus of all of the books published by the Sociological Imagination Group since 2001. It is depicted in Figure 1-1 of *Saving Society* as well as in *Beyond Sociology's Tower of Babel, The Invisible Crisis of Contemporary Society,* and *Armageddon or Evolution?* Of course, there are many other problems in modern society, but this one is particularly important because it is so broad and is largely invisible. And that aspirations-fulfillment or values-fulfillment gap is continuing to increase.

The Extraordinary Language of the Social Sciences

It was indeed a huge problem involving a struggle for over a decade to discover a small number of concepts—from among the hundreds of existing ones throughout the social sciences—that make up the extraordinary language. For those concepts must promise to penetrate deeply into the complexities of human behavior and to yield the basis for making progress on fundamental problems. Also, they must be linked together systematically so as to yield propositions or statements that specify the probable causes of problems. Further, they must cover the waterfront of "head," "heart," and "hand"—along with behavior that is widely shared throughout society—to take into account human complexity. Still further, that extraordinary language must take us far up language's ladder of abstraction so that we can learn to see the forest of our problems, and it must also take us far down that ladder so that we can come to see the trees as well.

The headings for Chapters 2 through 4 within the table of contents specify trees or concrete concepts within the extraordinary language that focus on a bureaucratic way of life. They describe behavior emphasizing "head," "heart," and "hand": "outward perception and thought," "emotional repression," and "conforming behavior," respectively. They are "situational" concepts, since they refer to behavior within a momentary scene. They occur within Part II of the book, titled "Extinction" because of evidence within *The Invisible Crisis* that they do in fact point toward an increasing values-fulfillment gap. Thus, Part II details a swing of the pendulum of the scientific method to the left, where we focus on fundamental problems of the individual and society.

By contrast, we have Part III with its swing of the pendulum to the right. This Part is titled "Evolution" because of evidence within *The Invisible Crisis* that the concepts within the headings for Chapters 5 through 7 point toward a decreasing values-fulfillment gap. These concepts also describe behavior emphasizing "head," "heart," and "hand": "inward-outward perception and thought," "emotional expression," and "deep action and deep interaction," respectively. These concepts are situational, just as are those in the headings of Part II. And all of these concepts illustrate our linguistic emphasis on dichotomy, as illustrated by the dichotomy between emotional repression and emotional expression. Yet it is these dichotomies that make it possible for us to see our behavior gradationally, as occurring somewhere between the two poles of a given dichotomy. And in this way we can point toward movement along the "head," "heart," and "hand" continua from a bureaucratic toward an evolutionary way of life.

Yet what is not to be found in these chapter headings are "structural" concepts that describe long-term behavior and that are discussed in the body of Chapters 2 through 7. It is when situational behavior is repeated over and over and over again that the result is structural behavior. And if there is a *change* in situational behavior that is repeated over and over and over again, then there is a corresponding *change* in structural behavior. Unfortunately, the emphasis throughout the social sciences has been on structural concepts rather than situational concepts. And the result has been a general failure to understand how structural changes, which are fundamental changes, can in fact occur. To explain such basic changes, one must make use of both situational and structural concepts.

Just as one can change from bureaucratic toward evolutionary situational behavior, so can one change from bureaucratic toward evolutionary structural behavior. These changes are discussed within Part III. As for "head," we can learn to move from a "bureaucratic self-image" and a "bureaucratic worldview" toward an "evolutionary self-image" and an "evolutionary worldview." With respect to "heart," we can come to move from a "wide values-fulfillment gap" toward a "narrow values-fulfillment gap." And with respect to "hand," we can learn to move from "bureaucratic rituals" like "stratification" and "bureaucracy"—including specialization with limited communication—toward "evolutionary rituals" like "deep dialogue" and "deep democracy." Of course, such structural changes are largely the result of the corresponding situational changes. But an understanding of the structural changes that those situational changes will yield over time provides a powerful image of the future that makes it easier to develop those situational changes.

Here, then, is a summary of our conclusions of the situational and structural changes involved in moving from a bureaucratic toward an evolutionary way of life:

Movement from outward toward inward-outward perception and thought

Movement from emotional repression toward emotional expression

Movement from conformity toward deep action and deep interaction

Movement from a bureaucratic toward an evolutionary self-image and worldview

Movement from a wide toward a narrow values-fulfillment gap

Movement from bureaucratic rituals like stratification and bureaucracy toward evolutionary rituals like deep dialogue and deep democracy

Given the power and reach of our bureaucratic worldview, it becomes essential to present many illustrations of each of these movements. And it is exactly this that we have attempted to do in Part III.

Achieving Fundamental Change Throughout Society

Although the focus of *Saving Society* is on situational and structural changes within the individual, those changes also imply changes throughout society. For such changes within "head," "heart," and "hand"—whether situational or structural—can come to be widely shared, granting the difficulties involved. Thomas Kuhn, a historian of science, wrote about this process in his *The Structure of Scientific Revolutions* (1962). Initially he focused on fundamental changes in the physical sciences, such as the shift within physics from Newton's laws of motion to Einstein's theory of relativity. Einstein's development of his theory promised to explain contradictions that had been discovered within Newton's laws with reference to the speed of light, thus yielding a vision of a better way of understanding the nature of motion throughout the universe. That vision, much like the movement of our pendulum far to the right, made it possible for physicists to gain the motivation and momentum to swing far to the left, where they were able to gain the awareness and commitment required to challenge their long-term assumptions about the truth of Newton's laws. And as they continued to conduct research on the speed of light, swinging their pendulum back and forth, they found more and more evidence supporting Einstein's theory of relativity. Thus, they were able to challenge their basic "paradigm" or fundamental assumptions about motion and move toward radically different assumptions, granting that this was no easy or short-term transition.

Kuhn speculated that much the same thing might occur with respect to a change in our cultural paradigm, and this is exactly what has been the focus of the publications of the Sociological Imagination Group. Our own evolutionary cultural paradigm promises to resolve the contradictions within our present bureaucratic cultural paradigm. For example, there is the scientific ideal calling for the integration of all knowledge relevant to a given problem, and there is our shattered social sciences that have erected barriers to such integration by burying bits and pieces of knowledge in our libraries. Let us recall here Gouldner's statement that social scientists "are from the beginning involved in creating a new culture." As a result of our swing of the pendulum far to the right, we gain the motivation and momentum for swinging it far to the left. There, we gain the awareness and commitment required to challenge such bureaucratic assumptions as to the necessity of patterns of specialization with limited communication and patterns of hierarchy that contradict egalitarian interaction. And then, over time, our own research and that of others can yield ever more evidence for the importance of changing our fundamental cultural structures from a bureaucratic toward an evolutionary way of life.

Having the Dream Come True

Is such a vast change really possible at this time in history? What is involved is not merely fundamental change within the social sciences but also fundamental change in society as a whole, and that includes the basic structures within the personality of the individual. Thornton Wilder's play, *The Skin of Our Teeth,* suggested that the entire history of the human race is a history of threats to the very survival of the human race that succeeded in motivating people to learn to face up to those threats and emerge with ways to solve their problems. We believe that this is our own situation at this time in history: we must learn to face up to increasing threats to our very survival. We believe that we have developed a direction for confronting those threats effectively by swinging our pendulum far to the right. We believe that this can encourage more and more of us to gain the awareness and commitment required to face up to those threats. And we believe that then, over time, we and others can learn to make progress on our problems and escape from those threats by "the skin of our teeth."

Alexander Pope, the eighteenth-century English poet, wrote, "A little learning is a dangerous thing." We are now experiencing the truth of Pope's poetry, for the "little learning" achieved within the physical and biological sciences—coupled with the limited development of understanding within the social sciences—is yielding nothing less than increasing threats to the very survival of the human race. C. Wright Mills—the sociologist whose *The Sociological Imagination* (1959) was the inspiration for this book—stated that the failure of social scientists to confront our threatening social problems "is surely the greatest human default being committed by privileged men in our times." We would extend his conclusion to the failure of the rest of us to confront our most threatening problems. Ours appears to be the greatest human default being committed by the human race throughout its history.

Yet following Thornton Wilder's *The Skin of Our Teeth,* we believe that awareness of the escalating problems that confront us can indeed motivate us to develop solutions, just as they have motivated the Sociological Imagination Group to develop a direction for changing from our bureaucratic toward an evolutionary way of life. Ralph Waldo Emerson wrote, "If a man write a better book, preach a better sermon, or make a better mouse-trap than his neighbor, tho' he build his house in the woods, the world will make a beaten path to his door." We believe that we have indeed written "a better book." Although our house is "in the woods," and although our voice is easily drowned out amidst the cacophony of our present-day mass media, we will persist in our efforts until we are in fact heard. For what we are offering is not only a direction for making progress on our threatening problems. Ours is a vision of the infinite potential of every single one of us to develop "head," "heart," and "hand," with no limit to how far we can go. Our dream is not only that "there will be a future for our children, our grandchildren, our great-grandchildren, and their great-grandchildren." Our dream is also that "one day we will all learn to be poets, philosophers and scientists."

* * *

We would like to acknowledge the important contributions of J. David Knottnerus to our basic ideas, especially his understanding of the concepts of ritual and social ritual. We also thank him for his timely reactions to each of our chapters despite a demanding schedule. We also wish to thank Harold Kincaid, Thomas J. Scheff, and Louis C. Johnston, whose efforts were essential for the origin and development of the sociological imagination group and who helped to shape our approach to the scientific method. This manuscript never would have seen the light of day without the continuing encouragement of Dean Birkenkamp, publisher of Paradigm. And we thank Louis Kontos and Christian Flores-Carignan, whose critical insights proved to be most useful. We are also grateful to those individuals who have given us their reactions to part of the manuscript and thus helped us to move outside of our own blinders: Hans Bakker, Stuart Bennett, Robert W. Fuller, John de Graaf, Douglas Hartmann, D. Paul Johnson, Louis C. Johnston, Vince Montes, Richard Moody, Hilarie Roseman, Thomas J. Scheff, Sandro Segre, Carl Slawski, Irwin Sperber, David Stearns, Emek Tanay, and Steven E. Wallis.

—Provincetown, Massachusetts, and Sarasota, Florida,
September 2010

PART I

Extinction or Evolution?

DOES SOCIETY REALLY NEED SAVING? Are our problems increasing at this time in history? Are we really heading for disaster? There is no question in our view but that this is indeed the present situation of the world. We are not attempting to promote a doom-and-gloom scenario or to hype existing problems in order to motivate interest in this book. We would much rather walk on the sunny side of the street. Yet the weight of scientific evidence for our conclusion—coming from both sources that are visible to everyone as well as from knowledge that is largely invisible—is overwhelming. This is not simply a question of nuclear terrorism, of the threat of war with weapons of mass destruction, of the continuing increase in the destructive power of those weapons, of global warming and environmental pollution, of our failure to understand the forces that are yielding these problems, of the increasing gap between the rich and the poor throughout the world, of a history of war without end and of ever more destructive ones, of the largely invisible problem of the growing gap between what people throughout the world want and what they are actually able to get, and of unfamiliar twenty-first-century horrors—like "engineered" airborne viruses, rogue nanomachines, and superintelligent computers—lurking just over the horizon. Rather, it is all of these problems—and many more—combined with one another and thus having an impact on one another.

We should have learned a lesson from the Holocaust. Here was a highly civilized nation that was led down a path using modern scientific and organizational procedures to send 6 million Jews and millions of others who were deemed to be not worthy of life to their deaths. Can we blame this on one evil man or on one evil society? Or should we, instead, look deeply into the nature of modern civilization itself? That is exactly what this book is about. The bureaucratic form of organization that was basic to the slaughtering of those millions of innocents is still alive and well and thriving all around us. The kind of civilization that created the gas chambers is much the same as modern civilization. And the human beings who pried the gold from the teeth of their prostrate victims and used their skin to construct lampshades are not particularly different from the rest of us. Not only have we learned very little from the Holocaust but we've learned very little from any of the wars throughout human history, for we have no clear direction for eliminating war. Neither do we have a clear direction for solving any of the other problems listed above.

Are we humans—with all of our medical, scientific, technological, and artistic accomplishments, and with all of the other efforts of so many of us to solve our problems—doomed to extinction? Have we, after all the years and all the generations that have gone before us, finally reached the end of the trail, if not today or tomorrow, then the day after tomorrow? Are we living on borrowed time, just waiting for the bombs to fall? We are convinced that there is indeed a way out for us, a way that leads not only to progress on our threatening problems but also a path that can take us beyond the fulfillment of our wildest dreams. It is a direction that can enable us to continue the long evolutionary journey that began some 14 billion years ago. This is not a question of the very long-term process of biological evolution, although we must succeed in building on our biological nature. Rather, it has to do with the evolution of the individual within his or her lifetime: the ability to think ("head"), to feel or express emotions ("heart"), and to act ever more effectively in confronting both personal and world problems ("hand"). It also has to do with the evolution of society: from our present bureaucratic groups that fail to make much use of human potential to groups that achieve individual evolution, or the continuing development of "head," "heart," and "hand." Here, we follow the vision of America's eminent philosopher and educator, John Dewey:

> Government, business, art, religion, all social institutions have a mean-
> ing, a purpose. That purpose is to set free and to develop the capacities
> of human individuals without respect to race, sex, class, or economic
> status. And this is all one with saying that the test of their value is the
> extent to which they educate every individual into the full stature of
> his possibility. Democracy has many meanings, but if it has a moral
> meaning, it is found in resolving that the supreme test of all political
> institutions and industrial arrangements shall be the contribution they

make to the all-around growth of every member of society (Dewey 1920/1948: 186).

Given the magnitude and scope of the problems that presently threaten us, and given the failures of our leaders and experts to develop a comprehensive direction for confronting effectively the full range of those problems, we tend to avoid the big picture of our overall situation and focus narrowly on this particular problem or that one. Our approach thus parallels the tunnel vision of the academic, business, and governmental worlds. We focus on this tree or that one, yet we fail to see the forest. This is the way bureaucratic organizations work, and this is also the way that each of us has learned to think, to feel, and to act. Yet if all of our social problems are indeed linked together, and if the result is that any one problem is extremely complex, then piecemeal "solutions" simply will not work. We humans have a long history of the "unanticipated consequences" of our efforts to solve big problems (Merton 1936; Raushenbush 1969; Phillips and Johnston 2007: 77–81). The unanticipated consequences of the war in Iraq by the Bush administration is no more than a recent example. The unanticipated consequences of the war in Vietnam by several U.S. administrations was another. A third was the bet by General Motors and Chrysler that SUVs were the wave of the future.

Yet the history of our accomplishments suggests that we humans have the capacity to do much better. Perhaps the greatest achievement of the social sciences—sociology, psychology, anthropology, political science, economics, and history—throughout the twentieth century has been learning the central importance of language in shaping human behavior. It is our complex language more than anything else that sharply distinguishes us humans from all other organisms throughout the known universe. It is language that enables each of us to learn from our experiences: to remember our past experiences and make use of them in the present. It is language that shapes the way we perceive the world. It is language that is fundamental to our emotional development. It is language that has proved to be our most powerful tool for solving problems. It is language that is basic to our ability to communicate with one another as well as with all those who are no longer with us. And it is this incredible tool of language that we have only just begun to understand, a tool that holds out to us the promise of our continuing development with no limit whatsoever once we learn to open up more of its potential.

The invention of writing became the basis for another tool, one that derives from language's possibilities: the scientific method. It is the scientific method—based on this ability to understand past knowledge—that enables us to stand on the shoulders of the giants of the past. It is the scientific method that has enabled us humans to shape the face of the globe over the past five centuries far beyond the technological achievements of the human race in all previous centuries. Yet it is our limited understanding of the scientific method, based on our limited understanding of language, that has yielded the two-edged sword of modern science. Our achievements in the physical and biological sciences are linked to "achievements" in the creation of weapons of mass destruction. And our scientific achievements have not taken us very far in the direction of understanding our complex human problems. Following the words of Alexander Pope, the eighteenth-century English poet, "A little learning is a dangerous thing."

However, we have the potential to broaden our understanding of the scientific method—just as in the case of our understanding of language—and build on our insights into human behavior no less than into the physical and biological universe. To understand just what language and the scientific method might do for us, it is necessary to consider the nature of the physical and biological universe. Ours is an interactive physical world, where no phenomenon can remain completely isolated from the rest of the world. There is no such thing as a perfect vacuum, for the walls of the container will transmit energy from the universe to what is inside the container, and vice-versa. Further, biological evolution is based on the interaction between organisms and their environments. It is as a result of long-term interaction that some species are able to adapt better than other species. Still further, the human being—with language and the scientific method—is the most interactive creature in the known universe. For those tools give us the capacity to learn to interact with ever more phenomena and even to create visions of possible futures that can become reality. Here, then, is a direction for us humans: to continue our evolutionary voyage by learning to continue to develop our interactive abilities.

This brief backward look at our entire 14-billion-year history suggests optimism about our future. For there appears to be no physical or biological barriers to our moving along an evolutionary path that would take us far beyond where we are. The idea of interaction gives us a direction, and the lack of those physical and biological barriers opens the door for us to move in that direction. No matter how difficult it might prove to be to make progress on our problems, it is most encouraging to realize that there is not only a direction that can take us toward solving them but also a direction that can take us toward our continuing development.

However, our bureaucratic way of life—by contrast with physical and biological forces—has erected barriers that work against our further interaction, and that limitation poses threats to our very survival. For example, the success of physical science and its technologies has yielded a thing-oriented materialistic world, with little room for learning how human beings can develop their infinite potential rather than destroy one another. Here we have an example of a bureaucratic failure: Given our focus on narrow specialization with limited communication throughout the academic world, a broad understanding of human behavior is neither achieved nor applied to creating a world emphasizing humanistic values like the ultimate worth of every single human being. Further, bureaucracy also fosters patterns of hierarchy that take away from people's ability to communicate with and learn from one another. This once again restricts our interactive possibilities.

If we focus on the nature of our bureaucratic personality—whether in Western or Eastern society—once again we find a dangerous failure to go beyond a certain degree of interaction. As for Western society—which has also succeeded in influencing the entire world due largely to the successes of its biophysical science and technology—its bureaucratic organizations demand the conformity of the individual. This also works against any form of emotional expression in the interest of maintaining conformity to fulfilling the goals of the organization rather than those of the individual. Largely as a result, Westerners learn to repress their emotions, thus building barriers preventing the interaction of "head" (or the mind) and "hand" (or actions) with "heart" (or emotions). As for Eastern society, there is indeed much more of a focus on the world of the individual, as is well illustrated by Buddhism. Yet once again emotional repression is encouraged, for the individual's emotional expression is seen as a species of "attachment" to or "thirst" for things or other goals that will inevitably lead to disappointment in fulfilling those desires. Thus, our very emotions—so fundamental to the nature of the human being—remain of limited use in helping us to solve our problems and to continue our evolutionary journey.

However, by opening up to the full potentials of language and the scientific method, we can learn—one step at a time—to address this problem of overcoming the barriers to our patterns of interaction, or to address just about any given problem. We might come to understand the potential of these two tools by means of an image or metaphor of a pendulum that can come to swing in ever-widening arcs, illustrating how the scientific method can work not only for professional scientists but also for the rest of us. The pendulum's swing to the left portrays the individual's awareness of and commitment to the problem of knocking down those barriers. The momentum that this achieves can enable the pendulum to swing far to the right. There we make progress on that problem by increasing our understanding of it and our ability to solve it, yielding greater weight to the pendulum. As a result, that swing to the right can yield the momentum for a swing even further to the left, and so on indefinitely. For with each swing weight can be added to the pendulum, with no limit to how far the pendulum can swing in both directions. This image suggests the infinite potential of the scientific method—building on the use of scientific concepts—for making progress on problems.

Is this vision no more than a naive dream, a fairy tale that fails to take into account the harsh reality of increasing problems throughout the world? Are we ignoring the incredible difficulties involved in changing ourselves and our world? As Fred Polak, a Dutch sociologist, argued, an image of the future can be the most powerful force that we humans can develop for actually creating the future (1973). Or, as the song from *South Pacific* goes—envisioning the special island of Bali Ha'i—"till you have a dream, how you gonna have a dream come true?" Yet our vision is far more than an idle dream. Its credibility is based on six books that we and our colleagues in the Sociological Imagination Group have published since 2001, including three volumes that collect the work of some twenty sociologists in nine annual conferences that started in 2000 (Phillips 2001; Phillips, Kincaid, and Scheff, eds. 2002; Phillips and Johnston 2007; Phillips, ed. 2007; Phillips 2009; Knottnerus and Phillips, eds. 2009). These books not only range widely over the social sciences but also make use of ideas from the physical and biological sciences, philosophy, literature, poetry, and applied fields like education and mass communication. Their focus is on opening up to the infinite potentials of language and the scientific method, and this book is an effort to build on whatever they have achieved.

Edna St. Vincent Millay, the American poet, has succeeded in describing what we believe to be a key problem that confronts us humans at this time in history

> Upon this gifted age, in its dark hour
> Rains from the sky, a meteoric shower
> Of facts ...
> They lie unquestioned, uncombined.
> Wisdom enough to leech us of our ill
> Is daily spun, but there exists no loom
> To weave into fabric.

Following Millay, there is little interaction among our "shower of facts." And that lack of integration in turn results in the one-sidedness and limitations of a great many of those "facts," Those ideas come not only from the full range of disciplines within the academic world, including what we have learned from all those who have gone before us. They also include knowledge from the worlds of business, government, religion, and the arts. These ideas also arise from journalists, educators, filmmakers, and dramatists, not to mention the rest of us, and they are all doomed to "lie unquestioned, uncombined." These ideas contain "wisdom enough to leech us of our ill." Yet they do not interact with one another: There is no "loom" to "weave" them together into a "fabric" so that we can come to understand the limitations of any given "fact" and then proceed to put these ideas to work in solving our problems. Yet we are convinced that the loom—of a broad scientific method that builds on the full potential of language—that we and our colleagues in the Sociological Imagination Group have constructed can weave together ever more of those ideas. Thus, our image of the future is a direction for us humans to break down the barriers preventing us from integrating our knowledge of the world and ourselves. It is those barriers that prevent us from learning how to confront the dangerous and increasing problems that threaten us and the rest of the human race at this time in history.

Part I sketches the general nature of a "bureaucratic way of life," of an "evolutionary way of life," and of how we can learn to move from the former to the latter. For example, exactly what is a bureaucratic group? Is there such a thing as a bureaucratic personality? How has a bureaucratic way of life prevented us from integrating our understanding of our problems? How can we learn to integrate our knowledge so as to achieve an ever-deeper understanding of these problems? How do we move from understanding to effective action on our problems? What is our image of the individual and society that points us toward a world where we not only learn to solve our problems but also continue to evolve with no limit whatsoever? In one chapter, of course, we can do no more than begin to answer such questions. In the book as a whole we can carry those ideas somewhat further. But no number of books can take us beyond a certain point. We must learn to put these ideas to work in our own lives—and that is advice for us authors no less than for readers—in order to move toward the vision that they embody.

It is a vision that is our own Bali Ha'i, a world like a special island that does not as yet exist. We have conveyed our vision in very general terms—calling it our "evolutionary manifesto"—on the website of the Sociological Imagination Group: www.sociological-imagination.org. In part of that manifesto we focus on the idea of "deep democracy," an idea based on the ideas in later chapters and elaborated in Chapter 8. Here is our Bali Ha'i:

> To begin to spell out just what "deep democracy" means to us, we might parallel the speech that Martin Luther King gave at the Civil Rights March in Washington on August 28, 1963: "I have a dream that one day on the red hills of Georgia the sons of former slaves and the sons of former slave owners will be able to sit down together at the table of brotherhood." We have a dream that:
>
> There will be a future for our children, our grandchildren, our great-grandchildren, and their great-grandchildren.
>
> One day we will all learn to see ourselves as children who are only just beginning to understand ourselves and our world, and we will also learn to dream about our infinite possibilities and move toward those visions one step at a time.

One day we will all learn to pay close attention to the accomplishments of all peoples throughout history as well as to our own personal accomplishments, and we will also learn to pay close attention to the failures of the human race and to our own personal failures.

One day we will be able to bring to the surface and reduce our stratified emotions like fear, shame, guilt, hate, envy, and greed, and we will learn to express ever more our evolutionary emotions like confidence, enthusiasm, happiness, joy, love, and empathy.

One day we will see peace on earth and fellowship among all humans.

One day we will no longer look down on any other human being.

One day we all will learn to be poets, philosophers, and scientists.

Bureaucratic Problems Versus Human Possibilities

The Potential of Language and the Scientific Method

WITHIN THE FIVE SECTIONS OF CHAPTER 1 we aim to carry further the above hints about our problems and directions for both solving them and continuing our evolutionary voyage. Our focus remains on the potentials of language and the scientific method. In "The Grocer and the Chief" we develop an example illustrating the change from preindustrial to modern society. And we also illustrate the problems and possibilities of contemporary society. "The Bureaucratic Way of Life" centers on those problems, and "The Evolutionary Way of Life: Language" focuses on those possibilities. Our fourth section, "The Evolutionary Way of Life: Language and the Scientific Method," introduces our direction for moving toward the infinite potentials of language and the scientific method. And in a final section, "Plan of the Book," we preview what is to come in the chapters that follow.

In our effort to communicate the abstract nature of our vision in a concrete way, we will put forward three figures in the first three sections of the chapter. We humans are not just creatures of language: We are also creatures, and our language builds on and transforms our biological nature. That nature includes our senses, with our vision being most important. Language can indeed invoke our senses to some extent, as illustrated by

9

the visual communication suggested by figures of speech or metaphors that convey images like the pendulum metaphor for the scientific method. Just as with the above introduction to Part I, we shall continue to make use of metaphors or images throughout this chapter and the book as a whole. The power of images is well illustrated by the enormous impact of television and film on our lives. Images can also help us to "go back to the future" by learning to build on our biological nature as creatures for whom sight is extremely important. A neglect of the individual's senses—part of the neglect of the individual—is characteristic of our bureaucratic way of life. In this book we do not intend to make that mistake.

The Grocer and the Chief

In the early spring of 1950 an interviewer named Tosun B. who lived in Turkey's capital city of Ankara drove for two hours on a dirt road to the tiny farming village of Balgat. Tosun was working together with many other interviewers on an international study directed by Daniel Lerner, a political scientist. Lerner was most interested in learning what was caus-ing the enormous change that he would later describe in *The Passing of Traditional Society* (1958). What motivates the individual to give up a way of life known since infancy for a completely different way of life? Why would an individual choose to risk everything by so doing? Changes in Turkey were a continuation of hundreds of years of change from farm to factory that were accompanying the long-term scientific and industrial revolution that had been transforming Europe's feudal societies. It is a transformation that continues throughout the world to this very day.

Tosun finally arrived in Balgat and found his way to the village chief, who proved to be most hospitable. He was a 63-year-old man whom Tosun later described as "the absolute dictator of this little village." He owned the only radio in Balgat, and villagers were invited to join him in his home as they learned about news from the outside world. After exchanging small talk, Tosun asked the chief how satisfied he was with life. He replied: "What could be asked more? God has brought me to this mature age without much pain, has given me sons and daughters, has put me at the head of my village, and has given me strength of brain and body at this age. Thanks be to Him" (Lerner 1958: 23-25 for this and subsequent quotes).

Then Tosun asked him to imagine himself as president of Turkey. What would he proceed to do? He responded that he would seek "help of money and seed for some of our farmers." Tosun continued with this question: "If you could not live in Turkey, where would you want to live?" The chief responded: "I was born here, grew old here, and hope God will permit me to die here."

Tosun later tracked down the village grocer, who presented a markedly different picture of his contentment. When Tosun inquired into how satisfied he was with life, he responded: "I have told you I want better things. I would have liked to have a bigger grocery shop in the city, have a nice house there, dress nice civilian clothes." He had seen a movie during one of his trips to Ankara that showed the kind of shop he wanted, with "round boxes, clean and all the same dressed, like soldiers in a great parade." But the grocer was also well aware of his limitations: "I am born a grocer and probably die that way. I have not the possibility in myself to get the things I want. They only bother me."

The village grocer was "the only unfarming person and the only merchant in the village." According to Tosun, "[H]e is considered by the villagers even less than the least farmer." In their eyes he had rejected the worth of the community and even the supreme authority of Allah. He responded to Tosun's question about what he would do as president of Turkey: "I would make roads for the villagers to come to towns to see the world and would not let them stay in their holes all their life." As for Tosun's question of where he would want to live if he could not live in Turkey, he responded: "America, because I have heard that it is a nice country and with possibilities to be rich even for the simplest persons."

The contrast between the grocer and the chief is most dramatic, with the grocer embodying industrial man and the chief embodying traditional or preindustrial man. The grocer stated, "I want better things ... a bigger grocery shop in the city, have a nice house there, dress nice civilian clothes." He was not a happy man: "I have not the possibility in myself to get the things I want. They only bother me." By contrast, there is the chief's "What could be asked more?" As president of Turkey, the grocer would not be limited to helping the farmers of Balgat: "I would make roads for the villagers to come to towns to see the world and would not let them stay in their holes all their life." Finally, although the chief could not imagine living outside of Turkey, the grocer had a ready answer: "America, because I have heard that it is a nice country and with possibilities to be rich even for the simplest persons."

These differences between the grocer and the chief—corresponding to the differences between industrial man and preindustrial man—may be understood more clearly by introducing the idea of the "revolution of rising expectations" that has accompanied the scientific and technological revolutions over the past five centuries. The phrase was coined in 1950 by Harlan Cleveland, an American governmental official, and has since then been picked up by many analysts of the change from preindustrial to contemporary society. The grocer's expectations or aspirations—by contrast with the chief's—have gone through the roof. Not only does he "want better things," suggesting materialistic desires, he also aspires to improve the material basis for nonmaterial aspirations, such as "roads for the villagers to come to towns to see the world."

It is these high expectations or aspirations that have become the basis for the grocer's unhappiness, for he is unable to fulfill them: "I have not the possibility in myself to get the things I want. They only bother me." In other words, he remains unable to close the gap between his expectations and the fulfillment of those expectations or aspirations. And it is exactly this aspirations-fulfillment gap—the gap between what people want and what they are actually able to get—that is fundamental to the major social problems of contemporary societies. Also, this is a gap that is largely invisible, as indicated in the first paragraph of the introduction to Part I, and this makes it far more difficult to confront. The result, as assessed in a book-length study (Phillips and Johnston 2007), is the threat named by that book's title: *The Invisible Crisis of Contemporary Society.* The threat's invisible nature derives from its source in the intangible phenomena of human aspirations and their fulfillment. And the crisis that it is causing derives from the increasing size of that gap with no end in sight. Emile Durkheim, a founder of the discipline of sociology, saw the danger of that gap in his monumental study of suicide: "From top to bottom of the [economic] ladder, greed is aroused without knowing where to find ultimate foothold. Nothing can calm it, for its goal is far beyond all it can attain" (1897/1951: 254–255).

Yet the grocer's aspirations are not just materialistic ones: They are nonmaterialistic as well. Let us recall that he wanted the villagers "to come to towns to see the world." More generally, the revolution of rising expectations throughout contemporary societies derives not just from the continuing scientific and technological revolutions. It also derives from long-term political changes that might be traced back to the American and French revolutions and linked to what has happened over the past two centuries. Most recently, for example, we have had the American civil rights movement, the women's movement, the gray panthers' movement, and the gay and lesbian movement. All of these political changes have encouraged more and more of us to aspire to such values as democracy, equality, freedom, and the ultimate worth of every single individual. Just as our material aspirations have increased in relation to our continuing scientific and technological revolutions, so have our nonmaterial aspirations increased as a result of continuing political movements. As a result, our revolution of rising expectations has come to include the full range of our material and nonmaterial values. And our aspirations-fulfillment gap—despite our successes both materially and nonmaterially in fulfilling our aspirations to some degree—continues to widen.

A schematic diagram is needed here to help us visualize the nature of the invisible crisis of contemporary society. As in the case of any problem, it is our awareness and understanding of the nature of the problem that is essential if we wish to solve it. Figure 1-1, The Invisible Crisis of Contemporary Society, can help us to gain that awareness, for it traces the relationship between both the revolution of rising expectations and the fulfillment of those expectations. In this way, we can see the growing gap between these two curves as we move from preindustrial society to contemporary society. We might note that the curve of the fulfillment of expectations does indeed increase as we move toward modern times. But that increase is as nothing compared to the increase in the curve of the revolution of rising expectations, yielding an increasing gap between what we want and what we are able to get. We might also note that these curves have to do with expectations or aspirations in general, including both material and nonmaterial aspirations.

Figure 1–1. The Invisible Crisis: The Escalating Gap between Expectations and Fulfillment

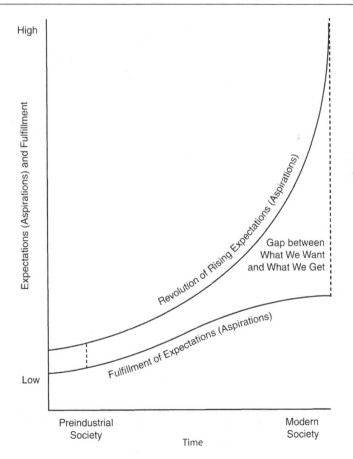

Seeing these curves in relation to the grocer and the chief of Balgat can help us to understand their significance more concretely. It is the chief, together with the farmers of Balgat, who are located on the left-hand side of the curves. The limited achievements of those farmers create no significant aspirations-fulfillment gap for them, since their aspirations or expectations are equally limited. For the grocer, on the right-hand side, the situation is much different, since he has experienced a revolution of rising expectations. He has visited Ankara many times and has seen what he is unable to have but has learned to desperately want. And he has nonmaterial aspirations as well, having seen the differences between an urban way of life and the life of the Balgat farmers, who have never visited Ankara. As for his resulting aspirations-fulfillment gap, he is not happy about it, yet he believes that he can do nothing about his situation.

Let us now focus on the significance of this growing and largely invisible aspirations-fulfillment gap in contemporary times, over half a century later than the study of the grocer and the chief. Given our continuing scientific and technological revolutions accompanied by our continuing political movements, that gap is continuing to widen. Our problems have multiplied and become increasingly serious, yielding new and deep aspirations for solving them. Yet our ability to make progress on them remains quite limited. For example, weapons of mass destruction can be launched by very small groups and not just nations; we have the serious problem of increases in global warming and environmental pollution; the revolution of rising expectations is becoming more and more of a worldwide phenomenon, illustrated by energy demands on the part of the vast populations of China and India; the gap between the rich and the poor continues to grow wider; and nuclear proliferation among nations along with sophisticated technologies for delivering such weapons continues to increase; and we have moved that much closer to the ultimate nightmares of engineered airborne viruses, rogue nanomachines, and superintelligent computers that could wreck havoc on billions of people. Our modern aspirations-fulfillment gap is, thus, far greater and far more serious than the gap experienced by the grocer of Balgat.

Most recently, we have experienced a financial meltdown and a deep worldwide recession. In our view this has been largely the result of yet other gaps between aspirations and their fulfillment. For example, many buyers of houses were unable to afford them without undertaking huge amounts of debt that they could only afford to repay under the best of circumstances. But circumstances changed, resulting in massive numbers of foreclosures. Those buyers had been encouraged by bankers who made large profits by leveraging their own cash reserves far beyond what would have been reasonable. Those bankers in turn were encouraged by others in the financial industry, who proceeded to package those questionable mortgages in what are called "derivatives," and who then leveraged the ratio of debt to cash reserves still further, making their own handsome profit. All the while the hands-off policy of the federal government yielded little or no oversight of what was happening within the huge housing market, failing to limit the degree of leveraging that was taking place. We might recall here Durkheim's analysis of the impact of industrialization at the close of the nineteenth century: "From top to bottom of the [economic] ladder, greed is aroused without knowing where to find ultimate foothold. Nothing can calm it, for its goal is far beyond all it can attain."

However, simply by seeing these problems as examples of the same aspirations-fulfillment gap linked to our continuing scientific and techno-logical revolutions, we have already made substantial progress not only in understanding their nature but also in developing a direction for making progress toward solutions. As for understanding, this gap embodies the full range of our aspirations, goals, or values, and it also embodies the impact of all of our actions on that range of aspirations. As a result, that gap is not limited just to the revolution of rising expectations associated with the scientific and technological revolutions—coupled with our long-term political movements—over the past five centuries. For that gap is itself a central factor that is involved in the full range of human problems.

Given this analysis of the importance of the aspirations-fulfillment gap, we can begin to focus on the forces that are generating those two curves in Figure 1-1 that result in this gap: the revolution of rising expec-tations, and the fulfillment of those expectations. Here, we can look to the systematic knowledge from the social sciences. In this one section of one chapter we can do little more than hint at how we propose to move in this direction throughout this book. In Part II we intend to show just how that increasing aspirations-fulfillment gap is linked to the repression of emotions. That repression occurs largely because the individual is un-able to maintain awareness of a large and growing gap between what he or she deeply aspires to and what he or she is able to achieve.

This analysis provides the basis in Part III for what we have come to call "the East-West strategy" for problem solving. This strategy employs a scientific method that makes use of language's potentials as a tool for help-ing us to become aware of the size of that gap as a basis for reducing it. The strategy involves a short-term effort to lower one's aspirations so that they move toward narrowing one's aspirations-fulfillment gap. As one succeeds in this effort, which follows a Buddhist orientation, one learns to raise up one's emotions from their repressed state and to express those emotions ever more fully. Metaphorically, one's emotions function like the engine of a car or plane: they are vital to achieving movement toward fulfilling one's goals or desires. Yet one must be careful not to repeat one's former situation of raising one's aspirations far beyond one's ability to fulfill them. And it is exactly here that the East-West strategy gives us a direction for raising aspirations as well as increasing our ability to fulfill them.

Yet why is it that we Westerners and Easterners—with all that we have achieved throughout history, and with all of the efforts of so many of us to solve our problems—find ourselves with our backs up against the wall? Granting this fundamental and largely invisible problem of an increasing aspirations-fulfillment gap, why haven't we figured out what is causing that gap and, as a result, taken decisive action to make progress on this problem? What are the forces that lie behind those two curves in Figure 1-1? Why do our experts and leaders continue to find themselves largely helpless in the face of growing problems? Why is all of this occurring at this particular time in history?

Many explanations have been offered, and most of them are partial truths, such as our shortsightedness with reference to environmental problems, leaders who have pursued their own personal agendas, the failure of educational systems, the supposed inevitability of technological "progress" in building weapons of mass destruction, and an economic system that favors the rich over the poor. Yet these are the trees and not the forest. What, then, is the nature of the forest? How are we to understand the development of this full range of problems, and why are they all coming together at this time? It is this kind of very broad analysis that we desperately require if we are to develop the understanding that we need to make progress not merely on this problem or on that one, but rather on the full range of our problems.

The Bureaucratic Way of Life

It is essential for us to probe the absolutely fundamental assumptions that provide the framework on which our way of life rests. William James, one of the founders of the philosophy of pragmatism—the philosophical basis for the scientific method—saw philosophy as yielding that framework, as he indicates in this passage:

> There are some people—and I am one of them—who think that the most practical and important thing about a man is still his view of the universe. We think that for a landlady considering a lodger, it is important to know his income, but still more important to know his philosophy. We think that for a general to fight an enemy, it is important to know the enemy's numbers, but still more important to know the enemy's philosophy (James 1907/1995: 1).

Following James's view, there are no ideas we have that are nearly as important as our philosophical assumptions. Indeed, those assumptions shape our ideas. Yet we all go along on our merry ways paying no attention to the nature of those deep beliefs that shape the full range of our behavior. There is a specialized area within philosophy that centers on these basic assumptions, namely, "metaphysics," or fundamental assumptions and beliefs about the nature of reality that shape all human behavior. However, despite the overarching importance of our metaphysical stance for understanding any and all aspects of our behavior, scientists—including social scientists—generally treat this area of knowledge as unscientific, much like angels dancing on the head of a pin. Metaphysics is seen as "mere speculation," by contrast with science, which supposedly focuses only on "hard facts" derived from scientific research. This rejection of the importance of our basic assumptions and beliefs about the nature of reality is tied to a historical view that genuinely scientific thinking emerged by rejecting the religious dogma and speculative thought of the feudal era in favor of experimentation and observation dealing with what we actually sense in the world. This focus on the hard facts deriving from experimentation and observation also became tied to a rejection of the social sciences as "true sciences," given their focus on intangible phenomena like human values, emotions, thought, and language.

Yet this view of metaphysics takes scientists away from understanding not only human behavior but also physical and biological phenomena. For they neglect to examine their own fundamental assumptions, and it is those very assumptions that shape every aspect of the research process. Those assumptions have an impact on the scientists' selection of a topic for research, procedures of observation or experimentation, the analysis of the data they collect, and the conclusions that they draw from an investigation. And metaphysical assumptions are by no means divorced from facts. Charles Peirce, the founder of pragmatism, understood the importance of this area of knowledge:

> There is and can be no doubt that this immature condition of Metaphysics has very greatly hampered the progress of ... psychology ... linguistics, anthropology, social science, etc. To my mind it is equally clear that defective and bad metaphysics has been almost as injurious to the physical sciences. . . . The common opinion has been that Metaphysics is backward because it is intrinsically beyond the reach of human cognition. . . . But metaphysics, even bad metaphysics, really rests on observations, whether consciously or not, and the only reason that this is not universally recognized is that it rests upon kinds of phenomena with which every man's experience is so saturated that he usually pays no particular attention to them (Peirce 1898/1955: 310–311).

To illustrate the importance of metaphysical assumptions, which are very largely invisible, let us assume that we live in a bureaucratic world yet remain unaware of this fact. We are so "saturated" with that bureaucratic way of life, following Peirce's analysis, that we pay no particular attention to it. From this perspective, we would fail to see the link between the use of bureaucratic procedures by the Nazis to perpetrate the Holocaust and our own bureaucratic way of life, as suggested in the second paragraph of the introduction to Part I. As a result, we would ignore the lessons that we ourselves might learn from the horrors of the Holocaust, as illustrated in this description of a scene by an SS officer:

> The train arrives. Two hundred Ukrainians fling open the doors and chase people out of the wagons with their leather whips ... Then the procession starts to move. They all go along the path with a very pretty girl in front, all naked ... They enter the death chambers.... The corpses are thrown out wet with sweat and urine, smeared with excrement and menstrual blood on their legs.... Two dozen dentists open mouths with hooks and look for gold.... Some of the workers check genitals and anus for gold, diamonds and valuables (Ferguson 2006: 507–508).

Here was perhaps the most wicked act in all of history, carried out under the leadership of a man who had come to power by democratic means, and accomplished by a death machine that made full use of bureaucratic patterns of organization. It was carried out by educated people within a society that illustrated the very height of modern cultural achievements. Yet our failure to pay attention to the bureaucratic metaphysical assumptions that lay behind the Holocaust—and that guide our own behavior as well—has blinded us to what we might learn from this historical tragedy. We say "never again," and we point the finger of blame at Hitler, at the Nazis, or at the German people, all the while failing to see the culpability of their bureaucratic worldview as well as our own. And if we cannot learn from the Holocaust, how can we expect to learn much from any of the wars throughout human history, or indeed from all of the tragedies—and all of the achievements as well—throughout history? For we are failing to take into account the most powerful force that continues to shape all human events: our metaphysical stance.

What, then, is the nature of our bureaucratic metaphysical stance? Here, let us shift our usage from the term "metaphysics" to the term "worldview," and thus inquire into the nature of our bureaucratic worldview. "Worldview" is a translation of the German word "*Weltanschauung*," a term used during sociology's initial development by scholars like Georg Simmel and Karl Mannheim whose vision of sociology was very broad. Our purpose here is twofold. On the one hand, "metaphysics" is a term that should certainly become important for scientists, but for our own purposes of communicating more widely it carries too much baggage suggesting that it is opposed to scientific analysis. "Worldview," by contrast, does not convey connotations of speculative ideas that oppose actual facts. Further, "worldview" suggests the importance of the sense of vision, thus pointing us in a concrete direction. Yet by shifting from metaphysical stance to worldview we do not abandon our efforts to develop a highly systematic and scientific approach to penetrating the complexities of human behavior and social problems. For us, our worldview is nothing less than our metaphysical stance or persisting image of the nature of reality.

A bit of background on the concept of worldview is in order, given its importance. Karl Mannheim, a sociologist known for his analysis of how ideas are developed within society—or the sociology of knowledge—gives us some insight into its breadth:

> Is it possible to determine the global outlook of an epoch in an objective, scientific fashion? . . . [T]heoretical philosophy is neither the creator nor the principal vehicle of the *Weltanschauung* of an epoch; it is merely only one of the channels through which a global factor—to be conceived as transcending the various cultural fields, its emanations—manifests itself. . . . If, on the other hand, we define *Weltanschauung* as something atheoretical with philosophy merely as one of its manifestations, and not the only one, we can widen our field of cultural studies . . . our search for a synthesis will then be in a position to encompass every single cultural field. The plastic arts, music, costumes, mores and customs, rituals, the tempo of living, expressive gestures and demeanor—all these no less than theoretical communications will become a decipherable language, adumbrating the underlying unitary whole of *Weltanschauung* (Mannheim 1952: 9, 13–14).

Mannheim takes pains to distinguish *Weltanschauung* or worldview from philosophy, with metaphysics being philosophy's concept that is closest to worldview. For Mannheim, *Weltanschauung* is an incredibly broad concept, including "every single cultural field" along with the ideas, feelings, and practices of ordinary people. Our own approach to worldview is more abstract or general, for we look to the worldview that has dominated not just one era but all previous eras, for we see a great deal of unity in the worldview of human beings throughout the entire history of the human race. More specifically, we see the worldview that has shaped human history as bureaucratic. We should note that Mannheim implies that it is indeed possible to approach *Weltanschauung* "in an objective, scientific fashion," and that is exactly the approach that we adopt.

It will be in Chapters 2, 3, and 4 that we will explore in some detail the nature of our bureaucratic worldview, building on the six earlier books of the Sociological Imagination Group. In this brief introduction to the present book, our focus will be on employing Figure 1-2 to introduce the general nature of this worldview. As indicated at the beginning of this chapter, images or figures will play an important role in conveying our ideas, helping us to go "back to the future" by making use of our biologically shaped senses along with language. In addition to the three figures or images in this introduction, a figure will be used in each of the chapters to follow.

To understand the significance of Figure 1–2, it is useful to draw contrasts between that figure and our description in the introduction to Part I of the interactive nature of all structures in our universe. With respect to physical structures, let us recall that all phenomena interact with one another, whether directly or indirectly, for there is no such thing as a perfect vacuum. Biological evolution requires long-term interaction between organisms and their environments. That interaction is speeded up in the lifetime of organisms, for they require relatively rapid interaction with the environment, such as the intake of oxygen and the exhaling of carbon dioxide as animals breathe. Further, with the tools of language and the scientific method, the human being has become the most interactive creature in the known universe. Yet Figure 1–2a's minimalist portrayal of the bureaucratic society starkly opposes the direction that our universe has been taking for over 14 billion years. On the one hand, we have its vertical lines dividing people and phenomena from one another, illustrating specialization with limited communication. On the other hand we have horizontal lines illustrating patterns of persisting hierarchy, reducing communication among individuals. Still further, the result of these horizontal and vertical barriers is to work against society's ability to make progress on the moment-to-moment problems resulting from the interaction of phenomena throughout the universe, given its rigidity and inability to adapt to change.

If we turn to Figure 1–2b, we find much the same contrast between our interactive universe and what the figure presents. For we have in that figure barriers between the individual's patterns of perception and thought ("head"), emotions ("heart"), and actions ("hand"), yielding what we have described in the introduction as the bureaucratic personality. More specifically, let us recall the Western and Eastern patterns of emotional repression working against the individual's ability to link perception or thought and action with emotion. Also, as discussed in the introduction, we make use of the potentials that language offers us only to a very limited degree, thus working to keep perception and thought apart from emotion and action. Further, our development of the scientific method accompanied with scientific technologies is also most limited, thus working to keep action apart from perception or thought and emotion. Yet all of these barriers to interaction should be expected, given the individual's residence within a bureaucratic society.

However, we should bear in mind that the bureaucratic way of life depicted by Figure 1–2 has been created by us human beings. It is certainly not a product of the nature of the universe and, indeed, stands directly opposed to the direction that the universe has been taking from the moment of its origin. Unfortunately, our bureaucratic worldview points us away from gaining understanding of our dangerous situation at this

Figure 1–2a. The Bureaucratic Way of Life

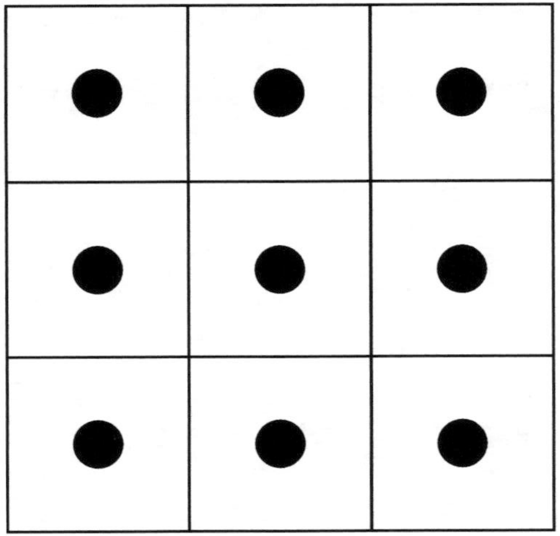

Figure 1–2b. The Bureaucratic Individual

Perception and Thought ("Head")	Emotion ("Heart")	Action ("Hand")

time in history, given the problems that have been developing over many years. For example, our limited understanding of the scientific method has yielded ever more powerful weapons of mass destruction and ever more effective methods for delivering those weapons. Yet that deficient understanding has failed to yield a social science that can confront our problems ever more effectively. However, with this understanding of our situation it becomes possible to achieve such progress. Let us turn, then, to considering an alternative way of life.

The Evolutionary Way of Life: Language

Just as Figure 1-2 portrays the bare bones of a bureaucratic way of life, so can Figure 1-3 portray the bare bones of an evolutionary way of life. Once again we have reference to the interactive nature of the universe, and once again we look to the direction of our universe toward ever more interaction, with the human being having an infinite potential for interaction with the aid of language and the scientific method. Figure 1-3 is divided into two parts, just as in the case of Figure 1a: 1-3a having to do with society, and 1-3b bearing on the individual. Focusing on Figure 1-3a, the arrows that are tying together the elements that were separated from one another in Figure 1-2a are meant to suggest two-way interaction. Actually, we might think of every element as interacting directly with every other element, but that is not depicted because it would yield a figure that is too complex for ease of understanding. We might note, then, that these interactive arrows replace—by comparison to bureaucratic society—both the vertical barriers that yield specialization with little communication as well as the horizontal barriers that yield persisting hierarchy with its limited communication. Further, all of this interaction results in the integration of knowledge along with communication among individuals, and this provides a basis for confronting problems in society ever more effectively.

To understand more fully the nature of an evolutionary—by contrast with a bureaucratic—way of life, it is essential to look to how the concept of evolution has been used in the past, distinguishing our own approach from prior ones. It was in his preface to *Armageddon or Evolution: The Scientific Method and Escalating World Problems* that Bernard Phillips looked back to earlier views of "evolution":

> The idea of evolution has been used in many different ways, and a number of them have hurt rather than helped our understanding of human behavior and have even contributed to our problems. We might think of Hitler's vision of Aryans as the "master race," and his mounting the Holocaust as a way of eliminating "inferiors" such as Jews and supposedly moving toward a higher development of the human race.

Figure 1–3a.   The Evolutionary Society

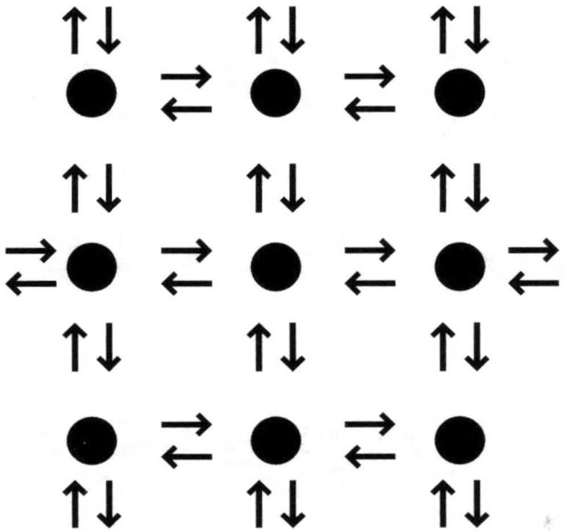

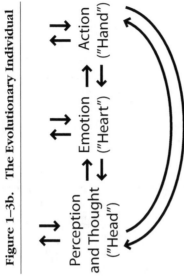

Figure 1–3b.   The Evolutionary Individual

Perception
and Thought → Emotion → Action
("Head")   ("Heart")   ("Hand")

We might think of Charles Darwin's theory of biological evolution as advancing our understanding of biology to an enormous degree. We might also think of Auguste Comte—the early founder of sociology—with his vision of the human race as necessarily going through three stages: theological, metaphysical, and positive, where the positive stage is the age of science and industrialism. Or there was Herbert Spencer's theory of necessary movement from homogeneity to heterogeneity or specialization. And we have another sociologist, Ferdinand Tonnies, and his view of necessary movement from *Gemeinschaft* or community to *Gesellschaft* or impersonal society, an evolutionary movement that is not in a progressive direction. More recent theories of evolution are illustrated by the anthropologist Leslie White and the sociologists Gerhard and Jean Lenski who emphasize the importance of technological development (Phillips 2009: xiv).

All of these efforts can contribute to our own understanding of evolution—even that of Hitler—provided that we are very careful in just which elements of these approaches we choose to build on. Hitler's destructive approach gives us an extreme version of a bureaucratic way of life, and thus it helps us to understand our own contrasting view of an evolutionary way of life. Also, his view illustrates a focus on the importance of the idea of evolution, an idea that we should by no means abandon just because of Hitler's interest in it: It is far too important for that. As for Darwin, his understanding of the process of biological evolution is central to our own approach, granting that we build on that approach and point as well toward the evolution of society and the individual. For one thing, biological evolution calls for the interaction between organisms and their environments, and it is this idea of interaction that is the basis for our own view of the evolution of all structures: physical, biological, social, and personal. For another thing, it is biological evolution that has yielded us large-brained primates—with the ability to emit a variety of sounds as a basis for speech and language—that is the basis for the situation of the human race as the most interactive creature in the known universe.

Comte's view of our present situation in the "positive" stage of evolution has led to very narrow "positivistic" and/or materialistic views of the nature of science and the scientific method, as illustrated by its rejection of the importance of metaphysics. Yet we can also applaud his interest in the importance of the idea that there is indeed an evolutionary process in society. Spencer's view of the importance of specialization is well taken, but only to the degree that specialization is also accompanied by the integration of knowledge along with communication. Unfortunately, however, what we have in the academic world and in society as a whole is specialization with minimal communication, yielding as a result a bureaucratic rather than an evolutionary worldview and way of life. As for White and the

Lenskis, technological developments have indeed been crucial throughout human history for the development of contemporary society, with all of our achievements and our failures. Yet we must also turn to the nature of the scientific method—the fundamental basis for technological developments over the past five centuries—for further understanding.

What all of these evolutionary theories lack is a focus on the idea of interaction—granting its generality—as central to the evolutionary process that has been taking place throughout the entire history of the universe. As outlined in the introduction, all phenomena throughout the physical universe interact with one another, whether directly or indirectly, and biological evolution requires interaction between organisms and their environments. As for the evolution of society and the individual, language has made us humans the most interactive creatures in the known universe. And if we learn to move away from our bureaucratic way of life with its barriers to fulfilling more of the potentials that language gives us, then we can continue on the evolutionary path that started with the Big Bang 14 billion years ago. Of course, progress along that path has by no means been continuous. For example, Riane Eisler—a student of our prehistory—has written of a change thousands of years ago from a "partnership model" of society to a "dominator model," analogous to a shift from an evolutionary to a bureaucratic way of life (1988). And some students of evolution, such as Ferdinand Tonnies, have also written about changes that have not been progressive. However, granting that we have no guarantee that we will overcome the bureaucratic barriers to further evolution, we nevertheless have the capacity to do so. This is Eisler's conviction as well, since she sees our earlier partnership model as helping to chart for us an evolutionary path that we can follow.

To build on these ideas, it is essential for us to focus on the nature of language and the potentials that it gives us humans, potentials for continuing to develop our interactive abilities with no limit whatsoever, just as we have come to believe that there is no limit to how far the scientific method can take us in understanding the world. It was in an earlier book that Phillips and a colleague put forward the idea of the three potentials of language:

> The *Babel* book, with its focus on the Web Approach to the scientific method, distinguished among the languages of social science, biophysical science and literature (Phillips 2001: 21-23). We might carry further our understanding of the role of language in human affairs by seeing these languages as emphasizing, respectively, three capacities of language: dichotomy, gradation or number, and figurative language or imagery. The social sciences have emphasized dichotomies, such as the distinction between equality and hierarchy or conformity and deviance. This goes back to the fundamental nature of all languages:

their division of the world into two categories. There is the phenomena denoted by a given word, on the one hand, and all other phenomena, on the other hand. Such a dichotomous perspective also appears to be the emphasis within everyday speech and thought.

The biophysical sciences, by contrast with the social sciences, have emphasized the gradational component of language. Here, we might see just about everything as a matter of degree, and we might even go so far as to designate a given phenomenon with a number and use that number as a basis for making predictions about the occurrence of that phenomenon. Following the title of a book by Tobias Dantzig, *Number: The Language of Science* (1954), the development of mathematics has been essential in the development of the biophysical sciences. . . .

Literature, by contrast, emphasizes imagery or figures of speech, which uses language to represent sense experiences. This takes us back to biological or perceptual experiences so fundamental that they precede the development of language, granting that language shapes those experiences and is in turn shaped by them. . . . Images from literature are, potentially, powerful means of communication. They can help the scientist to understand what he or she has learned, and they can also help the scientist communicate that knowledge. It is a focus on only one of these capacities of language—whether dichotomy, gradation, or imagery—which is a basis for a narrow, or what might be called a stratified, worldview or metaphysical stance. By contrast, a focus on all three is a basis for a broad, or what might be called an interactive, worldview (Phillips and Johnston 2007: 12-13).

Let us recall from the preceding section of this chapter on the bureaucratic way of life the three aspects of the bureaucratic society, as depicted by Figure 1-2a's grid pattern: (1) the vertical lines dividing people and phenomena from one another based on specialization with limited communication, (2) the horizontal lines preventing communication or the integration of diverse phenomena based on persisting hierarchy, and (3) the inability of society to make progress on its fundamental problems as a result of those barriers to interaction. If we focus now on (1), the above vision of the potentials that language holds out for us human beings replace those vertical lines with the interactive double arrows depicted in Figure 1-3a. More concretely, there is every reason why all of us have the capacity to become "renaissance" men and women by learning to turn those interactive capacities into interactive abilities, and continue without limit to develop our understanding of the social sciences, the biophysical sciences, and literature (or the arts in general).

Presently, not only are there the enormous barriers dividing these three broad fields of knowledge, but there are huge barriers within each of them, and there are even barriers within those barriers. For example, there is very little communication among the various social sciences: sociology, psychology, anthropology, history, political science, and economics. And still further, there are a great many specialized fields within each of these social sciences. For example, there are now no fewer than 46 specialized sections within the American Sociological Association, and counting, with minimal communication among them. To make matters much worse, there are some 400 articles representing 400 highly specialized fields—with minimal cross-references to other highly specialized fields to be found in those articles—listed in the *Encyclopedia of Sociology* (Borgatta and Montgomery 2000). Given our arguable assumption as to the complexity of human behavior, the failure of social scientists to follow through on their responsibility to penetrate that complexity—requiring, in our view, an approach that reaches out not just to those 400 specialized areas but also to biophysical science and to literature and the arts—becomes starkly evident. Given the fundamental, escalating, and highly threatening problems throughout the world at this time in history, the political irresponsibility of social scientists becomes what C. Wright Mills—the sociologist whose work became the basis for the Sociological Imagination Group—called, half a century ago, "the greatest human default being committed by privileged men in our times" (1959: 176).

There are two other aspects of a bureaucratic society in addition to those vertical lines that separate the pieces of knowledge that are developed within a given specialized area: the horizontal lines of Figure 1–2a, which invoke persisting hierarchy, and the ineffectiveness of a bureaucratic society in making progress on our basic problems that results from the grid's barriers to interaction and learning. This suggests that the bureaucratic worldview and way of life has been victimizing the human race throughout its history, working to prevent us from fulfilling our infinite capacities for learning and evolving. Fortunately our analysis of language can help us to integrate pieces of knowledge from the social sciences so that we can at least develop a direction for moving toward an evolutionary way of life. It is a direction that invokes a very broad approach to the scientific method, one that encompasses not just achievements in the social sciences but also what has been accomplished in the biophysical sciences as well as literature and the arts (or, more generally, the humanities). And it is also an approach to the scientific method that makes use of the incredible potentials that language has given us.

Given the above discussion of evolution, how do we define an evolutionary worldview by contrast with a bureaucratic worldview? First, it is a worldview, namely, a metaphysical stance or persisting image of the nature of reality. To carry our definition further we must anticipate what we shall write in Chapters 5, 6, and 7, which have to do with evolution. We might, then, define an evolutionary worldview so as to follow the headings of those chapters: a metaphysical stance that includes inward-outward perception and thought ("head"), emotional expression ("heart"), and deep action and deep interaction ("hand"). And we might also anticipate Chapters 2, 3, and 4 by using those chapter headings to define explicitly a bureaucratic worldview: a metaphysical stance that includes outward perception and thought ("head"), emotional repression ("heart"), and conforming behavior ("hand"). These definitions yield a dichotomy between the evolutionary and bureaucratic worldviews. Yet we can also envisage a continuum between them and see people's worldviews gradationally, located on a continuum between these two poles. Also, our definitions make use of language's metaphorical potential with their use of the images of "head," "heart," and "hand," thus invoking the third basic potential that language gives us.

The Evolutionary Way of Life: Language and the Scientific Method

For most of us, there is no question about the nature of the scientific method: It is the process that physical and biological scientists make use of as they proceed with their research. For we all know of their enormous accomplishments in learning about the nature of the universe. If anyone knows the nature of the scientific method, it is certainly those scientists, given their achievements. And we all know of the tremendous accomplishments of biophysical technologists like engineers and physicians— who also make use of the scientific method—in shaping the face of the globe and in conquering many diseases. As for "social scientists," they are obviously not real scientists, for what have they actually accomplished in solving the massive social problems throughout the world? However, we might allow them to masquerade as scientists by applying that term to themselves. Yet we all know deep down that there is no such thing as "social science." At best, social science is an intellectual effort, quite inferior to a genuine scientific approach, that may be useful for limited purposes and to a limited extent. That inferiority is well illustrated by the failure of those who study human behavior to develop a mathematical analysis that can yield accurate predictions of human behavior. Indeed, that failure most probably indicates that there will never be such an animal as "social science."

The above paragraph obviously was written tongue-in-cheek. It suggests the enormous prejudices that social scientists must confront as they go about their business in attempting to unravel the enormous complexity of human behavior and social problems. This introductory chapter is not the place to confront these various prejudices in any detailed way, although we expect to be able to do so in the chapters that follow. Yet in these times when—in our view—nothing less than the fate of the human race is at stake, it is exactly this kind of prejudice that merits the same indictment that Mills leveled at the political irresponsibility of social scientists: "the greatest human default being committed by privileged men in our times." If, indeed, we are correct in our assessment of the enormous complexity of human behavior and social problems, and if our own work indicates that there is indeed a direction for penetrating that complexity, then any failure to aid the continuing development of social science is an omission that is potentially far more deadly than the Holocaust. For such prejudice works to block the path to what we believe to be the only way out for the human race.

To briefly illustrate these prejudices, we turn to an analysis—by Susanna Hornig, a student of the mass media—of the award-winning PBS documentary science series *NOVA* to examine how the idea of science is being presented to the general public (1990). There is a clear hierarchy between the "hard sciences" like physics and chemistry and the "soft sciences" like botany. As for the social sciences, they are to be found at the very bottom of the scientific hierarchy, for they are almost completely ignored. Yet this is not merely a hierarchy: It is a hierarchy that continues to persist. The implication is that the soft sciences—and especially the social sciences—have no chance whatsoever to develop into "real" sciences: They are doomed to remain forever within their present low status. As for the nature of the scientific method, Hornig tells us of one episode in particular, "The Race for the Superconductor" (aired March 29, 1988), focusing on competition among researchers from Switzerland, Japan, and the United States to create a material that will lose almost no power to electrical resistance. Much of the presentation is taken up with "shots of complex laboratory equipment, chemicals in jars, blackboards complete with equations," a periodic chart where the elements appear to be taking off from the chart and flying toward the viewer, and bottles of liquids dripping through complicated arrangements of tubes. But there is little or no explanation of the nature of all this research.

NOVA, then, gives us a clear illustration of all three aspects of a bureaucratic society, by contrast with the scientific ideal of interaction as a basis for scientific progress. The horizontal lines in Figure 1-2a representing persisting hierarchy or social stratification are illustrated by the persisting hierarchy or social stratification among the different sciences, with social science running a distant last. And there is also a suggestion of persisting hierarchy with the focus of the episode on the superconductor as a competitive race, with the implication that it is the United States that is and should be superior to other nations in its scientific activities. This is a far cry from the scientific ideal of openness to communication from scientists across the globe. As for the vertical lines, just as social science is almost invariably ruled out of *NOVA*'s presentation of science, so is there no social science attention to the human behavior involved in the race for the superconductor or in the scientific activities depicted in other episodes. Questions that have to do with human behavior—such as the degree to which these investigators are illustrating harmful conformity to scientific ideas that are widely accepted and are as a result going around in circles—are never asked and as a result are never answered. As for the aspect of a bureaucratic society having to do with its effectiveness in solving problems, we have in *NOVA* an example of miseducation rather than education.

Among the many social scientists who have contributed to our understanding of the scientific method—granting that their work has not been integrated—we would like to single out two who provide the basis for building a broad scientific method on the potentials of language. C. Wright Mills, the sociologist quoted above with reference to the political irresponsibility of social scientists, wrote these words half a century ago:

> The sociological imagination enables us to grasp history and biography and the relations between the two within society. That is its task and its promise.... [T]hose who have been imaginatively aware of the promise of their work have consistently asked three sorts of questions: (1) What is the structure of this particular society as a whole? ... (2) Where does this society stand in human history? ... (3) What varieties of men and women now prevail in this society and in this period? ... Whether the point of interest is a great power state or a minor literary mood, a family, a prison, a creed—these are the kinds of questions the best social analysts have asked. They are the intellectual pivots of classic studies of man in society—and they are the questions inevitably raised by any mind possessing the sociological imagination. For that imagination is the capacity to shift from one perspective to another—from the political to the psychological; from examination of a single family to comparative assessment of the national budgets of the world; from the theological school to the military establishment; from considerations of an oil industry to studies of contemporary poetry. It is the capacity to range from the most impersonal and remote transformations to the most intimate features of the human self—and to see the relations between the two. Back of its use there is always the urge to know the social and historical meaning of the individual in the society and in the period in which he has his quality and his being (Mills 1959: 6- 7).

Although Mills called his vision for sociologists "the sociological imagination," this quote indicates that he was in fact writing about a social science imagination. For a start, "history" and "biography"—illustrating psychology, and including "the most intimate features of the human self"—are absolutely essential. As for "society," this quote covers the range of society's institutions: "family," "state," religion ("the theological school"), the "military," the economic institution ("the national budgets of the world" and "considerations of an oil industry"), and the educational institution ("studies of contemporary poetry").

Yet Mills proceeds beyond social science in his understanding of how the scientific method must build on the potentials of language. While still a graduate student at the University of Wisconsin, he analyzed some 50 textbooks on social problems to learn about "the style of reflection and the social-historical basis of American sociology." He was appalled at this discovery:

> The level of abstraction which characterizes these texts is so low that often they seem to be empirically confused for lack of abstraction to knit them together. They display bodies of meagerly connected facts, ranging from rape in rural districts to public housing, and intellectually sanction this low level of abstraction.... Collecting and dealing in a fragmentary way with scattered problems and facts of milieus, these books are not focused on larger stratifications or upon structured wholes (Mills 1943: 168).

It is this idea of "abstraction" that is fundamental to understanding how language actually works. What we see and what we come to believe "abstracts" from reality, or from whatever is actually out there that we can never know completely. In other words, the "map" of our vision and our concepts is never the same as the "territory" of the reality we are looking at. Given this distance between ourselves and reality, Alfred Korzybski, the founder of the field of general semantics (1933), stressed the importance of becoming "conscious of abstraction." More specifically, what we see and what we believe about what we see is a product of both what is in the world and what is in our own heads. Every image and every concept we have is, then, a result of the interaction between the individual and the world. To understand how language works, then, we must come to see it as an interactive process, just as interaction is so fundamental to all aspects of our world.

What Mills is writing about here is the importance for social scientists to avoid—in their efforts to explain phenomena—using concepts that are only at a "low" level of abstraction and, instead, to move up to concepts at a high level of abstraction like "stratifications." In other words, sociologists should take seriously the technical concepts—like "social stratification"—that are quite general and that differ from the far more specific concepts that we all use in everyday life, like "rape in rural districts." As another example of the failures of sociologists to move up from a low level of abstraction to a high level—or, metaphorically, to move up the "ladder" of abstraction—different sections of the American Sociological Association focus on different kinds of persisting hierarchy, as illustrated by such hierarchical behavior as racism, sexism, classism, ageism, and ethnocentrism.

By moving up the ladder we lose specificity but we gain generality. By moving down we gain specificity but lose generality. Yet by moving both up and down we gain both generality and specificity. Indeed, this is the way language works in general and not just in the academic world. When we move up from "rose" to "flower" we gain generality, and when we move down to "rose" we gain specificity.

Mills himself was explicit about the importance of such movement both up and down language's ladder of abstraction, as he made clear in his most influential book at the end of his career, *The Sociological Imagination*:

> One great lesson that we can learn from its systematic absence in the work of the grand theorists is that every self-conscious thinker must at all times be aware of—and hence be able to control—the levels of abstraction on which he is working. The capacity to shuttle between levels of abstraction, with ease and with clarity, is a signal mark of the imaginative and systematic thinker (1959: 34).

It was in that book that he castigated "grand theorists" for failing to come far down the ladder of abstraction. And, equally, he criticized "abstracted empiricists" for not moving far up that ladder.

We can make good use of Mills's idea of shuttling up and down language's ladder of abstraction by shuttling very far up that ladder, even to the fundamental assumptions that shape the scientific method itself, namely, our worldview. It is here that the scientist's focus is not limited to the examination of external phenomena but also includes his or her own assumptions and beliefs about the nature of reality. For example, researchers centering on sexism could learn to probe the nature of their own metaphysical assumptions and come to see how their bureaucratic worldview works against their understanding of sexism by not seeing that pattern of hierarchy in relation to other patterns of hierarchy: racism, ageism, classism, and ethnocentrism. In other words, they could come to see how their worldview works against the ideal of the scientific method that calls for their opening up to the full range of phenomena that are relevant to the problem they are investigating. And by so doing—assuming that they envision an alternative worldview that promises to follow that scientific ideal and help them with understanding sexism—they may move toward abandoning their bureaucratic worldview and toward adopting that alternative worldview.

Mills emphasized certain key sociological concepts, like social stratification, and he gave us a vision of an approach to sociology that is broad enough to encompass the various social sciences. Yet it is one thing to develop a broad approach to knowledge and quite another thing to develop the concepts that can actually achieve the breadth of understanding that Mills called for. What is required is nothing less than a systematic approach for integrating the shattered bits and pieces of knowledge buried in our libraries that make up the literature of the social sciences. More specifically, what we require is a system of general concepts deriving from the literature of sociology that are sufficiently integrated to penetrate the enormous complexity of human behavior and social problems. This is no simple matter, given the existence of 46 sections of the American Sociological Association, no less than 400 specialized areas within the discipline, and literally thousands of social science concepts. However, the 6 books developed by the Sociological Imagination Group over the past decade—all of which focus on movement toward an evolutionary worldview with its emphasis on the integration of knowledge—have given us a running start.

To understand more clearly the importance of a language of social science, we might compare it to the language of physics or chemistry. Without its technical concepts—like force, mass, valence, and nucleus— physical science would not get very far. Alvin W. Gouldner, a sociologist whose work overlapped with and also followed that of Mills, can help us to understand more clearly the importance of working with the language of social science. It is this language, following Mills's idea of shuttling up and down language's ladder of abstraction, that can take us far beyond our everyday concepts like "rape in rural districts."

In the following quote, Gouldner comments on the role of social science language two years after the publication of his *The Coming Crisis of Western Sociology* (1970), a book that pointed in an evolutionary direction:

> The pursuit of . . . understanding, however, cannot promise that men as we now find them, with their everyday language and understanding, will always be capable of further understanding and of liberating themselves. At decisive points the ordinary language and conventional understandings fail and must be transcended. It is essentially the task of the social sciences, more generally, to create new and "extraordinary" languages, to help men learn to speak them, and to mediate between the deficient understandings of ordinary language and the different and liberating perspectives of the extraordinary languages of social theory. . . . To say social theorists are concept-creators means that they are not merely in the knowledge-creating business, but also in the language-reform and language-creating business. In other words, they are from the beginning involved in creating a new culture (Gouldner 1972: 16).

Social science language, relative to ordinary language, is "extraordinary." For one thing, it is language that communicates the research within the social sciences. For another thing, it is generally more abstract than our everyday language, as illustrated by the concepts of bureaucracy and social stratification, and thus it can work to integrate a great deal of our knowledge. For yet another thing, it is sufficiently abstract so as to reach up to our invisible fundamental assumptions or worldview. And for still another thing, social science language can reach far down language's ladder of abstraction so as to relate to our everyday concepts. Yet it is by no means a replacement for ordinary language, which we may see as generally lower on language's ladder of abstraction. Rather, the social scientist shuttles up and down language's ladder of abstraction, following Mills's orientation. Not only is ordinary language "deficient" by itself, but social science language is also deficient by itself. However, by shuttling up and down that ladder we gain both generality and concreteness. We might note as well that Gouldner is not merely writing about the progress of social science. He is centered on the business of sociologists proceeding to "help men learn to speak" the extraordinary language of social science. It is in that way that we can all learn to use the broad approach to the scientific method that this language embodies. And the social scientist must learn to speak that language no less than everyone else.

The language of social science is, more specifically, the set of concepts together with their relationships that embody what social scientists have discovered about human behavior. Gouldner called that language an "extraordinary" language not only because it differs from the vernacular language that we use in everyday speech, but also because it carries with it insights about how we behave that social scientists have developed during the many years of their investigations. For example, we have emphasized the concept of "bureaucracy" in the above pages, a concept that includes the idea of persisting hierarchy or "social stratification," two of the important concepts within this language of social science. They both describe patterns of behavior to be found throughout any given society. Other concepts within the language of social science will be found in Figures 2-1, 3-1, 4-1, and 5-1. They have to do with the behavior of the individual, the group, and society as a whole, with some of these concepts focusing on the momentary situation and most of them emphasizing long-term patterns of behavior.

It is this extraordinary language of the social sciences that is fundamental to the way the scientific method works within these disciplines. If we return to the pendulum metaphor for the scientific method, it is that language that helps us to swing that pendulum far to the left, where we become aware of and committed to making progress on a problem. For that awareness and commitment requires that we build on what scientists have learned about that problem in the past. And the language of social science is equally important for our swing to the right, where we make progress toward solving that problem. For example, if our problem is understanding how persisting hierarchy might be reduced, then the concept of stratification is essential if we are to gain such understanding.

Given the importance of the scientific method for our argument throughout this book, it would be useful to define that method explicitly and not merely rely on the metaphor of a swinging pendulum. The scientific method is a procedure for solving problems that (1) defines problems so as to build on relevant previous knowledge; (2) develops ideas, hypotheses, or theories for making progress on those problems; (3) tests these ideas against experiences (such as available data, observations, or experiments); (4) assesses the researcher's impact on the research process; (5) uses procedures for analysis to develop conclusions about the applicability of those ideas, hypotheses, or theories; and (6) repeats this process as often as is required to make sufficient progress on the problem. Unfortunately, these high standards for the scientific method are rarely followed throughout the social sciences and even in the biophysical sciences. For example, "relevant knowledge" within (1) is almost invariably defined far too narrowly to confront the complexity of human behavior. As for (2) and (4), those ideas almost never include people's worldview or the worldview of the investigator. Concerning (5), a wide range of quantitative and qualitative procedures is rarely used.

The following section will outline our overall efforts to develop a direction in this book for moving from a bureaucratic to an evolutionary way of life in the remaining chapters. As for the nature of the "extraordinary" language of social science, that is central to our efforts in the chapters to follow, just as it was central to our efforts in previous books. Beyond our discussion of the incredible potential of language coupled with the scientific method, it is essential that we build on that discussion by demonstrating just how those tools can help us penetrate the complexity of human behavior and escalating social problems. More specifically, we must make use of the extraordinary language of social science within a scientific approach to those tasks. We learn any language because it proves to be useful in helping us to solve our problems. The scientific method is our best problem-solving technique, and the extraordinary language of social science is a crucial part of that method. We are convinced that by learning to use the scientific method in our everyday lives we can indeed learn to make steady progress in solving the escalating problems of modern society as well as our personal problems. And even beyond that, we can continue to develop our "head," "heart," and "hand" with no limit whatsoever. By so doing, the extraordinary language of social science will become part of our everyday language, for it will help us to fulfill our potential as human beings.

To illustrate further the importance of that extraordinary language, without the concept of bureaucracy—a key idea within that language— how far would we be able to go in understanding the combination of forces that are working against our movement toward ever greater interaction? Alternatively, we might use "bureaucracy" as a kind of swear word, invoking images such as that of long lines standing in front of us, or endless forms that we are required to fill out, or faceless clerks who refuse to take into account our personal situation as they proceed to behave inflexibly. But by so doing how would we be able to understand in a systematic way the several forces within an organization that come together to create those long lines, those forms, and those clerks? And how would we begin to understand the nature of a bureaucratic way of life? In Chapter 1 we have no more than begun to understand the nature of bureaucracy, and in the chapters to follow we shall open up to the nature of this concept in greater detail. Yet "bureaucracy" is no more than a single concept within the extraordinary language of social science, and its systematic links with other concepts from that language can carry our understanding of the forces operating within society and the individual much further.

Plan of the Book

In Part II, Chapters 2, 3, and 4, we will examine our bureaucratic way of life in greater detail with the aid of a broad scientific method that builds on an evolutionary worldview—as outlined in Figure 1-3—and makes use of social science's extraordinary language. More specifically, as suggested by the chapter headings in the table of contents, Chapter 2 will focus on the "head," Chapter 3 on the "heart," and Chapter 4 on the "hand." For we must move widely over the range of human behavior—by contrast with the highly specialized approach throughout the social sciences—in order to make progress in understanding the nature of our bureaucratic behavior. Following the interactive approach of a scientific method that follows scientific ideals, we shall move very far up language's ladder of abstraction—even up to the level of our worldview or metaphysical assumptions—and also move very far down that ladder to the concrete concepts that we all use in everyday life.

Our approach in Part III, Chapters 5, 6, and 7, where we look to the nature of an evolutionary way of life, will be much the same. It is in these chapters that we describe in some detail our overall approach to confronting our escalating problems. This involves using the scientific method within the context of what we have called "the East-West strategy" and "deep dialogue." That approach contrasts sharply with the Eastern or Western strategy that we presently use—involving emotional repression—along with a scientific method that fails to follow the ideals of that method, which calls for broad and interactive behavior. And it also contrasts with our present patterns of dialogue or conversation that fail to invoke our fundamental assumptions or worldview.

Both Part II and Part III build on the extraordinary language of social science. Let us not forget that it is our limited use of the infinite potential of language—and our limited use of a scientific method that builds on that potential—that has held all of us back from continuing on our evolutionary journey. This is the case not only for biophysical scientists and those in the humanities but for social scientists as well, and it is also the case for the rest of us. It is indeed difficult for us to understand the implications of our failure, a failure that can be traced to social scientists more than any other group. For our bureaucratic way of life works to prevent us from looking very deeply into the future and seeing what we believe to be nothing less than the end of our species. However, learning that language can help us not merely to move ever more deeply into understanding the complexities of human behavior and world problems, but also ever more deeply into pulling our own "head," "heart," and "hand" together. That integration of self is what C. Wright Mills was somehow able to achieve without the benefits of working with an extraordinary language or working with others like those in the Sociological Imagination Group. The emotional commitment that he achieved—building on his intellectual breadth—enabled him to prepare the way for the rest of us to stand on his shoulders. This book will introduce what we see as key elements of that extraordinary language, concepts that can become the basis for our learning to apply that language to personal and world problems, granting that others in the future will be able to do a better job than we can do at this time. Our task—both for readers and authors—lies beyond this book: learning to integrate that language into our everyday thoughts, feelings, and actions. That will be a never-ending task.

Part IV is our vision of Bali Ha'i: the idea that we can all learn to use a broad scientific method in our everyday lives. This is not an image of a static utopia but rather a vision of how we can move from where we presently are—with all of our problems—taking one step at a time toward the development of our human potential. It is here that we invoke our two most powerful tools, joined together: a scientific method that follows scientific ideals coupled with the infinite potentials of language. It is the East-West strategy that embodies this approach, a strategy not only for confronting personal and world problems but also for continuing to evolve far beyond our present problems, with no limit whatsoever to our continuing development. Although we humans presently are the most interactive creatures throughout the known universe, our bureaucratic worldview sharply limits our ability to move toward our infinite capacities. Yet we can learn to move toward an evolutionary worldview that will free us from those limitations. Granting the enormous and increasing problems confronting the human race at this time in history, we believe that growing awareness of those problems can succeed in motivating us to put our incredible human capacities to work on them.

PART TWO

Extinction

As we proceed to move further into understanding a bureaucratic way of life, we should continue to focus on the central problem linked to that way of life: the gap between our aspirations and their fulfillment. It is a gap that has to do with the full range of our desires or goals, impacting the full range of our problems. And if that gap continues to increase, it will reach a point of no return with catastrophic consequences throughout the world. If this problem were something visible—like the threat of war, nuclear proliferation, or environmental pollution—we could learn to confront it far more easily. Yet it is almost completely invisible and, as a result, it becomes most difficult to confront. This is why our learning to use the extraordinary language of social science is so vital. For that language—with its breadth and focus on human behavior—can help us to become aware of that gap.

It is in Chapters 2, 3, and 4 that we introduce the extraordinary language of social science with the aid of Figures 2-1, 3-1, and 4-1. Those figures cover the waterfront of human behavior, centering on "head," "heart," and "hand," respectively. But they are not limited to a focus on the individual, for they also have to do with perception or thought, emotion and action, respectively, that are widely shared throughout society. These concepts of the extraordinary language are sufficiently broad that we are able to integrate our ordinary language concepts within them. Here, then, is at least part of the "loom" that Edna St Vincent Millay called for in order to "weave into fabric" our "meteoric shower of facts."

It is the contrast between our ordinary language and this extraordinary language that can help us to understand more fully the contribution of the latter. A key idea we need is the distinction between situational behavior that is not repeated and behavior that is repeated in one situation after another. It is such repetition that is the nature of "structures," which have to do with the persistence of phenomena in scene after scene. The extraordinary language focuses on structures, and it contrasts with our focus on nonrepetitive situational language in our everyday speech. As a result, within that speech there is little interaction and integration among our ordinary concepts. Yet it is when we proceed to integrate those structural concepts from the language of social science with our everyday situationally oriented vocabulary that we succeed in integrating our knowledge of human behavior. It is this integration that promises to give us the tools that we need to confront ever more effectively our increasing aspirations-fulfillment gap.

By so doing, we follow Mills's strategy—as discussed in Chapter 1—of shuttling up and down language's ladder of abstraction. For example, there is the concept of social stratification that is higher up on the ladder of abstraction than the concepts of sexism, racism, ageism, classism, and ethnocentrism, yet "social stratification" has to do with all of those less abstract concepts through its focus on persisting hierarchy. By moving up and down from those less abstract concepts to the more abstract concept of social stratification, we come to understand more fully both the idea of social stratification and the ideas of those less abstract concepts. And in this way we move toward integrating the knowledge within the 46 sections of the American Sociological Association that presently remain divided from one another. In the same way, when we learn to move down language's ladder of abstraction from more abstract structural concepts within the extraordinary language to the situational language of our everyday vocabulary, we learn to integrate our social science knowledge with our everyday commonsense knowledge, yielding an ever deeper understanding of the problems that we face, such as our increasing aspirations-fulfillment gap.

Yet it is one thing to discuss the differences between the extraordinary language and our everyday language, and it is quite another thing to actually combine the two languages and employ both within our everyday behavior from one moment to the next. We have had a period of some five centuries during which—given the enormous successes of the physical and biological sciences—we have learned to pay attention to physical and biological structures by contrast with personality and social structures. It is our ordinary language that has come to emphasize physical and biological structures, while the extraordinary language emphasizes the reality of personality and social structures, a reality that we fail to emphasize. Chapters 2, 3, and 4 can help us begin to see what is ordinarily invisible, namely, basic personality and social structures that are invoked by the extraordinary language.

Here, the metaphors of "head," "heart," and "hand" can help, and those ideas will be our focus in chapters 2, 3, and 4, respectively. They apply to society—focusing on behavior that is widely shared—no less than to the individual. We can come to focus on those metaphors more easily by linking them to the classic 1939 film *The Wizard of Oz,* based on Lyman Frank Baum's *The Wonderful Wizard of Oz* (1900/2006). Ray Bolger appeared as the Scarecrow whose "head" was filled with straw; Jack Haley played the Tin Woodsman without a "heart"; and Bert Lahr was the Cowardly Lion without the courage to act, suggesting a failure of the "hand." And Judy Garland played Dorothy, whose understanding, commitment to return to Kansas, and caring relationships with her newfound friends merged to combine "head," "heart," and "hand."

CHAPTER 2

"Head"

Outward Perception and Thought

CHAPTER 1 PRESENTED A SHARP CONTRAST between a bureaucratic and an evolutionary way of life with its Figures 1-2 and 1-3. Yet before plunging ahead into Figure 2-1 with its presentation of the portion of the extraordinary language linked to the "head" and focused on a bureaucratic way of life, it would be most useful to present some details on that way of life as it has actually developed. For bureaucratic organizations have in fact achieved a certain degree of communication, by contrast with the lack of communication presented in Figure 1-2a, for otherwise they never would have attained at least their limited degree of success. And the same is true for us bureaucratic individuals, as presented in Figure 1-2b, for we would not be able to survive without at least some degree of integration of "head," "heart," and "hand." In this way we'll move into a position to understand just how we can make use of the extraordinary language of social science to take next steps in an evolutionary direction.

Max Weber—a founder of sociology whose *Economy and Society* (1964) was voted by the members of the International Sociology Association as the most influential book for sociologists throughout the entire twentieth century—has shaped most of the studies of bureaucracy since his time. To understand his view of bureaucracy we must adopt his long-term historical perspective, where he compared organizations in his own day of the late nineteenth and early twentieth centuries with European preindustrial organizations during the Middle Ages and in ancient times. Before the scientific revolution in Western Europe starting in the sixteenth century— and before the industrial revolution that followed it shortly afterwards— preindustrial organizations lacked the specialized scientific knowledge that came later along with the further development of universities. More generally, they lacked the newly developing scientific spirit that no longer bowed down to the authority of the church and the nobility as to what is true and false and what should and should not be done. Instead, organizations like universities, businesses, and armies came to be organized by people who had opened up to the new scientific spirit of the age. That spirit was reinforced by the invention of the printing press, by the explorers who discovered the New World of the Americas, by the Renaissance that recovered the learning of ancient Greece and Rome, and by the Protestant Reformation that questioned the authority of the church hierarchy.

Thus, although we can speak of preindustrial bureaucracy as well as modern bureaucracy, the modern type is substantially different in that it builds on—and fosters—the scientific and technological revolutions that are continuing to this day. By so doing, modern bureaucracy invokes the full knowledge and power that the biophysical sciences and their technologies have developed over the centuries. Yet Weber himself was aware of the limitations of modern bureaucracy, granted that he saw no alternative to it that would be more effective. In particular, he was much concerned by bureaucratic rigidity, the materialistic focus of a capitalistic economy, and the impact of that economy along with its bureaucratic organizations on those working within them. Near the end of his widely known *The Protestant Ethic and the Spirit of Capitalism* he wrote:

> In Baxter's view the care for external goods should only lie on the shoulders of the "saint like a light cloak, which can be thrown aside at any moment." But fate decreed that the cloak should become an *iron cage*. . . . No one knows who will live in this cage in the future, or whether at the end of this tremendous development entirely new prophets will arise, or there will be a great rebirth of old ideas and ideals, or, if neither, mechanized petrification, embellished with a sort of convulsive self-importance. For of the last stage of this cultural development, it might well be truly said: "Specialists without spirit, sensualists without heart; this nullity imagines that it has attained a level of civilization never before achieved" (Weber 1905/1958: 181–182; italics ours).

Although many social scientists since Weber's time have found fundamental problems with modern bureaucracies—such as failures at internal and external communication, ineffectiveness in efforts to solve problems, rigidity in the face of change, and insensitivity to the needs of those being served by the bureaucracy—little has been done to develop other forms of organization to replace bureaucracies. Yet despite all of the research indicating severe problems within our bureaucratic organizations—such as the failure of the CIA, the FBI, and the NSA to communicate with one another so as to anticipate the 9/11 catastrophe—no new kind of group has emerged to replace them. Instead, for example, the report of the 9/11 Commission not only failed to suggest the replacement of federal bureaucracies with a more communicative kind of group, but it also failed to cite social science research on the limitations of bureaucracies or on anything else. Yet it is little wonder that, for all of the research indicating the failures of bureaucracies, no effort to eliminate them in favor of a more effective type of group has as yet proved to be successful. For if bureaucracies reflect both our bureaucratic worldview as well as our own bureaucratic personalities, then we can expect no elimination of our bureaucracies unless we succeed in changing our bureaucratic worldview.

However, two researchers, Helen Constas (1958) and Stanley Udy (1959; see also Phillips 2008: 135–136) have charted a different or non-bureaucratic kind of organization that we might simply call a "group." A group is an aggregate or collection of individuals who repeatedly interact with one another directly or indirectly. Udy, whose research was based on the earlier analyses of Constas, focused on the 7 characteristics of bureaucracy that Weber had specified, selecting 150 organizations producing material goods from 150 societies. Those seven characteristics were divided into two sets: Three of them were, in his view, bureaucratic, yielding a substantial division of labor, an extensive hierarchy involving three or more levels, and rewards distributed according to one's position in the hierarchy. The other four characteristics were, in his view, "rational" or "scientific": They had limited objectives so as to enable the organization to achieve a focus; an emphasis on performance so that rewards are dependent on achievement; specification of limitations on the involvement of those within the organization on external commitments; and rewards given to those with lower authority in return for their participation. He found that that the three bureaucratic characteristics tended to occur when the four scientific characteristics did not, and vice-versa, and he concluded that the bureaucratic characteristics were opposed to the scientific ones, revealing the contradictory nature of bureaucracies, not only as Weber defined them but also as they presently exist throughout the world.

There is a parallel here between what Weber found to be a key basis for the advantages of modern over preindustrial bureaucracies, on the one hand, and what Constas and Udy found to be the most effective aspects of bureaucracies, on the other hand. It is the scientific aspects of modern bureaucracies that give them their effectiveness. Yet neither Weber nor Constas nor Udy was aware of the importance of linking the scientific method with its usage of language, just as Mills succeeded in doing with his focus on the importance of shuttling up and down the ladder of abstraction, and just as we have emphasized in Chapter 1. The languages of physical and biological science are well integrated, as illustrated by their usage—especially within physical science—of mathematics to link phenomena in a highly systematic way. And if we combine the relative simplicity of physical and biological structures—by contrast with social and personality structures—together with this integrated approach to language, we can begin to understand the enormous successes of the physical and biological sciences. We can also understand the importance of an approach to the scientific method that pays close attention to that method's orientation to language.

Does this analysis overturn our description of bureaucracies as characterized by the isolation of phenomena—as portrayed in Figure 1-2—by contrast with their interaction? Only partly. We can see that our previous analysis was too one-sided. We emphasized a dichotomous approach in that initial analysis of bureaucracy, and by so doing we ignored a more detailed or sophisticated gradational analysis. Yet it has been and still is the failure of physical and biological science to pay serious attention to human behavior—and in particular the findings of social scientists—that conveys their limited approach to integrating knowledge, granting their successes with physical and biological structures. The barriers between the phenomena depicted in Figure 1-2a still apply to these sciences once we see them as barriers between biophysical phenomena and human behavior.

Yet despite this limitation, the successes of those sciences have much to teach us about the importance of the systematic integration of phenomena as well as the importance of the approach to language within the scientific method. From this perspective, it is not just physical and biological science that excludes the social sciences from consideration: It is contemporary bureaucracy as well. And if it is indeed attention to science that has given present-day bureaucracies their effectiveness over preindustrial bureaucracies—as implied by the work of Weber, Constas, and Udy—then we might expect that their inclusion of attention to social science will yield greater effectiveness.

However, let us not forget here the importance for bureaucratic organizations of using the metaphorical language of the humanities for achieving the integration of knowledge along with effective communication. It was in Chapter 1 that we distinguished among the dichotomous emphasis within social science, gradational emphasis within biophysical science, and the metaphorical or figurative emphasis within the humanities, concluding that all three are important for the progress of science. Yet just as bureaucratic organizations generally exclude social science language, so do they generally do much the same in the case of the metaphorical language of the humanities. Here again, Figure 1-2a describes the situation of bureaucracies. Granting their ability to integrate knowledge of physical and biological phenomena, metaphorical language could help them to do a better job of integration.

Our analysis of bureaucracy in these few pages can give us a more realistic view of its accomplishments, by contrast with a completely negative and stereotypical understanding of it. Yet its strengths with respect to an understanding and use of physical and biological science—coupled with its weaknesses with respect to human behavior—have produced an increasingly dangerous situation for all of us. In the chapters to follow we shall probe the nature of those dangers in greater detail. In this chapter our focus will be on those dangers with respect to the "head," including such phenomena as our perception and thought. We shall focus in particular on introducing related concepts within the extraordinary language of social science. We begin with a section on outward perception and thought—by contrast with inward-outward perception and thought—that is fundamental to a bureaucratic way of life, given that perception is what we all do from one moment to the next. We continue with a section on self-image, a concept that meshes hand-in-glove with our worldview, the title of our third section. It is these two very abstract concepts, working together, that provide the most general framework for our bureaucratic way of life. For example, if our bureaucratic worldview orients our perception outward, then this orients our self-image toward seeing ourselves as quite limited. Correspondingly, a limited view of self encourages us to look outward. Our final section, the scientific method—linked closely to language, the human being's most powerful tool—probes our limited procedures for understanding our world and ourselves. Our aim throughout this chapter is to demonstrate the power of the concepts we introduce—within the extraordinary language of social science—for yielding understanding of our bureaucratic way of life, and also for opening us up to an alternative.

Before proceeding to these sections, it would be most useful to have in mind the general picture of the extraordinary language insofar as it bears on the "head." To this end, Figure 2-1 presents that language. Although the concepts in Figure 2-1 will be explained and illustrated in the sections of Chapter 2, a few general remarks can help to introduce them. For one thing, all of these concepts are structures in that they involve repetitive behavior and in that they are relatively abstract. Further, they are all linked together systematically, just as individual worldview is tied to cultural worldview, beliefs and assumptions are tied to cultural norms, and personality structure is tied to social structure As a result, we can use these concepts from the extraordinary language of social science to work toward integrating the concepts that we all use in everyday life—concepts that generally are more concrete and situational and that generally are not integrated—so as to develop our understanding to an increasing extent. At first, we can do that intellectually in this book with its focus on the "head." Beyond this book, we can proceed to develop "heart" and "hand" by becoming committed to using them in everyday life and actually using them to demonstrate their ability to help us solve problems.

Figure 2–1. "Head": Outward Perception and Thought and Other Structures

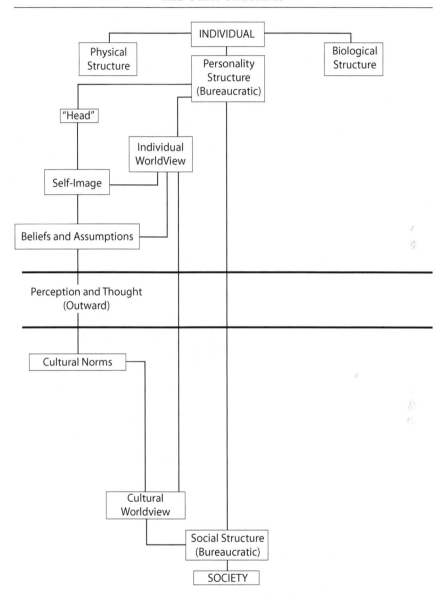

By contrast with this approach, the bureaucratic worldview operating throughout society fails to pay attention to these structural concepts and to how they are related to one another, keeping social science knowledge in the libraries rather than in the heads of political leaders and the rest of us. As a result, we all remain most limited in our ability to integrate knowledge and, as a result, in our ability to understand how to solve problems. Social scientists have at least developed these structural concepts that have the potential to integrate our knowledge. However, given the operation of their bureaucratic worldview—and ours as well—they have not proceeded to integrate those concepts systematically and, in addition, worked toward using them as a basis for integrating them with our everyday commonsense knowledge. In this book, by contrast, we hope to illustrate such integration and demonstrate its problem-solving potential.

Our first order of business, however, is to understand where we are before we can move forward. That is why our focus in Part II is on extinction rather than on evolution. The abstract concepts in Figure 2-1 and their relationships to one another point to where we are at the present time, namely, to our bureaucratic way of life. But those concepts in Figure 2-1 that we are using as tools to understand our present situation along with their relationships can help us gain the understanding that we require to move toward a different way of life. They are part of an image of a possible future for all of us, assuming that they can in fact help us to solve our growing problems. By contrast, intellectually, emotionally, and in our actions we are shattered souls, unable to integrate more than a tiny portion of the knowledge available to us and, as a result, at the mercy of escalating problems that threaten our very survival. Awareness of this situation is vital if we are to pay sufficient attention to Figure 2-1 along with the words in this book so as to give them a chance to help us at this time in history. How are we, then, to understand the forces that have propelled us—and are continuing to propel us—into our bureaucratic way of life? Granting our efforts over centuries to counter the limitations of that way of life, why have they proved to have been largely unsuccessful? What are the key concepts from social science's extraordinary language that can help us to understand our situation, and how are they related to one another?

Outward Perception and Thought

Just as Alvin Gouldner alerted us to the importance of the extraordinary language of social science—as discussed in Chapter 1—so did he alert sociologists to the importance of what he called "a reflexive sociology":

> What sociologists now most require from a Reflexive Sociology, however, is not just one more specialization, not just another topic for

panel meetings at professional conventions.... The historical mission of a Reflexive Sociology as I conceive it, however, would be to transform the sociologist, to penetrate deeply into his daily life and work, enriching them with new sensitivities, and to raise the sociologist's self-awareness to a new historical level.... A Reflexive Sociology means that we sociologists must—at the very least—acquire the ingrained habit of viewing our own beliefs as we now view those held by others ... (Gouldner 1970: 487).

A broad approach to the scientific method requires that the researcher look to his or her own impact on every phase of the research process. This appears to be a most obvious idea, especially for sociologists who focus much of their work on learning about the impact of people on one another. Strangely enough, however, sociologists and other social scientists only rarely attempt to assess what we may call the "investigator effect." However, this lack of reflexivity appears to be a general phenomenon to be found throughout society and not just among social scientists. Some 2,500 years ago, Socrates claimed that "the unexamined life is not worth living." We also have a similar idea from the Bible: "Physician, heal thyself." Much the same idea was put forward by Walt Kelly's comic-strip character, the opossum Pogo, upon seeing litter under a tree: "We have met the enemy, and he is us," Kelly took off on Commodore Oliver Hazard Perry's report of his victory over the British in the battle of Lake Erie: "We have met the enemy, and they are ours."

Despite such ideas pointing up the importance of a reflexive orientation, it appears that we all have great difficulty in looking inward and paying attention to ourselves for any length of time. It should be no surprise that we have developed no more than a limited ability to look inward rather than outward for more than tiny stretches of time. This was the thesis of Gurdjieff, a Russian scholar of the early twentieth century who was much influenced by Eastern thought, particularly Indian and Buddhist teachings. P.D. Ouspensky, a student of Gurdjieff, recorded his teachings as including the idea of "identification": that "we become too absorbed in things, too lost in things ... We identify with things" (Ouspensky 1957/1971: 12). For example, this appears to be what we do while watching film or plays, or when we read novels: We identify with the hero or heroine.

Gurdjieff and Ouspensky focused on Eastern thought. Ouspensky's presentation of Gurdjieff's ideas can yield further insight into the nature of our outward orientation to our perception and thought:

> The chief idea of this system was that we do not use even a small part of our powers and our forces.... If we begin to study ourselves we first of all come up against one word which we use more than any other and

that is the word "I." We say "I am doing," "I am sitting," "I feel," "I like," "I dislike" and so on. This is our chief illusion ... we consider ourselves one ... and we suppose that we refer to the same thing all the time when in reality we are divided into hundreds of different "I"s.... So in self-observation.... generally you do not *remember yourself*.... because you cannot remember yourself, you cannot concentrate, and ... you have no will. If you could remember yourself, you would have will and could do what you liked .... You may sometimes have will for a short time, but it turns to something else and you forget about it....

[W]e become too absorbed in things, too lost in things .... This is called identification .... The idea of identification exists in Indian writings and the Buddhists speak of attachment and nonattachment.... For me personally, in the beginning, the most interesting idea was that of self-remembering. I simply could not understand how people could miss such a thing. All European philosophy and psychology just missed this point.... we are really asleep. We only imagine that we are awake. So when we try to remember ourselves it means only one thing—we try to awake. And we do awake for a second but then we fall asleep again.... This group I met in Moscow used oriental metaphors and parables, and one of the things they liked to speak about was prison—that man is in prison ... he can wish for only one thing—to escape. (Ouspensky 1957/1971: 3-4, 12-13).

Although the focus of this excerpt is on the problem of moving toward inward perception and thought—and away from our overriding emphasis on outward perception and thought—it begins with the idea of the incredible potential of the human being. And it is also optimistic near the end, when Gurdjieff claims the following: "We can awake only if we correct many things ... and if we work very persistently on this idea of awaking, and for a long time (Ouspensky 1957/1971: 13). His reference to oriental thought, and Buddhism in particular, reminds us of the importance of Eastern thought in moving toward inward perception and ideas. The overall emphasis of the excerpt is on the immense difficulty of such movement, and of our continuing focus on outward thought. For example, we remain unable to remember ourselves for extended periods of time, and as a result we have no will, that is, we cannot motivate ourselves to solve any given problem we want to solve. Further, when we use "I" to refer to ourselves, although we like to think that we are a unitary being, in fact we are nothing of the kind: We are shattered into hundreds of pieces. Metaphorically, we continue to be asleep, or alternatively, we continue to remain in prison. And Western psychology and philosophy—along with our own understanding—has almost completely avoided awareness of our true situation as individual human beings.

If we look to Figure 1-2a, we can see the bureaucratic basis for our failure to pay attention to ourselves as we experience life in one scene after another: That way of life and the language that it emphasizes works toward separating phenomena from one another and against tying them together, such as an ability to see ourselves seeing external phenomena and not just seeing either external phenomena or seeing ourselves. The failure of social scientists to investigate the investigator effect is a case in point, for that would require them to link their own behavior with the behavior of those they are studying. And if social scientists—who should know better, given their professional orientation—fail to accomplish this, then this fact speaks worlds about the inability of the rest of us to link the inner with the outer. We might, then, see the advice of Socrates, of Gouldner, and of Pogo as very limited efforts to counter forces that are incredibly powerful, forces linked to our bureaucratic way of life.

We might also look to Figure 1-2b for further insight into our orientation to outward perception and thought. In that figure we may note the barrier between perception and thought, on the one hand, and emotions, on the other hand. Ouspensky refers to this by claiming that our outward orientation results in a lack of "will" and an inability to act: "because you cannot remember yourself, you cannot concentrate, and ... you have no will. If you could remember yourself, you would have will and could do what you liked.... You may sometimes have will for a short time, but it turns to something else and you forget about it...." Thus, "head" affects both "heart" and "hand." Yet this impact of our outward orientation is not limited to the personality of the individual, as we can see to some extent in Figure 1-2a: It also has a profound impact on society as a whole. For society is made up of individuals with an outward orientation, and as a result social structures have developed that emphasize such an orientation.

Given the importance of the extraordinary language for helping us to understand our situation, and given the illustrations that we now have, let us turn to Figure 2-1. The prevalence of our outward orientation to perception and thought suggests that there are indeed powerful forces shaping that orientation. We have been arguing that it is our bureaucratic worldview, which has succeeded in shaping nothing less than personality and social structures, that lies behind that outward orientation. Here, we might distinguish between perception and thought. Perception has to do with an individual's sensations derived from sight, hearing, touching, tasting, and smelling. By contrast, ideas or thoughts are based on language. Animals other than humans have no complex language, so that it is their perceptions that guide their motivations and actions. For us humans with a complex language, however, our situation is far more complicated, since our perceptions are affected by our thoughts, and vice-versa. That is why we have lumped the two together. More generally, our biological structure has shaped our patterns of perception, but so have our experiences as individuals in society. This suggests that our outward orientation has been and can be shaped by our experiences in society. Granting that our bureaucratic worldview has pointed us outward, such behavior is not fixed for all time. Indeed, Gurdjieff and Ouspensky argued that it can be changed, although that would take considerable effort. Our own view is much the same. It will be in Part Three that we will focus on procedures for achieving that change. Yet those procedures require, first and foremost, awareness of our present situation of an orientation to outward perception and thought.

Figure 2–1 is arranged so that the lowest level on the ladder of abstraction is located within the pair of horizontal lines, namely, perception and thought. As we move up from those lines we move toward more abstract concepts, and as we move down from those lines we also move toward more abstract concepts. Thus, we have two ladders of abstraction that point in opposite directions, with the lowest rung of each ladder located within those lines. Using this metaphor, "beliefs and assumptions" are located at the next rung of the ladder pointing upward, and "cultural norms" are located at the next rung of the ladder pointing downward. Given our outward orientation to perception and thought, it is the phenomena depicted by the upper ladder that escape our attention. By contrast, within an evolutionary worldview with its orientation both inward and outward, the phenomena invoked by both ladders become important.

As for that next rung of the ladder pointing upward—beliefs and assumptions—these are repetitive behaviors or structures, by comparison with the situational behavior invoked by "perception and thought." We have placed situational behavior within those horizontal lines to emphasize its distinction from the structures to be found outside of those lines. Yet these concepts from the extraordinary language within those horizontal lines of Figure 2-1 are structures, granting that they invoke our everyday situational behavior. In order to understand how change comes about, it is essential for us to take into account both situational and structural behavior. For a structure, like a given belief, results from the repetition of experiences within one scene after another, and that structure in turn works to shape what happens within a new situation. Social scientists have emphasized structural behavior at the expense of situational behavior, and that has helped them to integrate phenomena. Yet it is also important both to link structural to situational behavior as well as to link structural behavior together in order to penetrate the complexity of human behavior.

As for the nature of beliefs and assumptions, these are elementary concepts that invoke relatively simple rather than complex behavior. We reserve belief in a bureaucratic worldview for the concept of worldview, which opens up to complexity. Just as beliefs and assumptions are elemental illustrations of the "head," so are emotions and actions—to be taken up in Chapters 3 and 4, respectively, elemental illustrations of the "heart" and the "hand." We believe that it is important to distinguish between beliefs and assumptions, granting that both concepts are structures. Beliefs are persisting thoughts, ideas, or opinions of an individual or group, whereas assumptions are beliefs that may be invisible to the individual or group. Assumptions may become invisible as a result of their clashing with beliefs that are dear to us, given an overall situation where we remain unable to face up to this contradiction or conflict. For example, we know of billions of people throughout the world living on the edge of starvation, and we are also aware of multibillionaires, all of which is linked to present-day political and economic systems. If we remain unable to come up with alternative systems then we learn to repress the contradiction between humanistic cultural values and our support of our present way of life.

A key problem with our focus on outward versus inward-outward perception and thought is its attention to physical and biological structures by contrast with social and personality structures. From one moment to the next those former structures are what we sense, and those latter structures are what we fail to sense. And we remain unaware that we are being shaped in the direction of not seeing the importance of human beings. Given this situation, how can we possibly follow the advice of Socrates or Gouldner or Pogo or our own advice to work toward our own evolution and the evolution of society? How can we learn to pay attention to the extraordinary language of social science, as illustrated by Figure 2-1, if we have learned that those concepts refer to phenomena that are not real by comparison with physical and biological structures? It is exactly here, however, that we can invoke other elements of the extraordinary language of social science—to be discussed in the next three sections of this chapter—to help us. Our discussion of self-image can help us to see ourselves from one moment to the next as the most interactive creatures within the known universe, entities far superior—in this sense—than the entire physical universe with all of its galaxies. From this perspective, we might proceed to define physical structures as no more than structures—or persisting systems of elements—that interact to a relatively limited extent with their environments. And we might define biological structures as structures that interact to a relatively moderate extent with their environments. Let us recall here our discussion of language in Chapter 1, illustrating our infinite potential.

Presently, especially given our large and increasing aspirations-fulfillment gap—as is well illustrated by problems like environmental pollution, terrorism, war, and a financial meltdown that we are unable to solve—it is indeed most difficult for us to see ourselves as having unlimited possibilities for our own evolution. Yet we maintain that it is our bureaucratic worldview, coupled with our self-image and much more as indicated by our extraordinary language, that lies behind these and many other problems. Although we have begun to gain a glimpse of that worldview in Chapter 1, in another section of this chapter we shall probe its nature more fully. Not only do we have a very limited understanding of who we are, as indicated by our present self-images, but we also have limited understanding of the bureaucratic forces that presently are shaping our problems.

And in a final section on the scientific method, we can learn more fully just how we have failed to make use of its incredible potential for helping us to make progress on our pressing problems, and we can gain insight into how we can proceed to tap that potential. For example, we can come to see our emphasis on perceiving physical and biological phenomena from one moment to the next as a fundamental problem that is closely linked to the rest of our problems. Following the enormous optimism linked to the scientific method—given its successes over the past five centuries—we can proceed to swing our pendulum of the scientific method in ever widening arcs so as to make progress on that problem.

As we proceed to take up the concept of self-image within the extraordinary language, let us continue with our emphasis on problems more than on solutions. For this is our focus in Part II with our treatment of the possibility of our own extinction. The above paragraphs outlining solutions are important, for if indeed we are to face up to our problems we must be able to approach them with confidence in our ability to make progress on them. Otherwise we would not risk facing up to those problems. Yet it is essential that we dig much more deeply into the nature of our problems in Part Two if indeed we expect to emerge with directions for solutions in Part Three that are in fact effective.

Self-image

We may define self-image simply as an individual's view of self, where "self" includes one's biological structure along with one's personality structure, and also one's memories of the full range of one's experiences. Yet there is a serious problem here, a problem that Gurdjieff and Ouspensky alerted us to in a previous quotation in this chapter. They maintain that if the individual is to have "will" or command of his or her motivation so as to be able to do whatever he or she wanted to do, then the individual must remain aware of self at all times. But if the individual continues to be distracted by one experience after another, then there is no such continuing awareness and, as a result, no will power that can be harnessed to attain goals or solve problems. Our example above of perceiving physical and biological structures from one moment to the next illustrates their point. For the result of such perception is that a continuing sense of self flies out the window.

It appears that external distractions from awareness of self have been increasing due to the technological developments within modern society, as illustrated by television, cell phones, ipods, and computers. Here we can bring forward another concept within the extraordinary language: "cultural norms," or widely shared expectations, beliefs, and assumptions throughout society. Those cultural norms, following our bureaucratic worldview, point us outward. Watching television, talking on our cell phones or taking pictures with them, listening to our ipods, working with our computers or using them to e-mail others—these activities are very widely shared. And it has come to be expected that we engage in these activities, that is, that we conform to the "norms" of doing these things. We have come to believe that all of this is valuable. Yet these activities are also distractions from paying attention to ourselves. At the same time, our revolution of rising expectations—that has been accompanying our scientific and political revolutions over the past five centuries—calls for increasing emphasis on such nonmaterial values as the ultimate worth of the individual. Thus, although we want more and more attention to our own individual worth and importance, we appear to be getting less and less. This is the overall point of our emphasis on our increasing aspirations-fulfillment gap: We are getting less and less of what we want, and we want more and more.

A further illustration of an outward orientation that takes us away from paying attention to ourselves comes from a problem that has been given the label "attention deficit hyperactivity disorder," or "attention deficit disorder"—also labeled ADD, for short. A recent article in the *Boston Sunday Globe* points up the problem:

> In the fast-paced, distraction-plagued arena of modern life, perhaps nothing has come under more assault than the simple faculty of attention. We bemoan the tug of war for our focus, joke uneasily about our attention-deficit lifestyles, and worry about the seeming epidemic of attention disorders among children. The ability to pay careful attention isn't important just for students and air traffic controllers. Researchers are finding that attention is crucial to a host of other, sometimes surprising, life skills: the ability to sort through conflicting evidence, to connect more deeply with other people, and even to develop a conscience. But for all that, attention remains one of the most poorly understood human faculties.... Children with attention problems are medicated; harried adults struggle to "pay attention." ... But with the field of attention training still in its infancy, scientists don't yet understand if any current teaching has long-lasting gains—or, for that matter, which practices work best (Jackson 2008: D1-D2).

Given our revolution of rising expectations, and given our increasing emphasis on what has become known as "multitasking," it is little wonder that attention deficit disorder has become an increasing problem not only for children but also for adults. Our cultural norms are calling on us to become involved in more and more activities that point to the fulfillment of increasing desires. The emphasis of the article is on the scientific progress that has been made along with the increasing scientific attention devoted to ADD. Yet as we can see from the last sentence, there is an admission that "scientists don't yet understand if any current teaching has long-lasting gains—or, for that matter, which practices work best." Our own view is that studies of ADD fail to address much of the complexity of the forces contributing to ADD, such as our bureaucratic worldview, our aspirations-fulfillment gap, and the limited approach by social scientists to the scientific method. We believe that the problem of attention deficit disorder will continue to increase along with our increasing aspirations-fulfillment gap, for we see the two as closely related. And research by the senior author and a colleague found "substantial evidence" in support of the hypothesis that "[t]he gap between aspirations and their fulfillment is in fact increasing in contemporary society" (Phillips and Johnston 2007: 234-235). One result of increasing ADD will be the individual's decreasing attention to self. For attention to self has to do with the development of one's personality structure. And the development of a structure requires behavior in a given direction that persists from one moment to the next, behavior that is quite at odds with attention deficit disorder.

For a contrast to ADD, we might look to Polonius' advice to his son Laertes in Shakespeare's *Hamlet,* just before Laertes embarks on a journey:

> This above all: to thine own self be true,
> And it must follow, as the night the day,
> Thou canst not then be false to any man.
> (1601: Act 1, Scene 3, Line 78)

Shakespeare is suggesting that a unitary self-image is the basis for achieving good relationships with others, that is, a well-formed personality structure can yield desirable social structures. By contrast, students' attention deficit disorders make it difficult for them to relate to their teachers as well as to other students along with their parents.

As we can see from the above discussion, the concept of self-image is on a par with the concept of worldview—in its generality and its links to a wide range of behavior—and this is why we have depicted the two concepts at the same level of abstraction in Figure 2-1. Feelings of humiliation and shame—which attack one's self-esteem—have been studied over many years by Thomas Scheff, a cofounder of the Sociological Imagination Group. For Scheff, it is the failure to acknowledge feelings of shame, the failure to bring those feelings up to the surface, that can yield problems for the individual and for society. Scheff analyzed the Old Testament and the New Testament for their references to shame and pride, and he found a striking difference that suggests a long-term change from preindustrial to contemporary society:

> The Old Testament contains many, many references to pride and shame but very few to guilt. The New Testament reverses the balance.... It is possible that the role of shame in social control has not decreased but has gone underground instead.... For example, we say, "It was an awkward moment for me ... " It contains two movements that disguise emotion: *denial* of inner feeling and projection of it onto the outer world. *I* was not embarrassed; it was the *moment* that was awkward (Scheff 1994: 43).

If we can generalize from Scheff's study to changes in society, then it appears that shame and pride have gone underground, and it is guilt that has come to the fore. These changes all indicate a lowered self-esteem. We can understand the failure to acknowledge shame by looking to our increasing aspirations-fulfillment gap coupled with a lack of understanding of how to narrow that gap. Here, then, is a dramatically threatening problem that we are unable to solve. Burying it, and burying our feelings of shame along with it, can help some of us in the short run to go on with our lives. But it can create increasingly serious problems for others. And it can also create increasingly serious problems for society as a whole, since we will remain unable to address a problem that we cannot see, a problem that will continue to escalate.

Granting that our negative views of ourselves are linked to a growing aspirations-fulfillment gap, that gap in turn is closely linked to our worldview, a concept that we have begun to examine in Chapter 1. Let us turn to that concept once again at this point, for its central importance demands much further study. We might recall that, for Karl Mannheim, *Weltanschauung* was a most fundamental concept, including "every single cultural field" together with the ideas, feelings, and practices of ordinary people. In Figure 2–1 we have located "individual worldview" above "beliefs and assumptions"—in common with self-image—indicating its greater generality or higher level of abstraction. Correspondingly, we have located "cultural worldview" below "cultural norms," indicating the same thing, for we conceive of a ladder of abstraction pointing downward as well as upward. As for the concept of culture itself, that will be taken up in Chapter 3. At this point, we can understand culture to focus on what is shared widely throughout society that is linked to both "head" and "heart." Thus, it will be located between the "head" and "heart" columns of Figure 2–1, just as in the case of "cultural worldview," yet it will be more abstract or general in that it will appear closer to "social structure."

Worldview

In carrying further our understanding of worldview—including both individual worldview and cultural worldview, as depicted in Figure 2-1—our emphasis will be on developing our insights into the nature of language. For it is our usage of language that not only distinguishes us from all other organisms within the known universe but also places us on a stairway that can lead to ever more interaction with the phenomena within the universe, including our own past experiences. Our usage, then, shapes the nature of our worldview, just as the reverse occurs. This is illustrated in Figure 2-1 by the line tying together beliefs and assumptions, on the one hand, and individual worldview, on the other hand. It is also illustrated by the line tying together cultural norms and cultural worldview. In our view our understanding of language is limited, since our bureaucratic worldview teaches us to see phenomena as relatively isolated from one another—by contrast with seeing them in interaction—just as is illustrated by Figure 1-2. Yet once we become aware of this problem we can learn to pull together our pieces of knowledge about language and move toward an increasing understanding of this incredibly powerful tool for solving problems.

In Chapter 1 we defined worldview as a metaphysical stance or persisting image of the nature of reality. And in referring to Mannheim's discussion of *Weltanschauung,* we were careful to indicate that the concept is broad enough to include every single cultural field along with references to the ideas, feelings, and actions of all of us. Thus, philosophical discussions of metaphysical assumptions point to only one aspect of worldview. Further, the concept of worldview is broad enough to point toward our senses and not just to what language has taught us, since "view" is part of the concept.

To gain further understanding of worldview, let us now dig more deeply into how language works. A crucial idea from Chapter 1 is the importance of shuttling up and down language's ladder of abstraction— an idea put forward by Mills—since we must shuttle very far up that ladder to reach the concept of worldview. Lev Vygotsky, a Russian analyst of language and child development who wrote in the early part of the twentieth century, gave us some insight into how people learn to move up and down that ladder:

The following example may illustrate the function of varying degrees of generality in the emergence of a system: A child learns the word *flower,* and shortly afterwards the word *rose;* for a long time the concept "flower," though more widely applicable than "rose," cannot be said to be more general for the child. It does not include and subordinate "rose"—the two are interchangeable and juxtaposed. When "flower" becomes generalized, the relationship of "flower" and "rose," as well as of "flower" and other subordinate concepts, also changes in the child's mind. A system is taking shape (Vygotsky 1962: 93).

To illustrate the impact of our failure to take into account our bureaucratic worldview, let us return to the example of the worldwide financial meltdown presented in Chapter 1. It was economists and not other social scientists who were summoned by President-elect Obama to confront the financial crisis that had dried up loans throughout the world. However, by so doing the newly elected administration failed to learn about many of the complex forces that have created this economic crisis, Those forces include the role of our worldview in generating a growing aspirations-fulfillment gap that was in turn a key basis for the collapse. Granting that economists have crucial knowledge about the intricate workings of the world's financial system, they have little or no knowledge of the impact of our worldview. And neither do they have the long-range perspective that is required to understand the genesis—over five centuries—of our aspirations-fulfillment gap

Following Vygotsky, being able to shuttle up and down language's ladder of abstraction is a learning process, and such learning takes time. Following our bureaucratic worldview, we have succeeded in such learning with respect to the concepts we use in ordinary speech. Yet we fail to have developed a linguistic "system" of concepts that takes into account the knowledge throughout our many specialized fields of knowledge and thus covers the full range of our experiences. By contrast, there are specialized groups—just like those within the 46 sections of the American Sociological Association—that have developed their own linguistic systems that focus on a relatively narrow area of phenomena.

Yet this is exactly what the extraordinary language of social science promises to accomplish. For in this way we can at least begin to understand just what all of our specialized groups are doing, granting that we don't learn to use their specialized concepts in our own lives. The result would be improved highways of communication among all of us, along with greater understanding and appreciation of what we are all attempting to accomplish. But even far more than this would be accomplished. The very idea of the scientific method calls on us to stand on the shoulders of giants, building on whatever knowledge has already been developed. An extraordinary language would enable the scientist to stand on far more shoulders and thus greatly improve his or her ability to solve problems. Still further, the rest of us can learn to use the scientific method in our own lives to an increasing extent, and we can learn to do much the same thing. Here, then, is a vision of an evolutionary way of life, based on making ever more use of the potentials of language and the scientific method. Of course, this is a vision that is very far from what is now going on within our present bureaucratic way of life.

To understand more fully the possibilities of an extraordinary language, it would be most helpful to explore its opposite: a language that teaches us to be less able to communicate with, understand, and appreciate the work of others, and also to be less and less able to develop as human beings and learn to solve personal and world problems. Newspeak, illustrating this kind of language, was developed by George Orwell in his classic novel *Nineteen Eighty-Four* (1949; see also Phillips and Johnston 2007: 208-210; Phillips 2008: 188-294). Orwell's nightmarish vision of Big Brother was based on Joseph Stalin, and his Oceania was modeled after Stalin's USSR. But Orwell carried his vision much further in a totalitarian direction than the USSR. For example, there are two-way "telescreens" in every home, school, workplace, and even on the streets, and the Thought Police are watching everyone to see just how enthusiastic they are in supporting Big Brother.

Winston Smith, Orwell's hero—who is attempting to fight the system that Big Brother has created—works in the Ministry of Truth, an extremely bureaucratic organization that follows the party's three slogans: "WAR IS PEACE, FREEDOM IS SLAVERY, and IGNORANCE IS STRENGTH." These slogans indicate the focus of Big Brother: for war, against freedom, and for ignorance. Winston's colleague, Syme—who is compiling a definitive edition of the Newspeak dictionary—explains to Winston how Newspeak is changing from one edition of the dictionary to the next, and also the nature of Newspeak:

> You think, I dare say, that our chief job is inventing new words. But not a bit of it! We're destroying words—scores of them, hundreds of them every day.... Do you know that Newspeak is the only language in the world whose vocabulary gets smaller every year? ... Don't you see that the whole aim of Newspeak is to narrow the range of thought? In the end we shall make thoughtcrime literally impossible, because there will be no words in which to express it.... Every year fewer and fewer words, and the range of consciousness always a little smaller.... By 2050—earlier, probably—all real knowledge of Oldspeak will have disappeared. The whole literature of the past will have been destroyed. Chaucer, Shakespeare, Milton, Byron—they'll exist only in Newspeak versions, not merely changed into something different, but actually changed into something contradictory of what they used to be. Even the literature of the Party will change. Even the slogans will change. How could you have a slogan like "freedom is slavery" when the concept of freedom has been abolished? The whole climate of thought will be different. In fact there will be no thought, as we understand it now. Orthodoxy means not thinking—not needing to think. Orthodoxy is unconsciousness" [1949: 45-47].

Newspeak does a good job of illustrating the bureaucratic society and the bureaucratic individual, as depicted by Figure 1-2. As the concepts in Newspeak are destroyed, the language's ability to help speakers interact with phenomena and tie together their own experiences continues to decrease. Newspeak's movement toward allowing no thought whatsoever means that the linguistic advantage that humans have over all other forms of life—an advantage that makes possible the human being's continuing development—comes to be lost. The link between ideas, on the one hand, and emotions and actions, on the other hand—as illustrated in Figure 1-3b—comes to be eliminated. Yet Newspeak also points up and yields insight into the problems that are occurring throughout our own bureaucratic way of life, problems that are not merely located within a science-fiction novel. For example, publishers generally are being confronted by a situation where serious reading is declining in association with increasing addiction to watching television. Increasing use of our new technological gadgetry—such as computers, cell phones, electronic cameras, and ipods—are also doing a job on reading. At the same time, there is at present no strong movement throughout the academic world that points a direction toward helping the ordinary individual make use of the vast amount of knowledge buried in our libraries. Indeed, specialization is continuing apace, and more and more walls are being constructed that work to divide knowledge. In addition, the escalating aspirations-fulfillment gap throughout the world makes it increasingly difficult for people to take the time to look at themselves and figure out just what is happening to them and to society at this time in history. And that same gap also influences us to repress our emotions, so that our confidence and motivation to confront growing problems—such as our inability to understand what is going on in the world—continues to decline. Newspeak, then, suggests nothing less than the direction that we moderns are taking in the contemporary world.

The anthropologists Benjamin Lee Whorf and Edward Sapir have helped us to understand just how powerful is the impact of language on human behavior by formulating what the called the "linguistic relativity hypothesis": the idea that language causes people to understand the world in a certain way (Whorf 1963). This hypothesis was well illustrated in a novel by Jack Vance, *The Languages of Pao* (1958; see also Phillips 2008: 195-199). Beran Panasper, ruler on the planet Pao in the far future, decides on a plan to counter the invasion of the warlike Brumbo clan of the planet Batmarsh as well as to counter extortion by the materialistic rulers of the planet Mercantile who are demanding enormous sums in return for the privilege of trading with them. In addition, there is the threat from the wizards on the planet Breakness, whose superior knowledge is being used to steal women from Pao and use them as concubines for the wizards. Beran succeeds in altering the mental framework of three groups of Paonese children, whom he locates on three of Pao's continents by teaching them Valiant (emphasizing the "hand"), Technicant ("heart"), and Cogitant ("head").

As a result, we have a most happy ending for Beran and the planet Pao. After a single generation, the Valiants develop their own warrior traditions and vanquish the Brumbos of Batmarsh. The Technicants build their own fleet of trading vessels, and the traders of Mercantile prove to be no match for these newly developed entrepreneurs. And the Paonese Cogitants oppose successfully the wizards of Breakness who had planned to take over Pao and convert it into an authoritarian regime. Yet Beran faces a rebellion by the Valiants, Technicants, and Cogitants, who are unable to communicate with one another or with the Paonese people at large, with each group demanding control of the planet. However, Beran is able to trump them, since their lack of ability to communicate outside their own groups makes this desire impossible to fulfill. Beran proceeds to institute a new language for these groups as well as for all of the Paonese people: Pastiche, a patchwork tongue made up of bits and pieces of Valiant, Technicant, and Cogitant. And he proceeds to dissolve the separate enclaves that housed those three groups. By so doing, everyone learns over time this new language, teaching valor, entrepreneurial ability, and wisdom to everyone.

Stepping outside of Vance's novel, we can gain further understanding of the linguistic relativity hypothesis of Whorf and Sapir. It is indeed reasonable to believe that if three groups of children were isolated for a generation and were taught Valiant, Technicant, and Cogitant, respectively, they would learn to emphasize valor, entrepreneurial ability, and wisdom, respectively. Further, we can understand more fully the incredibly powerful role that language plays in the shaping of the individual and of society and, in particular, the nature of our worldview. We can also gain further insight into the bureaucratic aspects of our own language by examining the languages of Valiant, Technicant, and Cogitant, with their narrow orientations to "hand," "heart" and "head," respectively. For example, we can see their links to Figures 1-2a and 1-2b. And we can also understand the importance of the language of Pastiche, with its union of "head," "heart," and "hand," and with its ties to Figures 1-3a and 1-3b. Granting the happy ending in Vance's novel, our own situation at this time in history is far more problematic. In our view we cannot even wait for an entire generation to make serious progress on our problems.

Granting the incredible potential of language to give us the basis for developing fundamental changes in every aspect of our world, this suggests the equal potential of a scientific method that makes full use of that potential as a springboard for helping us move toward those changes. It was the promise of the Enlightenment era of the eighteenth century that science could enable societies—after many thousands of years of unsolved problems—to make desperately needed progress on their most difficult problems, such as war and poverty. That promise still lives throughout contemporary societies and has been an important basis for the development of democracies throughout the world. Yet, unfortunately, the scientific method—as presently practiced—has not lived up to its potential. Why? What is wrong with present practices?

We have taken some basic steps—in Chapter 1 and in this chapter—toward probing the reasons for the failures of the sciences as they are presently practiced. In Chapter 1, we portrayed the nature of a bureaucratic society and individual in Figure 1-2. It was in that chapter that we indicated how a bureaucratic worldview, with its limited approach to language, is powerful enough to trump scientific and humanistic ideals. Thus, for example, Mills's idea of shuttling up and down language's ladder of abstraction—or a vision of opening up to language's dichotomous, gradational, and metaphorical potentials, or taking responsibility for investigating "head," "heart," and "hand"—falls by the wayside. And in Chapter 2, we have begun to present the extraordinary language of social science. By so doing, we can begin to see how situational patterns of behavior linked to a bureaucratic way of life—like outward perception and thought—take us far away from the ability to confront our problems effectively. And we can also begin to see how structural patterns of behavior—like our bureaucratic worldview and self-image—work to enforce outward perception and thought, by contrast with the reflexive visions of Socrates, Gouldner, and Pogo.

Yet there is a great deal more to the story of the failures of science in the modern world, granting all of its achievements. The following section will give us yet another chapter in that story, but no more than a chapter. Our question has been only partially answered: Why has science failed us? What is wrong with the way science is practiced in contemporary societies? What is the nature of those forces that have prevented scientists from fulfilling the ideals of the scientific method? Is there any way out of our present situation where science not only remains helpless to make progress on our problems, but science is also a problem in itself, given its continuing creation of weapons of mass destruction?

The Scientific Method

Just as in the previous section we turned to probing further into the nature of language in order to understand our bureaucratic worldview, so will we turn to probing further into the history of Western philosophy in this section in order to understand present scientific practices. For it has been philosophers no less than scientists themselves who have shaped our understanding of the nature of the scientific method. Given our bureaucratic culture, scientists—especially in recent years with our increased specialization—generally do not see themselves as able to criticize what is happening in philosophy, yet they proceed to conform to the conclusions of philosophers. This is the situation throughout social science no less than physical and biological science. For example, philosophers over the years—given the enormous successes of the physical and biological sciences—generally have seen the use of mathematics as the epitome of the scientific method. This relegates social science to a very low status, as was illustrated in Chapter 1's description of the television show *NOVA*. Of course, in this one section we can do no more than touch on a few ideas from the history of Western philosophy, yet we shall add to those ideas in the chapters to follow. Our focus here is not on the enormous contributions of Western philosophy to the development of our ideals for the scientific method as well as to the successes of the physical and biological sciences. Rather, we are centering on the negative impact of philosophy on scientific practice.

Although it appears to be an impossible task to do justice to the history of Western philosophy in a few pages that focus on its failures relative to its vision of the scientific method, that task has been made possible by Abraham Kaplan, a philosopher whose focus has been on pragmatism, the one philosophy that is closest to scientific ideals. In this passage he focuses on the failures of key movements within Western philosophy:

> There is no doubt that far and away the most significant development in Western culture in the past three or four centuries has been the rise of modern science and the transformation of civilization by the technology based on that science. But in the course of this transformation, a radical bifurcation has grown up between man and nature, value and fact, which confronts us with the dilemma of either turning our backs on science or else resigning ourselves to living in a world without human meaning or purpose. Pragmatism conceives the task of philosophy for modern man to be nothing other than finding a way out of this dilemma.
>
> The history of modern philosophy is, for pragmatism, a history of successive attempts to cope with this problem, and the elaborate constructions of epistemologists and metaphysicians are to be understood in terms of their bearing on this fundamental cultural crisis. On one side we have science and technology, on the other side, religion, morals, politics, and art. The tradition of realism and empiricism—from John Locke and David Hume to Bertrand Russell—has turned largely in the direction of science, and has provided for human values no more solid a foundation than a subjective emotional involvement. The idealist tradition—represented most influentially by Hegel and the conventional

religionists—may do justice to human aspirations but cannot give any intelligible account of science and scientific method consistent with its own presuppositions. Other philosophies—like those of Descartes, Immanuel Kant, and contemporary neo-orthodoxy—try to resolve the dilemma simply by accepting it, thinking to settle the conflict between science and religion, between rational good sense and emotional sensibility, by assigning to each its own domain within which its sovereignty is to be undisputed (Kaplan 1961: 16-17).

Kaplan is suggesting that modern Western philosophy—other than pragmatism—is either one-sided in the face of the rise of science and technology or else reaches toward a dualism that fails to address the problem of achieving human meaning or purpose in combination with the impact of science and technology. Thus, it is realism and empiricism (Locke, Hume, and Russell) that sides with science; it is idealism (Hegel, conventional religionists) that sides with human aspirations; and it is dualistic philosophies (Descartes, Kant, contemporary neo-orthodoxy) that avoid the problem. We might add to Kaplan's argument by citing existentialism—illustrated by Kierkegaard, Nietzsche, and Sartre—as giving us more of a one-sided idealism. And we might add phenomenology—illustrated by Husserl and Heidegger—to that idealistic approach. Further, we might cite logical positivism and analytic philosophy—heirs to British empiricism—as continuing to side with the pole of science. Of course, the history of Western philosophy is not quite as neat as this analysis suggests. For example, Karl Marx dips into realism or empiricism—granting his ideological commitment to revolution—in his fundamental contributions to social science. And his orientation to equality takes him as well into the camp of idealism, granting his view that religion is the opium of the people.

By turning to our own contrast between a bureaucratic and an evolutionary worldview, we can achieve further understanding of the history of Western philosophy. For example, we can see the one-sided philosophies of idealism and empiricism or realism as illustrating a bureaucratic worldview. Yet at the same time we should not ignore their contribution to the integration of phenomena, as illustrated by an interactive worldview: gradationally, they have achieved some movement toward an evolutionary worldview. As for the dualism of Descartes and Kant, we can see that in much the same way: as bureaucratic in its failure to achieve interaction between mind and body. Further, if we consider other figures throughout the history of Western philosophy—such as Plato and Saint Thomas Aquinas—we can also see both their one-sidedness or failure to achieve interaction between dichotomized areas, and we can also see their contributions to understanding the interaction among phenomena.

As for pragmatism, that philosophy stands apart as taking us very far toward illustrating an evolutionary worldview, although Kaplan's analysis is deficient in its failure to take into account the contributions of social science. Kaplan states the aims of pragmatism, pointing toward a broad scientific method, in the following:

> Pragmatism cannot rest content with either of the one-sided philosophies, which simply ignore the problem, nor yet with any dualistic philosophy, which mistakes a formulation of the problem for its solution. As against the scientific philosophies of our time, the pragmatist is determined to restore man to the position of centrality which is rightfully his—not because the world is mindful of man, but because it is the human mind with which we inescapably look out on our world. As against the several idealisms, the pragmatist insists on the realities of conditions and consequences, causes and effects, in which ideals must be grounded if they are to have any impact on human life. And as against the philosophies which compartmentalize experience, the pragmatist argues that man cannot live divided against himself, affirming in the name of religion or morality what he must deny in the name of science. By circumscribing for each its own sphere of influence, we do not forestall conflict but only mark out the battle lines (Kaplan 1961: 17).

Yet T. S. Eliot wrote:

> Between the idea
> And the reality
> Between the motion
> And the act
> Falls the Shadow.
> From "The Hollow Men," 1925

Between the wish of pragmatists like Kaplan and the fulfillment of that wish—much the same as the aspirations-fulfillment gap of Figure 1-1—"falls the shadow." It is exactly here that the philosophy of pragmatism is deficient, granting that Kaplan's ability to define the problem at hand is most useful. And it is exactly here that the extraordinary language of social science, coupled with a broad approach to the scientific method, can make progress on that problem.

Overall, then, our brief examination of the history of Western philosophy reveals a failure to move beyond a certain point in integrating existing knowledge of phenomena. And that failure even includes the philosophy of pragmatism to some degree, given its very limited usage of the extraordinary language of social science. As a result, the history of Western philosophy has worked to influence social scientists in a bureaucratic direction, limiting their ability to follow scientific ideals. We have seen this, for example, in the push of logical positivists and analytic philosophers toward a narrow emphasis on mathematics and quantitative social science, ignoring the importance of qualitative social science along with the limitations of mathematics and computers. An exception is recent work in the philosophy of social science, as illustrated by the publications of Harold Kincaid (1996; Kincaid, Dupre, and Wylie 2007). Yet pragmatism can indeed be integrated with social science, as we shall see in Part III. And that integration can give social science and the scientific method a broad and systematic philosophical foundation that points toward the development of an evolutionary social science and an evolutionary society. However, we still have much more to learn about the nature of our bureaucratic society. Chapter 3 will focus on phenomena relating to the "heart," an area of knowledge that is no less fundamental than the "head" and the "hand."

CHAPTER 3

"Heart"

Emotional Repression

IT WOULD BE MOST DIFFICULT to overestimate the importance of our ability to understand our own emotional lives and those of others to probe the nature of the escalating problems throughout the world. This quote from Hitler's *Mein Kampf* illustrates the link between his emotions and what subsequently happened to the European Jews along with others deemed not worthy of life:

> There is ground for pride in our people only if we no longer need be ashamed of any class. But a people, half of which is wretched and careworn, or even deprived, offers so sorry a picture that no one should feel any pride in it. Only when a nation is healthy in all its members, in body and soul, can every man's joy in belonging to it rightly be magnified to that high sentiment which we designate as national pride. and this highest pride will only be felt by the man who knows the greatness of his nation.... Particularly our German people which today lies broken and defenseless, exposed to the kicks of all the world, needs that suggestive force that lies in self-confidence....
>
> If at the beginning of the War and during the War twelve or fifteen thousand of these Hebrew corrupters of the people had been held under poison gas, as happened to hundreds of thousands of our very best German workers in the field, the sacrifice of millions at the front would not have been in vain. On the contrary, twelve thousand scoundrels eliminated in time might have saved the lives of a million

real Germans, valuable for the future (Quoted in Scheff 1994: 114, 116-117).

The horror of the Holocaust was arguably the worst experience of the human race in contemporary times. For here was a modern nation with its leader democratically elected and its widely recognized cultural achievements in the arts and sciences that nevertheless proceeded to deliberately slaughter millions whose only crime was that they were Jewish. From *Mein Kampf* we can see the role of emotions like shame and pride in the genesis of the Holocaust, tied to Hitler's own personality as well as the humiliation of Germany fostered by the Treaty of Versailles after World I, the massive inflation that followed, and the Great Depression of 1929. The poison gas that Hitler wished to release on the "Hebrew corrupters of the people" actually was released on his millions of Jewish victims—and millions of others whom he believed to be not worthy of life—years later, with the aid of modern technological procedures employed by bureaucratic organizations.

Yet how could this have happened? How could a nation at the highest level of civilization have proceeded to engage in mass murder with the aid of the very technology that was instrumental in the development of their civilization? How could the many thousands of years of effort and achievement by the human race have led to something to which lower forms of life would never stoop? Thomas Scheff, along with other social scientists, has given us some initial answers. Those answers include the Treaty of Versailles along with the huge inflation and worldwide depression that followed. They also include Scheff's finding of consistent and substantial evidence for Hitler's having developed a great deal of hidden shame and for his having become prone to continuing shame-rage cycles. It is those very cycles that Scheff has labeled "a feeling trap," where negative emotions—especially shame and rage—work together in a never-ending feedback relationship yielding ever-increasing shame and rage. Those cycles occur throughout society—and certainly are not unique to Hitler—when negative emotions continue to be repressed. Let us recall here Scheff's analysis of the decline of references to shame in the New Testament, by contrast with the Old Testament, in our discussion of self-image in Chapter 2. Apparently the repression of shame has occurred throughout contemporary society, yielding a basis for shame-rage cycles.

It appears, then, that social scientists do at least have partial answers for what is arguably the greatest crime against humanity ever to have been perpetrated. What we have learned is that there are forces afoot in society—forces that have never been tamed—that can unleash another Holocaust as well as the lesser problems that are now continuing to plague modern society. Further, those other problems that include war and terrorism—when coupled with our ever-greater ability to destroy ourselves with weapons of mass destruction—can yield not only the murder of many millions of innocents. The probability is continuing to increase, as our weapons become ever more deadly and ever more available, that we humans will succeed in completely destroying ourselves.

However, we still have remaining to us a window of opportunity for building on our understanding of human behavior and human problems, granting that time is short. The crucial questions we must answer are these: Can we develop that understanding in time? Can we win the race between understanding and destruction, between education and war, between the forces for human evolution and the forces let loose by our bureaucratic way of life? Can we learn to tap our incredible potential as human beings for solving problems before that potential is wiped out? Can we become sufficiently aware of the dangers we face in time to avert catastrophe? Can we succeed in developing further the understanding already achieved by the social sciences so that we become able to make continuing progress toward solving our fundamental problems?

Our own answers to these questions are all affirmative. Our direction in this book is to continue to build on Chapters 1 and 2, focusing on the human being's two most powerful tools: language and the scientific method. More specifically, we shall carry further our initial presentation of the extraordinary language of social science. Our next step is a focus on Figure 3-1, where we add an analysis of "heart" to our previous examination of "head." What is at stake here is nothing less than our ability to probe the dark forces that were at work in Hitler—both from personality structure and social structure—and that are also at work in the rest of us. We are convinced that we can all learn the extraordinary language of social science, that we can learn to use that language in our everyday lives, and that the result will be a clear demonstration of its effectiveness in helping us make progress on personal and world problems.

Values, Cultural Values, Institutions, Culture

Is it true that we moderns are emotional cripples who have great difficulty in understanding our emotions, let alone those of others? If so, then this is yet another huge gap—just as Figure 1-1 portrayed—between our aspirations and their fulfillment. Elie Wiesel, the American Nobel Prize winner and Auschwitz survivor, put forward the importance of emotions in these words:

> The opposite of love is not hate, it's indifference.
> The opposite of art is not ugliness, it's indifference.
> The opposite of faith is not heresy, it's indifference.
> The opposite of life is not death, it's indifference.
> (Quoted in Knowles 2004: 834, No. 13).

Figure 3–1. "Head" and "Heart": Outward Perception and Thought, Emotional Repression, and Other Structures

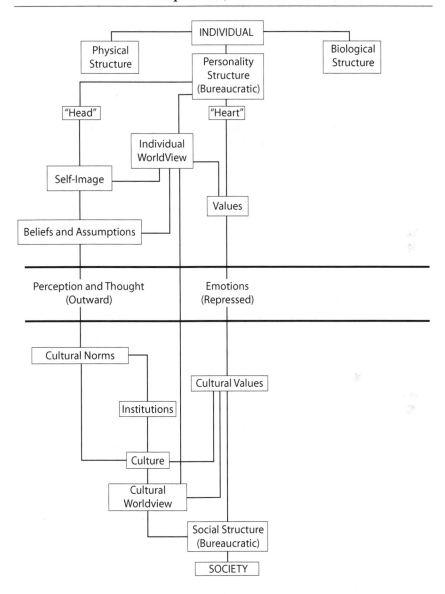

It was indifference to the fate of 6 million Jews and millions of others that paved the way for the Holocaust. It is indifference to our increasing aspirations-fulfillment gap that makes possible escalating problems throughout the world with no solutions in sight. Yet if we are to move away from indifference, we require the linguistic tools that can help us to bring it to the surface where we will be able to confront it. Here the concepts of "values" and "cultural values" can prove to be most important. We might define values simply as the persisting goals, ideals, interests, or motives of an individual or group, granting that some of our values are repressed because they represent a dark side of our emotional commitments. And when values are widely shared throughout society, we might speak of cultural values. These concepts might appear to be of little importance, since we already have literally thousands of other concepts at our beck and call. Yet we fail to integrate those thousands of concepts, and our thoughts and speech jump from one concept to another, failing to make use of much of the knowledge that is available to us as we are confronted by one problem after another.

By contrast, the concepts of value and cultural value are part of the extraordinary language of social science, as we can see from Figure 3-1. As a result, they are tied systematically to a number of other concepts, as depicted by the lines linking all of the concepts in Figure 3-1 together. In addition, that system of concepts embodies a vast amount of research achieved throughout the history of the social sciences. Further, those concepts are all quite abstract or general, giving them the ability to encompass the thousands of concepts that we all use in our everyday lives. Thus, they are not simply just a few words with little significance.

But let us note that those concepts vary in their degree of abstraction or generality. For example, with respect to the individual, values generally cover more ground or more phenomena than beliefs or assumptions, as indicated in Figure 3-1 by its placement at a higher level. The same is the case for cultural values and cultural norms, as indicated in Figure 3-1 by its placement at a lower level. All of these concepts within the extraordinary language constitute a challenge: Can we begin to link them with our own everyday thought, speech, and writing? Can we, as a result, proceed to test their effectiveness in helping us confront personal and world problems? Can we, assuming that they pass muster, make them part of our automatic patterns of thinking, speaking, and writing?

What social scientists have discovered is that social structures—like cultural values—are so powerful that they exert enormous influence on every single one of us. As a result, cultural values are most effective in shaping our own individual values, granting that each of us also develops—as a result of our own unique experiences—a set of values that are not widely shared throughout society and are not shared by many groups. Thus, if we learn the nature of cultural values, then this gives us a shortcut to understanding the nature of perhaps the most important values of almost every individual within that society. This is much like a psychoanalysis of every member of society without having to get involved in that nearly impossible task. Of course, people do vary in their degree of commitment to any given cultural value, but that variation is limited.

Although one might wonder why people vary so much in their behavior if indeed their cultural values are much the same, let us bear in mind that human situations are most complex, and so is any given individual. Thus, for example, two individuals with the same values might behave quite differently as a result of the impact of other factors. A man who commits murder might hold much the same cultural values as his victim, yet circumstances might have resulted in murder despite that similarity. Those Germans who conformed to Hitler's murderous orders in all probability shared the cultural values of those Germans who were not part of the bureaucracies directly involved in the Holocaust. Let us also bear in mind that, again following T. S. Eliot, between the idea and the reality falls the shadow. From Figure 1-1 we note that there is a substantial gap between aspirations and their fulfillment, or between cultural values and actions—to be taken up in Chapter 4—that indicates the individual's failure to fulfill them.

As for the nature of an "institution," note its location in Figure 3-1 straddling "head" and "heart" as well as "cultural norms" and "cultural values." That straddling is taken into account in the definition of institution as a system of cultural values and norms focused on solving certain problems within society as a whole. Just as cultural values and cultural norms are shared throughout society, so do institutions bear on society as a whole. This differs from ordinary usage, where we may see any organization that has been around for a great many years as an institution. The sociological definition is not as loose, for the several institutions are seen as dividing up and focusing on the fundamental problems of society as a whole. In this way it becomes possible to evaluate society's institutions, that is, to raise the question as to how well they are doing in addressing their problems.

For the institution of science, its problem is developing understanding of the universe, including physical, biological, social, and personality structures. For the institution of education, the problem is communicating that understanding throughout society. For the political institution it is the development, distribution, and use of power. For the economic institution the problem is the production, distribution, and consumption of whatever society has come to value. The religious institution aims at developing and communicating the ultimate meaning and significance or worth of life, and it also has much to do with helping the individual achieve emotional expression through its rituals. And the family's problems are the continuation of life as well as the achievement of intimate or close social relationships. Within our own view, given the increasing aspirations-fulfillment gap throughout contemporary societies—as portrayed in Figure 1-1—all of our institutions are making no more than limited progress on their problems. And they will be failing us increasingly as that gap continues to increase.

As for culture, its placement within Figure 3-1 indicates its definition: It is at a more abstract or general level than society's system of institutions, each of which has to do with a portion of culture. And it is society's system of cultural values and norms that are at a lower level of abstraction than its institutions, for it is those cultural values and norms that form the basis of those institutions. Granting culture's higher level of generality or abstraction than institutions along with cultural values and norms, culture is in turn organized around its cultural worldview, which is at a still higher level of abstraction or generality, a level that is paralleled by individual worldview at the other end of Figure 3-1. All of these new concepts—values, cultural values, institutions, and culture—are quite abstract, given that they do vary in their levels of abstraction. Let us note once again that, whereas for the top half of Figure 3-1 it is movement upward that yields a higher level of abstraction or generality, for the bottom half of Figure 3-1 it is movement downward that yields a higher level of abstraction or generality. However, it is most difficult to understand the significance of these concepts without understanding how they are interrelated and also the nature of concepts at a lower level of abstraction.

The key concept that can help us here is cultural values. For they are central to the other concepts. For one thing, they are the basic values that every individual develops, granting that there is some variation for any given individual. For another thing, they are central to the definitions of institutions and culture. And for still another thing, it is our ability to open up to the full range of our cultural values—versus our failure to achieve such interaction—that points us toward an evolutionary cultural worldview versus a bureaucratic cultural worldview. Of course, cultural norms are involved as well in the definitions of institutions and culture. Yet cultural norms, by contrast, are more specific—as indicated by their position in Figure 3-1—just as beliefs and assumptions are more specific than values. For example, we might look for the set of beliefs and assumptions that bear on any given cultural value, just as—with reference to the individual—we might look for the set of beliefs and assumptions that bear on any given value. Thus, let us now proceed to come down language's ladder of abstraction. What, then, is the nature of our cultural values? Answering this question will help us not only to understand the nature of our cultural norms, our institutions, our culture, and our cultural worldview. it will also help each of us to understand the nature of his or her own values as well as the values of others.

Unfortunately, there has been little attention to the overriding importance of determining the nature of our cultural values by social scientists. Sociologists have focused their attention, by contrast, on the "hand," partly in order to distinguish themselves from anthropologists with their emphasis on the "head" and the "heart," or on culture. Psychologists have centered on the individual, with little concern for social structures. And historians along with political scientists generally have not adopted any systematic orientation to discovering the nature of our cultural values. However, there is an exception to this lack of attention to cultural values: the work of Robin M. Williams Jr., published in a textbook, *American Society* (1970). Given the bureaucratic orientation to knowledge within sociology no less than the rest of the academic world, textbooks have low status within the pantheon of scientific research and thus are largely ignored. Yet Williams's achievement goes beyond a systematic understanding of American cultural values, given the continuing worldwide scientific and technological revolutions, the penetration of the mass media along with computer technology, American influence, and economic globalization. American cultural values indicate, with some variation, the nature of cultural values throughout the world.

Yet as we proceed to examine American cultural values, we must give full recognition to the historical roots of those values, illustrating the interaction among societies throughout the world. America's cultural values were shaped by a great many forces, such as the developments within Greek and Roman civilizations, Judeo-Christian ideals, the invention of the printing press and the university, Islamic intellectual developments linked to Greco-Roman civilizations, the Renaissance and Reformation in Europe, the journeys of exploration throughout the world, the French eighteenth-century Enlightenment era, and much much more. However, these few words neglect the enormous impact of earlier developments in the Middle East and the Far East as well as in other areas of the world. Indeed, given an evolutionary worldview we cannot ignore the impact of any human action anywhere in the world throughout all of human history on American cultural values, granting that our knowledge of the nature of those impacts is extremely limited.

As for the nature of American cultural values, Williams focuses on only major values, excluding the many relatively minor ones. Those major cultural values include the following eight that we have divided into two groups: people-oriented cultural values and work-related cultural values. People-oriented values are closely linked to the values emphasized by the French Enlightenment, and also to the ideals associated with the American Revolution and the beginning of the French Revolution. They focus on the political institution. As for work-related cultural values, they are most closely associated with the scientific and technological revolutions. Their focus, by contrast, is on the economic institution or the world of work. However, both people-oriented and work-related cultural values also pervade the other institutions: science, education, religion, and the family. We might see all of these cultural values as specifying a substantial portion of the aspirations within the upper curve of Figure 1-1. They are important in themselves, granting that we cannot use their existence to determine the degree to which such values are in fact fulfilled, as indicated by the lower curve of Figure 1-1. Indeed, as we have indicated, evidence indicates that the aspirations-fulfillment gap with respect to the full range of our cultural values is continuing to grow. The following are excerpts from Williams's analysis, based on the many publications that he analyzed as a basis for his conclusions:

People-Oriented Cultural Values

Equality

At the level of explicit doctrine, intrinsic equality is widespread in American culture ... in the form of a specifically religious conception (the equality of souls before God. ... At the level of overt interpersonal relations, adherence to a sense of intrinsic human value is discernible ... by an extraordinary informality, directness, and lack of status consciousness in person-to-person contacts. ... A second major type of equality consists of specific formal rights and obligations ... from military service to voting, from public education to taxation—representing not only freedom but also equality (Williams 1970: 475–476).

Freedom

Always the demand was for freedom from some existing restraint ... a tendency to think of rights rather than duties ... a distrust of central government. ... American spokesmen emphasize freedom of speech and assembly, a multiparty, representative political system, private enterprise, freedom to change residence and employment ... it has seemed to make a great difference whether the individual receives a certain income or has a certain type of occupation as a result of an apparently impersonal, anonymous, diffuse, competitive process, as against "being forced" to accept that employment or remuneration by law or by the command of a visible social authority (Williams 1970: 480–481).

Democracy

Along with majority rule, representative institutions, and the rejection of ... monarchical and aristocratic principles ... American democracy stressed the reservation of certain "inalienable rights" as unalterable by majority rule.... The new system was devised in such a way as to limit and check centralized governmental power and to establish an ordered pattern for agreeing to disagree.... Its ... fundamental assumption is the worth and dignity and creative capacity of the individual, so that the chief aim of government is the maximum of individual self-direction, the chief means to that end the minimum of compulsion by the state (Williams 1970: 493–494).

Individual Personality

[W]e note a large number of important legal provisions [for] ... the protection of personal freedom or the physical or social integrity of the person ... illegality of slavery ... illegality of imprisonment for debt ... prohibitions against personal defamation (libel and slander); prohibition of "improper search and seizure;" prohibition of "cruel and unusual punishment;" right of habeas corpus.... The "value of individual personality" as impressionistically conceived represents ... uniqueness, self-direction, autonomy of choice, self-regulation, emotional indepen-dence, spontaneity, privacy, respect for other persons, defense of the self, and many others (Williams 1970: 496–497).

Work-Related Cultural Values

Achievement and Success

American culture is marked by a central stress upon personal achieve-ment, especially secular occupational achievement. The "success story" and the respect accorded to the self-made man are distinctly American, if anything is. Our society has been highly competitive—a society in which ascribed status in the form of fixed, hereditary social stratification has been minimized. It has endorsed Horatio Alger and has glorified the rail splitter who becomes president (Williams 1970: 454).

[Economic] Progress

By the late nineteenth century ... [p]rogress could now become a slogan to defend the course of technological innovation and economic rationalization and concentration.... Progress became identified with "free private enterprise" ... a belief in the positive value of ever-increas-ing quantities of goods and services, as illustrated in the dogma that ever-increasing per capita gross national product is the touchstone of progress toward "abundance" (Williams 1970: 469).

Material Comfort

[A] certain kind of materialism may emerge in a society, even though it is not initially a primary criterion of desirability—in the sense that the sheer availability of creature comforts and the incessant advertising used to sell them creates a social pressure to concentrate effort and attention upon them.... the objective opportunity to secure material comforts elicits, in the long run, a desire for them. Once a high standard of living has been enjoyed ... it is extremely difficult to reduce the level of sensation (Williams 1970: 471).

Science and Secular Rationality

Applied science is highly esteemed as a tool for controlling nature. Significant here is the interest in order, control, and calculability—the passion for an engineering civilization.... But the prime quality of "science" is not in its applications but in its basic method of approaching problems—a way of thought and a set of procedures for interpreting experience.... Science is disciplined, rational, functional, active; it requires systematic diligence and honesty; it is congruent with the "means" emphasis of the culture—the focus of interest upon pragmatism and efficiency and the tendency to minimize absolutes ... (Williams 1970: 487-488).

As we proceed to examine these eight cultural values, let us keep in mind their link to Figure 1-1, for they make up a good portion of the aspirations within the top curve of that figure. Further, we must not forget the importance of cultural values even when they are not being fulfilled. As we shall see in the next section on emotional repression, unfulfilled values do not disappear. Rather, they lie buried within us. Given the opportunity, they can come to life. Yet if they fail to be fulfilled, then they can have extremely negative repercussions on the individual and society, as is well indicated by our discussion of the Holocaust at the beginning of this chapter. For example, intolerable gaps between cultural values—such as material comfort, progress, achievement and success, freedom and individual personality—and people's ability to fulfill them developed throughout Germany, gaps that Hitler proceeded to exploit for his own purposes. It is here that we can bring forward Hitler's extremely bureaucratic individual worldview—and the prevailing bureaucratic cultural worldview as well—in helping us to understand the events that followed.

That bureaucratic cultural worldview can also help us understand the conflicts among these cultural values, for that worldview works to separate phenomena, just as is indicated by Figure 1-3. And that failure to achieve interaction is a breeding ground for the development of conflict and, in this case, conflicts among cultural values. Karen Horney—a neo-

Freudian psychoanalyst who paid serious attention to culture by contrast with Freud—discussed such conflicts in her *The Neurotic Personality of Our Time* (1937). She cites a number of contradictions among cultural values, such as that "between competition and success on the one hand, and brotherly love and humility on the other." This contradiction may be illustrated by the contradiction between the values of "achievement and success" and "material comfort," on the one hand, and the values of "equality" and "individual personality," on the other hand. More generally, we also have the contradictions between work-related cultural values and people-oriented cultural values.

Horney saw no way out of these contradictions "within the normal range" other than either "to take one of these strivings seriously and discard the other" " or "to take both seriously with the result that the individual is seriously inhibited in both directions."

But there is indeed a third alternative. For her two alternatives derive from a bureaucratic worldview within which there is a continuing failure to achieve interaction between work-related and people-oriented cultural values. By contrast, within an evolutionary worldview our own success need not threaten others but rather might help them learn how to achieve their own success (Phillips and Johnston 2007: 93; Phillips 2008: 60–61).

More specifically, such a change from a bureaucratic to an evolutionary worldview would involve a broadening of the cultural value of "science and secular rationality." Science would come to be defined not merely by biophysical science, but rather would come to include social science as well. As a result, that cultural value would no longer encourage our emphasis on "an engineering civilization," on "material comfort" and on a materialistic civilization. "Achievement and success" would be broadened far beyond our present-day narrow view of occupational achievement as the major direction for advancing humanity. By contrast, people-oriented values would become ever more important. Here, we assume that a broader approach to science that would give social science its due would help us all to work more effectively toward fulfilling those cultural values. Further, our overriding emphasis on the political sphere of life would be broadened if indeed we extended our approach to social science into practicing the scientific method in our everyday lives. It is one thing to have a democratic form of government. But it would be quite another thing to see democracy practiced within all of our institutions, including the worlds of work, science, education, religion, and the family.

It is important that we do not limit our understanding of the nature of cultural values to only those eight listed above and derived from Williams's analysis. His focus was on the major cultural values that had developed in modern times, such as the rise of science and secular rationality, the scientific and technological revolutions' emphasis on achievement and success along with material comfort and progress, and the focus of political revolutions and modern social movements on equality, freedom, democracy, and the worth of the individual. In our efforts to understand the nature of contemporary cultural values we should also take into account what we can learn from society's institutions. For example, our contemporary institutions give us additional orientations to the nature of our cultural values. Those institutions, conceived of as systems of cultural values and norms that focus on the organization of society and the solution of its major problems, thus give us a set of values that overlap with the ones derived from Williams's analysis.

More specifically, there is the institution of education with its focus on the cultural value of achieving understanding of the world. There is the institution of science, which is also concerned with understanding, and which in addition—given its close links to technology—is oriented to the very general cultural value of solving problems great and small. Yet that focus up to now has largely excluded solutions to the problems of human behavior. There are the family's commitments to the cultural values of the continuation of life as well as the achievement of intimate and close relationships. Religion suggests the cultural values of ultimate meaning and a sense of self-worth for the individual, and it also suggests the cultural value of emotional expression. The political institution, given its bureaucratic orientation, has been oriented to the cultural value of the achievement of power over other people, suggesting the hierarchical pattern of behavior that is so basic to the present organization of society. And it also joins the institution of science in its orientation to solving the problems of society. As for the economic institution, there is its present bureaucratic focus on material comfort, achievement and success, and progress.

It is useful to integrate these institutional cultural values with the eight derived from Williams's research so that we begin to understand the full range of cultural values operating throughout society. We should bear in mind that those eight values remain in full force throughout our institutions, and that the institutional values we have specified are additional values operating within those institutions. As for education, there is the cultural value of understanding the world. And there is the scientific value of solving problems, joined with the political institution's emphasis on the same value. The family gives us the value of the continuation of life as well as the value of intimate and close relationships. Religion gives us the value of ultimate meaning, and it also joins with Williams's listing of the value of individual personality in its focus on self-worth and emotional expression for the individual. And the economic institution overlaps with Williams's listing of the values of material comfort, achievement and success, and progress. Thus, we have five additional cultural values: one each from education and religion, one from science joined with the political institution, and two from the family.

In addition, just as there is emotional repression throughout contemporary society, and just as our assumptions—displayed in Figure 3-1 along with beliefs—include beliefs that are repressed, so do we moderns have cultural values that we repress, values linked to our bureaucratic worldview. Williams includes these major cultural values by listing "racism and related group-superiority themes," "nationalism and patriotism," and "external conformity." We can combine the first two, since nationalism and patriotism illustrates a focus on group superiority, which is close to such patterns of behavior as sexism, ageism, ethnocentrism, and classism. We can also see this value of group superiority as including the orientation of the political institution to the value of achieving power over other people. Few of us would be willing to acknowledge such values.

As for the cultural value of external conformity—given the values of individual personality, freedom, achievement and success, and progress—few of us would acknowledge any commitment to that value. Yet along with the cultural value of group superiority, external conformity is an integral part of our bureaucratic worldview. Group superiority and conformity are head and tail of the same coin of social stratification or patterns of hierarchy. Conformity is closely tied to the outward perception and thought that is emphasized within a bureaucratic way of life. As we shall see in Chapter 4 emphasizing "hand," actual patterns of conformity—and not just the repressed cultural value of external conformity—are central to our bureaucratic patterns of action and interaction within the momentary scenes of our lives. Thus, it is useful to conceive of a total of 15 major cultural values that operate as powerful forces throughout contemporary society. There are those derived from Williams's analysis, including the four people-oriented cultural values (equality, freedom, democracy, and individual personality), the four work-related cultural values (achievement and success, progress, material comfort, and science and secular rationality), the five additional institutional values (understanding the world, solving problems, the continuation of life, intimate and close relationships, and ultimate meaning), and there are also the two repressed cultural values (group superiority and external conformity). It is our ability to come down language's ladder of abstraction so as to gain awareness of these major cultural values that can help us to develop insight into the impact of culture on the individual and society

The fulfillment of cultural values rests, of course, on the individual's fulfillment of them, since culture has to do with what is widely shared by individuals throughout society. A key factor in such individual fulfillment is the individual's ability to express his or her emotions, a factor that we shall focus on in Part III with its orientation to an evolutionary way of life. Here in Part II, however, our emphasis is on understanding our bureaucratic way of life, a way of life that structures emotional repression rather than emotional expression. The development of our cultural values is a fundamental achievement of contemporary society, yet the focus of bureaucratic society on emotional repression is a powerful barrier to our fulfillment of those values. It is in the next section on emotional repression that we shall proceed to probe the forces producing emotional repression. Figure 1-3b with its depiction of the separation of the individual's "head," "heart," and "hand" within a bureaucratic way of life has already given us a very general view of the forces that yield emotional repression, which works against the interaction of the "heart" with the "head" and the "hand." Those forces are tied to our bureaucratic way of life. Yet Figure 1-3b—and Figure 1-3a as well, with its focus on the barriers to interaction within bureaucratic society—tell us little about the specific forces involved in emotional repression. How are we to understand those specifics? What are the arguments for the development of emotional repression throughout modern society? Such understanding can help us learn how to move away from emotional repression.

Emotional Repression

If we return to previous materials, we have already suggested the importance of emotional repression within our bureaucratic way of life. For example, Figure 1-3b in Chapter 1, depicting the bureaucratic individual, separates emotion from perception and thought as well as from action. In Chapter 2 we have Scheff's analysis of a change from the Old Testament to the New Testament, indicating that shame has moved underground and as a result points us toward an increase in shame-rage cycles, as illustrated in Chapter 3 by the rise of Hitler. We also have in this chapter Elie Wiesel's conclusion that the opposite of love, art, faith and life is not hate, ugliness, heresy, or death, but rather indifference. In addition, we have our examples of repressed major cultural values: group superiority and external conformity. It appears, then, that emotional repression is absolutely central to our present bureaucratic way of life. Yet what are the specific forces that propel it forward, granting that we have already touched on them? Why do we choose to bury our shame rather than bring it to the surface where we have the opportunity to deal with it? What about our other negative emotions, like fear and hate? Are we free to express our positive emotions like love and pride in oneself or self-confidence? Why have social scientists done so little to help us understand our emotions? Is it possible that we can learn to express our emotions ever more fully, given the forces for repression that presently exist?

The idea of emotional repression is linked closely to Sigmund Freud's idea that within every individual there is such a thing as an "unconscious mind," a place within us where we repress—and thus avoid awareness of—ideas and feelings that we are unable to tolerate. This idea is linked to our assumptions—as depicted within "beliefs and assumptions" in Figure 3-1—since assumptions may be unconscious. Correspondingly, "cultural norms"—also to be found in Figure 3-1—can include widely shared unconscious assumptions. Just as Scheff writes about the repression of shame and its resulting in shame-rage cycles, so does Freud write about the repression of conflicts that we are unable to deal with consciously, conflicts that emerge in disguised form within our dream lives. These conflicts, for Freud, become the basis for mental problems like neurosis if we fail to bring them up to the surface and deal with them. We might see our process of repression as much like closing the spout of a teapot and clamping down its lid all the while that water is continuing to boil. At some point the pressure of the steam within the teapot will become so great as to cause an explosion of the teapot. Or if we do allow a bit of steam to escape here and there to avoid that explosion, our efforts will be diverted from the opportunity to lead a normal life by continually working to prevent most of that steam from escaping. As a result, our neurosis, based on emotional repression, will work to distract us from paying attention to our everyday situations.

Freud's concept of the unconscious and his idea of the repression of problems that we are unable to address are absolutely central to his overall contributions to understanding human behavior. As for where those problems come from, he blames culture for making impossible demands on the individual, demands that ignore the nature of human behavior and human possibilities, as illustrated in his most well-known book, *Civilization and Its Discontents*:

> The cultural super-ego [culture] has developed its ideals [cultural values] and set up its demands.... It issues a command and does not ask whether it is possible for people to obey it. On the contrary, it assumes that a man's ego is psychologically capable of anything that is required of it, that his ego has unlimited mastery over his id [sexual and emotional instincts or drives]. This is a mistake; and even in what are known as normal people the id cannot be controlled beyond certain limits. If more is demanded of him, a revolt will be produced in him or a neurosis, or he will be made unhappy. The commandment, "Love thy neighbour as thyself," is the strongest defence against human aggressiveness and an excellent example of the unpsychological proceedings of the cultural super-ego. The commandment is impossible to fulfil ... (Freud 1930/1989: 107-109).

There is a parallel between Freud's view of the "cultural super-ego" or culture that existed in Europe and our own understanding of the nature of the bureaucratic society, for both make demands on the individual that cause enormous problems. For Freud, those problems lead to either revolt, neurosis, or unhappiness. Our metaphor of the teapot illustrates such results, where the explosion of the teapot is analogous to revolt, and where continually guarding against allowing more than a small amount of steam to emerge is analogous to neurosis or unhappiness. Freud's diagnosis of the negative impact of civilization—illustrated by the European culture of his day—even went so far as to suggest the neurotic nature of civilization itself: "[M]ay we not be justified in reaching the diagnosis that, under the influence of cultural urges, some civilizations, or some epochs of civilization—possibly the whole of mankind—have become 'neurotic'?" (110). In our own view, not only do the problems that Freud labeled neurotic extend throughout modern society but they are increasing, as illustrated by our increasing aspirations-fulfillment gap. Freud's view of the cultural demands of society on the individual are much the same as our own view of cultural values or aspirations. And his view of the inability of individuals to fulfill those demands is another way of referring to the aspirations-fulfillment gap.

As we have seen in our reference within the preceding section to the work of Karen Horney in her *The Neurotic Personality of Our Time* (1937)—a book published two years before Freud's death—she was able to carry further Freud's ideas. She was not burdened by Freud's focus on vague biological instincts that are fixed within our biological makeup, like the "life instinct" and the "death instinct," for social research had come to question the usefulness of the concept of instinct that emphasizes behavior that is biologically fixed for all time. Alternatively, Horney was aware of the enormous impact of culture in shaping the behavior of the individual.

Given her insights into the nature and importance of culture, Horney put forward her ideas, building on Freud's analysis, of the forces producing neurosis, forces that can readily lead to emotional repression:

> When we remember that in every neurosis there are contradictory tendencies which the neurotic is unable to reconcile, the question arises as to whether there are not likewise certain definite contradictions in our culture, which underlie the typical neurotic conflicts. The first contradiction to be mentioned is that between competition and success on the one hand, and brotherly love and humility on the other. On the one hand everything is done to spur us toward success, which means that we must be not only assertive but aggressive, able to push others out of the way. On the other hand we are deeply imbued with Christian ideals which declare that it is selfish to want anything for ourselves, that we should be humble, turn the other cheek, be yielding. For this contradiction there are only two solutions within the normal range: to take one of these strivings seriously and discard the other; or to take both seriously with the result that the individual is seriously inhibited in both directions.

The second contradiction is that between the stimulation of our needs and our factual frustrations in satisfying them. For economic reasons needs are constantly being stimulated in our culture by such means as advertisements, "conspicuous consumption," the ideal of "keeping up with the Joneses." For the great majority, however, the actual fulfillment of these needs is closely restricted. The psychic consequence for the individual is a constant discrepancy between his desires and their fulfillment (Horney 1937: 287-288).

What Horney succeeded in achieving in her analysis is nothing less than a union of anthropology's concern with culture, sociology's focus on patterns of behavior in society, and psychology's focus on the behavior and the problems of the individual. Her first contradiction has to do with the contradiction between cultural values, as indicated in the preceding section. Her focus on the contradiction "between competition and success on the one hand, and brotherly love and humility on the other" is also a contradiction between the cultural values of "achievement and success" and "material comfort," on the one hand, and "equality" and "individual personality," on the other hand. Another example of the contradictions among cultural values is that between the repressed cultural value of group superiority and the value of equality. And still another example is the contradiction between external conformity and individual personality.

Horney's second contradiction—"between the stimulation of our needs and our factual frustrations in satisfying them"—refers to what we have emphasized in this book as well as earlier publications. It is the gap between our aspirations and their fulfillment, a gap that works to shape our major visible social problems, and a gap that appears to be increasing. Overall, Horney's first and second contradictions have substantial impacts on the mental health of the individual, as indicated by the title of Horney's book: *The Neurotic Personality of Our Time*. For they work to teach the individual to repress fundamental goals, interests, motives, or ideals. And since what is at stake is nothing less than major cultural values, we are truly able to speak—following Freud's and Horney's analyses—of a neurotic society.

Given her broad approach to knowledge, especially taking into account the appearance of her book over 70 years ago, Horney's publication well illustrates an evolutionary worldview. She practiced psychoanalysis in Berlin before settling down in New York, where she continued to practice and also taught at the New School for Social Research. But her emphasis on the importance of culture in the origins of neurosis—even though Freud himself had referred to culture ("the cultural super-ego") in his *Civilization and Its Discontents*—led to her expulsion from the New York Psychoanalytic Institute. Here we have a classic example of the bureaucratic worldview:

Each discipline focusing on human behavior is supposedly sufficient unto itself, and no external disciplines need apply.

Freud himself was not to blame for this arrogant trashing of the scientific method. Yet his followers at the New York Psychoanalytic Institute were by no means acting much differently from other students of human behavior, granting that their approach was less subtle. For example, there is the critique of Horney's treatment of culture by Robert Merton, a former president of the American Sociological Association and a major figure in contemporary sociology for decades:

> Despite her consistent concern with "culture" ... Horney does not explore differences in the impact of this culture upon farmer, worker and businessman, upon lower-, middle-, and upper-class individuals, upon members of various ethnic and racial groups, etc. As a result, the role of "inconsistencies in culture" is not located in its differential impact upon diversely situated groups. Culture becomes a kind of blanket covering all members of the society equally, apart from their idiosyncratic differences in life-history (Merton 1949: 379).

Merton is correct that culture can have a different impact on different groups in society, yet to criticize the importance of culture for understanding the behavior of groups and of the individual is to adopt a most one-sided defense of the importance of groups at the expense of culture. Culture has been widely demonstrated—by sociologists no less the anthropologists—to be an extremely powerful force in the shaping of human behavior, *and also* it is important to take into account differences among the groups in society. Anthropological knowledge—as illustrated by the key anthropological concept of culture—is important, and so is sociological knowledge. By ignoring one kind of knowledge in an effort to emphasize another kind, we become victims of a bureaucratic way of life. Social scientists like Merton should be the very first to understand just how far this exclusionary stance departs from our ideals for the scientific method, ideals that exemplify an evolutionary worldview.

Merton is illustrating deep biases throughout the social sciences that exclude related disciplines, just as Figure 1-2 depicts. Another example from sociology has to do with Figure 3-1, where culture is linked to social structure in a subordinate way. This view of social structure differs from the generally accepted one of excluding culture from social structure, with social structure centering only on the "hand," illustrated by such concepts as social stratification, bureaucracy, and social interaction. In this way, "culture" becomes a less important concept for sociologists, and this helps to explain why sociologists generally have ignored the concept of cultural values. This approach is generally adopted by sociologists despite the widely understood view of structures as persisting patterns of behavior, and surely culture is a persisting pattern of behavior. Anthropologists generally go along with this approach, for they would not wish to see "culture," their most important concept, subordinated to "social structure." By so doing, however, they prevent culture from being given its due by sociologists, and they also work against the integration of "head," "heart," and "hand" by anthropologists. By contrast, Figure 3-1 enables us to achieve that integration by paying serious attention to culture. And in this way social scientists and the rest of us can also learn to pay more attention to cultural values along with emotional repression.

Such exclusionary behavior on the part of psychiatrists, sociologists, and anthropologists suggests their own patterns of emotional repression. Just like physical and biological scientists who ignore the social sciences, these students of human behavior—as prisoners of a bureaucratic worldview—have little understanding of how they might proceed to follow scientific ideals and integrate their different studies so as to penetrate the complexity of human behavior. Given the many hundreds of social science concepts and many thousands of social science studies, their lack of a vision of how to integrate social science knowledge is, from the perspective of the pendulum metaphor introduced in Chapter 1, a failure to see how to move the pendulum far to the right. And if the pendulum cannot swing far to the right, neither can it develop momentum for swinging far to the left, where they would address the problem of how to integrate social science knowledge. As a result, they repress awareness of and interest in this problem that is so fundamental to the progress of the social sciences, given the complexity of human behavior. In other words, a failure to see how a problem can be solved yields a failure to address that problem.

Readers should bear in mind that our focus in Part II is on problems outside and inside of social science and the academic world, and that it is social scientists who have developed most of our understanding of the nature of human behavior. It will be in Part III that we will shift that focus from problems to directions for solutions. With this in mind, we continue with our view of anthropologists, who have indeed taught us a great deal about the diversity of human cultures, both at present and historically. Yet teaching us about that diversity tells us little about the nature of human behavior in general, that is, what all of us share. And what we all share is exactly what we tried to emphasize in the above section emphasizing cultural values and contemporary institutions, given our interest in confronting world problems.

Donald Brown, an anthropologist interested in what is universal to the human species, has commented on this failure of anthropologists:

> Although they were sent into the field with the charge of getting the whole picture, so that they could come back relieved of parochial views and thus tell the world what people are really like, anthropologists have

failed to give a true report of their findings. They have dwelt on the differences between peoples while saying too little about the similarities (similarities that they rely upon at every turn in order to do their work).... The more those [sociocultural] differences can be shown to exist ... the more sociocultural anthropologists (or sociologists) can justify their role in the world of intellect and practical human affairs and thus get their salaries paid, their lectures attended, their research funded, and their essays read (1991: 154).

What Brown is suggesting is a failure of many of those anthropologists who emphasized the diversity of human cultures to be reflexive about themselves, their own values, and their own impact on their research. This has to do with their emphasis on "outward perception and thought" by contrast with "inward-outward perception and thought," as discussed in Chapter 2. They justified their own approach with the argument that they were being "value neutral," that is, that they were supposedly avoiding any impact on the peoples they studied that would bias their results. But in the process of adopting a value-neutral stance, they failed to help us learn about human behavior in general, and not just about behavior within this culture or that one. We need knowledge of human behavior in general if we are to find ways to make progress on problems throughout the world, problems that require actions by the world population as a whole.

The approach of those anthropologists is much the same as the claim of an interviewer that he or she is being neutral so that the interviewee will be completely free to come up with opinions that are not influenced by the interviewer. A commitment to the idea of value neutrality is not limited to those anthropologists studying exotic cultures. Rather, it is a stance that presently dominates social science. More specifically, the principle of value neutrality requires the scientist to remain uncommitted to any particular cultural value, staying completely neutral. According to this idea, the scientist should simply present the facts and let others decide how to make use of them, a process requiring others to be concerned with cultural values while the scientist attempts to ignore them. From this perspective, facts and values are quite distinct entities, and scientists who attempt to combine them will present no more than ideas revealing their own biases in favor of their own values, and not genuine facts. As a result, following the arguments of those in support of a value-neutral stance, science will no longer move us ever closer toward understanding phenomena. Rather, it will be the scene of competing political ideas, and deepening knowledge will go out the window.

Yet a recent collection of the work of 11 contemporary philosophers of science suggests that those arguments are invalid:

All the chapters in this book raise doubts about the ideal of a value-free science. That ideal takes science to be objective and rational and to tell us about the way things are, but not the way they should be. That ideal has dominated our conception of science for centuries. Critics of the value-free ideal are clearly challenging deeply held assumptions about a key institution of the modern era....

If the critics of the value-free science ideal are right, then these traditional claims about science not only are ungrounded but also can have pernicious consequences. If the *content* of science—not just its application—can and must involve values, then presenting scientific results as entirely neutral is deceptive. It means ignoring the value assumptions that go into science and the value implications of scientific results. Important value assumptions will be hidden behind a cloak of neutrality in public debates over policy and morality. If scientific results concerning IQ and race, free markets and growth, or environmental emissions and planetary weather make value assumptions, treating them as entirely neutral is misleading at best.... (Kincaid, Dupre, and Wylie, eds. 2007: 3-5).

These well-known philosophers have joined with what social scientists have discovered about human beings: that the individual has a heart no less than a head and a hand, and that the only way to get rid of our values is to kill us, just as the removal of a heart will accomplish that. And since the scientist is a human being just like the rest of us, the emphasis on value neutrality of our traditional approach to the scientific method yields emotional repression. Granting the impossibility of achieving value neutrality, these philosophers also argue for the pernicious consequences of this doctrine: "Important value assumptions will be hidden behind a cloak of neutrality in public debates over policy and morality." Thus, value neutrality is neither possible nor desirable for the progress of scientific research.

Another pernicious consequence of the doctrine of value neutrality has to do with our understanding of the way in which the scientific method is supposed to work. How is the scientist to develop deep commitment to scientific investigation—involving a long period of work with limited financial rewards—yet also maintain a value-neutral stance with its accompanying emotional repression? The colorless language of sociologists in their articles and books illustrates that repression, yet what is desperately required is emotional expression linked to deep emotional commitment to the tasks of science. Especially in these times of escalating social problems, the emotional commitment of social scientists is of paramount importance. Without such commitment, how can the social scientist possibly communicate to people outside of the academic world, and also communicate the sense of urgency that the times require? The scientific method itself, as discussed in the preceding chapters, requires awareness and commitment to a problem as its initial step, as illustrated by the pendulum metaphor, yet the doctrine of value neutrality yields no more than lip service to that most important step.

These philosophers raise an important question: How are we to preserve the ideal behind the doctrine of value neutrality, namely, keeping science free from bias and corruption? Of course, value neutrality does itself have pernicious consequences in hiding values behind a cloak of neutrality. But how are we, then, to avoid a science that comes to resemble a political debate between opposing values rather than the cumulative development of understanding? In our own view, the problem of achieving that movement toward ever greater understanding can be addressed by shifting toward inward-outward perception and—more generally—toward an evolutionary worldview. By so doing, the investigator opens up to his or her own basic assumptions and, as a result, can study his or her impact on the research process, namely, the nature of "investigator effects." In that way, the pretense of value neutrality is abandoned. The scientific community will, as a result, be in a position to take into account more of the complexity of what is actually going on within scientific communication. Attention would be paid, within scientific communication, not only to the scientist's own values but also to the possible impact of those values on every phase of the process of scientific investigation: the selection of a problem, the methods used to investigate it, the interpretation of the results, and the wider implications of the study.

In addition, however, it becomes essential for the scientist to open up to a very wide range of cultural values in order to avoid narrow political debates by scientists with narrow and opposing values. Here once again an evolutionary versus a bureaucratic worldview becomes most important. For that worldview points the scientist toward such breadth as well as toward egalitarian interaction with other scientists, enabling them to open up to one another's values. By contrast, the present worldview of scientists—as depicted in Figure 1-2—points away from both breadth and interaction. Following an evolutionary worldview, scientists can work together—by contrast with having divisive political debates—on developing the kind of understanding of human behavior that will help all of us to fulfill the range of our widely shared cultural values, such as those eight cultural values taken from Williams's analysis and outlined in the above section.

Granting the role of value neutrality, the role of value conflicts, and the role of a bureaucratic worldview in the development of emotional repression, let us now proceed to focus on the fundamental problem of the growing aspirations-fulfillment gap in contemporary society. Freud discussed this in the context of culture's unrealistic demands on the individual, and Horney discussed this as her second contradiction. This is the fundamental problem that has been the focus of the publications of the Sociological Imagination Group. It is clear in general that the individual cannot easily tolerate awareness of a large gap between his or her aspirations and their fulfillment. And it is most reasonable to believe that in a situation where the individual sees no direction for narrowing that gap, the individual will as a result repress awareness of it, that is, engage in emotional repression. Yet we need more understanding, based on more illustrations, of this process of emotional repression.

Arthur J. Vidich and Joseph Bensman studied the people of "Springdale" in the late 1950s, a town in upper New York State given that fictitious name. Their results were published in *Small Town in Mass Society: Class, Power, and Religion in a Rural Community* (1960). This small farming town had lost its local independence as a result of outside dominance by large corporations and the federal government. The town had been passed by, economically, by the industrial revolution, and a great many Sprindalers had seen their earlier dreams of economic success shattered. Much like the grocer of Balgat—as discussed in Chapter 1—they were experiencing a large aspirations-fulfillment gap. Vidich and Bensman attempted to answer the question of how the Springdalers managed to cope with this situation:

> *The technique of particularization* is one of the most pervasive ways of avoiding reality. It operates to make possible not only the failure to recognize dependence but also the avoidance of the realities of social class and inequalities. The Springdaler is able to maintain his equalitarian ideology because he avoids generalizing about class differences. The attributes of class are seen only in terms of the particular behavior of particular persons....
>
> The realization of lack of fulfillment of aspiration and ambition might pose an unsolvable personal problem if *the falsification of memory* did not occur, and if the hopes and ambitions of a past decade or two remained salient in the present perspective. But the individual, as he passes through time, does not live in spans of decades or years. Rather, he lives in terms of seasons, days and hours and the focus of his attention is turned to immediate pressures, pleasures and events.... As they [hopes and aspirations] are in process of disappearing, other thoughts of a more concrete and specific nature occupy the individual's attention, and new goals are unconsciously substituted for those that are being abandoned.... As a consequence, his present self, instead of entertaining the youthful dream of a 500-acre farm, entertains the plan to buy a home freezer by the fall (Vidich and Bensman 1960: 299, 303; italics ours).

It is, then, these two processes—the technique of particularization and the falsification of memory—that help the Springdalers, and perhaps the rest of us as well, to cope with their large aspirations-fulfillment gap.

The technique of particularization on an individual level is paralleled by bureaucratic specialization with limited communication at the level of the group or society as a whole. This is illustrated by the specialization and subspecialization throughout the social sciences. And the falsification of memory is illustrated by the repression of the goals of the founders of sociology to help solve society's basic problems.

Vidich and Bensman are able to give us more insight into just how the Springdalers manage to deal with their situation:

> Because they do not recognize their defeat, they are not defeated. The compromises, the self-deception and the self-avoidance are mechanisms which work; for, in operating on the basis of contradictory, illogical and conflicting assumptions, they are able to cope in their day-to-day lives with their immediate problems in a way that permits some degree of satisfaction, recognition and achievement (1960: 311–320).

Here, then, is the Springdalers' reaction to their large aspirations-fulfillment gap: repression of this problem, thus permitting "some degree of satisfaction, recognition and achievement." We see much the same thing in the behavior of contemporary social scientists. They go about their day-to-day business of teaching (although many social scientists are not teachers), meeting with students, giving examinations, doing research, writing, publishing, having discussions with colleagues, going to meetings in their organizations, going to professional meetings, serving on committees, corresponding with other social scientists, giving recommendations, accepting honors, gaining promotions, winning awards, corresponding with colleagues, and so on. By using the technique of particularization and the falsification of memory they continue to repress the big picture of increasingly threatening social problems throughout the world. And they also succeed in repressing their own failure to make substantial progress on understanding those problems and providing ideas for how to solve them.

Our focus on cultural values and emotional repression in this chapter adds an orientation to "heart" to the orientation to "head" in Chapter 2. It is in Chapter 4 that we shall complete our broad introduction to escalating problems in society with a focus on the "hand." It is also in Chapter 4 that we shall complete, with Figure 4-1, our introduction to the extraordinary language of social science. We shall focus on such questions as: How do our actions or interactions—such as our patterns of conformity—contribute to our bureaucratic way of life? How do the new concepts to be introduced relate to one another and to the other concepts within the extraordinary language? Can that language yield fundamental understanding of society's escalating problems?

CHAPTER 4

"Hand"

Conforming Behavior

It is in this chapter that we complete our initial presentation of the extraordinary language of social science with our focus on the "hand," although "heart" and "head" must be included as well. An evolutionary approach requires a building operation that must continue after the last sentence of this book is read if indeed these ideas are not just to prove somewhat meaningful to the reader but also to become genuine tools for solving problems. Thus, they must be put to work in one's everyday life to test whether or not they can help the reader understand human behavior and confront effectively personal and world problems.

Figure 4-1—Hand": Outward Perception and Thought, Emotional Repression, Conformity (Situational Behavior) Joined with Individual and Social Structures—presents our continuing introduction to the extraordinary language. In addition to the concepts presented in Figures 2-1 and 3-1, it includes new concepts: action or social interaction (with a focus on conformity), individual rituals, social rituals, groups, stratification, bureaucracy, and social organization. To the reader, these new concepts combined with the old ones might appear to be more than can be easily learned, and that is indeed the case: They cannot be easily learned, but they can be learned, especially when we have already learned to use literally thousands of concepts.

Starting with the most abstract new concept, "social organization," we can come far down the ladder of abstraction to define it as persisting and shared patterns of action or interaction within a group. By so doing,

Figure 4–1. "Head," "Heart," and "Hand": Outward Perception and Thought, Emotional Repression, Conformity, and Other Structures

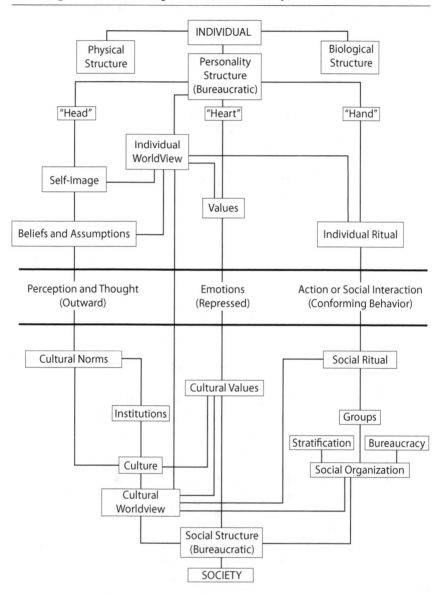

social organization comes to include the other concepts that are on the way down that ladder—social stratification, bureaucracy, groups, and social rituals—for they all also are based on patterns of action or interaction within a group. Note, as indicated by the arrow on the lower left side of Figure 4-1, that when we move up from social organization to these other concepts, we are in fact moving toward a lower level of abstraction.

From Figure 4-1 we can see that social organization is at the same level of abstraction as culture, granting that "cultural worldview" is a still more abstract focus on the key elements of culture. Thus, it is social organization and culture—with their orientations to "hand" and to "head" and "heart," respectively, that give us the two basic parts of social structure. Like love and marriage they are supposed to go together, but the bureaucratic worldview and way of life keeps them apart. As a result, sociologists generally fail to pay much attention to culture, and anthropologists generally fail to pay much attention to social organization. We noted an example of this in Chapter 3's quote from Robert Merton that centered on the limitations of the concept of culture.

In Chapter 2 we examined the nature of the bureaucratic society as well as the bureaucratic individual, with their barriers to hierarchical and horizontal communication and their resulting limited effectiveness as portrayed in Figure 1-2. And it was also in Chapter 2 that we advanced the idea—based on the work of Constas and Udy—that it is the narrow approach to science that works to limit the effectiveness of bureaucratic organizations and individuals. As for the concept of social stratification with its focus on persisting hierarchy within or among groups, we can see that pattern of social organization as fundamental to bureaucratic organizations and to society as a whole as well as to the bureaucratic individual. With respect to the concepts of social and individual rituals, these have to do with persisting patterns of action or interaction, whether within a group or society as a whole or within the individual. They are related to the term "habit," used by some psychologists along with the rest of us. But they differ in that they imply meaningful and expressive actions or interactions, thus linking the "hand" behavior of rituals with the "head" and the "heart." By contrast, habits usually are thought of in isolation from "head" and "heart." We might note also that most of us think of rituals as having to do exclusively with religion, but our own usage of the term opens it up to the full range of human behavior.

We begin this chapter with a section on the extraordinary language of social science, for we have yet to explain and illustrate much about Figure 4-1 and its implications. We follow this with a section on social organization, proceeding next to a section on culture and, finally, to a section on institutions. We shall discover that the 15 cultural values introduced in Chapter 3 are most important within all of these sections. Indeed, we might well see them as a missing link that can help us to connect the concepts of the extraordinary language of social science to the concrete concepts located between the lines at the center of Figure 4-1. Those concrete concepts are closely linked to our momentary sensory experiences, and it is those concepts that are widely used in fiction and film as well as by all of us in everyday life. We might also see the six institutions discussed in Chapter 3—political, economic, scientific, educational, religious, and family—as yet another missing link between the abstract ideas within the extraordinary language and the concrete ideas that we all use in one scene after another. In this way we will also work to tie key concepts having to do with culture together with key concepts having to do with patterns of social organization.

The Extraordinary Language

Neil Postman's analysis of Orwell's *Nineteen Eighty-Four* (discussed in Chapter 2) and Aldous Huxley's *Brave New World* (1939) in his *Amusing Ourselves to Death: Public Discourse in the Age of Show Business* (1985) can help us understand the relationship between social organization and culture:

> We were keeping our eye on 1984. When the year came and the prophecy didn't, thoughtful Americans sang softly in praise of themselves. The roots of liberal democracy had held. Wherever else the terror had happened, we, at least, had not been visited by Orwellian nightmares.
>
> But we had forgotten that alongside Orwell's dark vision, there was another—slightly older, slightly less well known, equally chilling: Aldous Huxley's *Brave New World*. Contrary to common belief even among the educated, Huxley and Orwell did not prophesy the same thing. Orwell warns that we will be overcome by an externally imposed oppression. But in Huxley's vision, no Big Brother is required to deprive people of their autonomy, maturity and history. As he saw it, people will come to love their oppression, to adore the technologies that undo their capacities to think (Postman 1985: vii-viii).

As a psychologist, Postman's background does not prepare him to pay much attention to social structure, much less to the concepts of culture and social organization, so we can understand his failure to use those concepts in his analysis. His reading of Orwell has led him to view *Nineteen Eighty-Four* as centering on patterns of social organization rather than on culture. For example, he cites the "externally imposed oppression" of Big Brother, who proceeds to "deprive people of their autonomy, maturity and history," Big Brother's banning of books, depriving us of information, and concealing the truth. All of this is related to an extreme pattern of stratification, which is a part of a bureaucratic pattern of social organization. By contrast, Postman saw *Brave New World* as "centering on culture, where people will come to love their oppression, to adore the technologies that undo their capacities to think" as a result of changes in cultural values. He focuses on such aspects of American culture as people's lack of desire to read books, passivity, egoism, and triviality.

Yet students of society understand that social organization and culture go hand in hand, just as "hand" must accompany "head" and "heart." It would be most difficult for Orwell in his nightmare vision of Oceania to neglect culture, just as it would be most difficult for Huxley to neglect social organization. Indeed, our own treatment of *Nineteen Eighty-Four* focused on language, a key aspect of culture. And Huxley's *Brave New World* included a description of the Controllers—with their patterns of stratification—who use eugenics and drugs to construct a population that can be easily manipulated. Granting that Huxley emphasizes culture, he also has a good deal to say about social organization. Yet Postman's point is an important one: Culture has to do with intangibles that are not easily recognized, and culture is incredibly powerful in shaping human behavior.

Postman explains more fully his contrast between Orwell and Huxley:

> What Huxley teaches us is that . . . when a population becomes distracted by trivia, when cultural life is redefined as a perpetual round of entertainments, when serious public conversation becomes a form of baby-talk, when, in short, a people becomes an audience and their public business a vaudeville act, then a nation finds itself at risk: culture-death is a clear possibility. . . . An Orwellian world is much easier to recognize, and to oppose, than a Huxleyan. Everything in our background has prepared us to know and resist a prison when the gates begin to close around us. . . . But what if there are no cries of anguish to be heard? Who is prepared to take arms against a sea of amusements? . . . Without a vote. Without polemics. Without guerrilla resistance. Here is ideology, pure if not serene. Here is ideology without words, and all the more powerful for their absence. All that is required to make it stick is a population that devoutly believes in the inevitability of progress (1985: 155–158).

From Postman's perspective, "An Orwellian world is much easier to recognize, and to oppose, than a Huxleyan." Yet there are less extreme examples of social stratification—such as what exists throughout the entire world—that also pose serious threats for modern society. For example, there is the problem of the increasing aspirations-fulfillment gap throughout the world. That gap results in large measure from patterns of social stratification and bureaucracy that make it most difficult to fulfill the cultural values or aspirations that prevail throughout societies. And that gap is no less invisible than the cultural values that Postman claims are not easy to recognize. Thus, it is no less difficult to oppose these patterns of social organization than patterns of culture, opposing Postman's claim that an Orwellian world—which includes relatively invisible as well as visible patterns of social stratification—is much easier to recognize and oppose than a Huxleyan world.

If we look to both culture and social organization, then we can more easily understand the basis for our aspirations-fulfillment gap, for "head," "heart," and "hand" are all involved. More specifically, we see our cultural values as shaping our aspirations, and we see our patterns of bureaucracy and stratification as shaping our ability to fulfill those values. Thus, we differ with Postman's statement that "Huxley, not Orwell, was right." In our view, Huxley *and* Orwell were right about the problems that were developing in modern society. For both were concerned with social organization as well as culture. And emerging problems—as illustrated by the growing aspirations-fulfillment gap—have to do with both culture and social organization. And patterns of stratification and bureaucracy, granting that they lack the intangibility of culture, are also very largely invisible. Since they are all around us—just like the water surrounding a goldfish in a goldfish bowl—we take them for granted, and they become invisible. Yet in our view they are fundamental forces in generating the escalating problems of modern society.

Given our focus in this section on social organization, we can clarify the implications of both books by looking to the cultural values within modern society—as discussed in Chapter 3—that would be affected by the patterns of social organization that they describe. On the one hand, the two cultural values that we are not proud of and work to suppress—group superiority and external conformity—are emphasized by the patterns of social organization described in both dark visions of the future. On the other hand, those patterns of social organization work against the fulfillment of a wide range of our other cultural values, although the emphasis of those two authors differs. For example, as we saw from Chapter 3's description of Newspeak in *Nineteen Eighty-Four,* Orwell focuses on how to trash the cultural values of understanding the world and ultimate meaning. But the book as a whole is a vision of how to prevent the fulfillment of the full range of other cultural values described in Chapter 3. As for *Brave New World,* the above-quoted excerpts emphasize Huxley's particular concern with our failure to fulfill the cultural values of understanding the world, solving problems, ultimate meaning, achievement and success, and progress.

Returning to Figure 4-1, let us proceed at this point to take up other new concepts within the extraordinary language. There is the concept of bureaucracy, which is the basis for our focus in Part II on a bureaucratic way of life. It was in Figure 1-2 of Chapter 1 that we depicted the bureaucratic society and the bureaucratic individual, focusing on three factors:

(1) ersisting hierarchy or social stratification, (2) barriers to communication, that is, specialization with little interaction across specialized areas, and (3) relative ineffectiveness in solving problems, given the existence of (1) and (2). In Chapter 2 we presented a more realistic view of bureaucracy, by contrast with an extreme view of those three characteristics. Historically, given the scientific revolution and the development of the educational institution in Western Europe, new bureaucracies proved to be more effective than preindustrial bureaucracies, granting their continuing limitations. We might proceed to define a bureaucracy or a bureaucratic organization as a group with an extensive hierarchy and division of labor with limited ability to interact internally and to solve problems. By contrast, the more general concept of "group" is broad enough to include both bureaucratic organizations as well as aggregates of individuals who interact to a great extent, such as families and friendship groups.

It remains to examine Figure 4-1's concept of "stratification," an idea that we have yet to focus on, for it is perhaps the best-researched concept throughout sociology. We did, however, pave the way for a more thorough treatment of social stratification. For example, in Chapter 1 we have Figure 1-1 with its widening aspirations-fulfillment gap, opening the way for the existence of forces—such as social stratification—that work against the fulfillment of those aspirations. Also, Figure 1-2a, with its barriers to interaction up and down hierarchies, suggests that stratification is an integral part of our bureaucratic society. As for Chapter 2, its details on the nature of contemporary bureaucratic organizations also details the existence of patterns of stratification that form an integral part of bureaucratic organizations. Further, the presentation of the nature of individual and cultural worldviews that are bureaucratic also included a presentation of patterns of social stratification that are envisioned within those worldviews. And Chapter 3 presents the repressed cultural value of group superiority, which gives legitimacy to patterns of social stratification. We might also note the focus within the political institution on the distribution of power, defined as power over other people, including coercion and not merely influence. Here again we have support for patterns of stratification.

We might define social stratification simply as a persisting hierarchy or pattern of inequality within a group or among groups. It is a pattern that is closely tied to bureaucratic organizations. But given our bureaucratic worldview and way of life, we claim it to be a pattern to be found—to somewhat varying degrees—throughout the many groups in society. However, our awareness of the prevalence of such patterns throughout society remains quite limited, as is evidenced by our repression of the cultural value of group superiority. After all, the cultural value of equality is a very important one, and it is directly opposed by the value of group superiority. Here, then, is a further argument supporting the idea that our Orwellian world of social organization—focusing on all kinds of stratification and not just the kinds suggested by Hitler and Stalin—is no less invisible and no easier to oppose than our Huxleyan world of culture.

Moving further down the ladder of abstraction, we come to "social ritual" and, correspondingly, "individual ritual." We might define the latter as an individual's persisting pattern of action that is meaningful and expressive to some degree, where a ritual's meaningfulness links it to "head" and its expressiveness ties it to "heart." This contrasts with the concept of habit, which we generally see as an isolated pattern of behavior. A social ritual is, then, no more than a ritual that is widely shared, such as decorating a Christmas tree or eating turkey during a Thanksgiving-day dinner, rituals that are both meaningful and expressive of cultural values such as close relationships. Although we ordinarily think of rituals as necessarily linked to religion, these definitions open up to a much broader use of the concept.

In common with the concept of cultural values, ritual and social ritual appear to be missing links within the abstract concepts of sociology. For the sociologist's focus has been on more general concepts like stratification and bureaucracy, concepts that focus on major forces shaping society. Psychologists avoid this concept, perhaps because of its social ties or because they already have the concept of habit. And anthropologists are less interested in specific patterns of action than in culture. Yet the concept of ritual—given its closeness to momentary actions and interactions as well as its relationships to culture—helps us approach human complexity with a framework broad enough to encompass "head," "heart," and "hand." An example of a bureaucratic individual ritual is addiction to, say, smoking. This is a persisting pattern of action that is expressive of a bureaucratic personality. Such a personality is oriented outward versus inward and outward, and is prone to emphasizing conflicting values, such as material comfort versus individual personality.

Continuing with our focus on bureaucratic patterns of behavior, we come to the very concrete concept of conformity as a species of action or social interaction. Conformity refers to an individual's situational or momentary behavior that follows the requirements of the norms or values of others. A basic question here is whether or not conforming behavior violates the individual's own values, such as "individual personality," "freedom," or "equality." If so, then conformity becomes an example of bureaucratic behavior, going along with patterns of stratification or bureaucracy yet failing to fulfill the values of the individual. We might also note that such conformity encourages outward perception versus inward-outward perception. Yet conformity need not violate one's own values and, thus, does not necessarily illustrate bureaucratic behavior. In a close relationship, for example, we might choose to conform to the wishes of the other person in order to foster the continuation of that relationship even when such conformity goes against our own desires, Yet we may do this because the value of that relationship substantially exceeds the values linked to following those desires, and thus such conformity goes along with—rather than follows—our own basic values.

To achieve further clarity on the nature of action and social interaction, we might refer to the glossary at the conclusion of this book. Action and social interaction are instances of human behavior, by contrast with the concept of interaction, which is broad enough to include both human and inanimate behavior. That general concept of interaction is most important, since it invokes the nature of our interactive universe. Yet concepts like action and social interaction point up our human situation as the most interactive creatures within the known universe. Focusing on these latter two concepts having to do with human behavior, action is sufficiently general so as to include social interaction, yet it also includes the behavior of individuals in isolated situations. Let us not forget the focus of our bureaucratic worldview on outward perception and thought, a focus that favors an emphasis on social interaction as distinct from the individual's action in isolated situations which, we believe, is at least as important.

This extraordinary language follows Gouldner's vision—presented in Chapter 1—that "At decisive points the ordinary language and conventional understandings fail and must be transcended." Just as mathematics is used in physical and biological science to achieve highly integrated relationships among physical and biological phenomena, so do we believe that the extraordinary language can accomplish much the same thing for human phenomena as a result of the logical relationships among concepts. Neither do we rule out the future development of mathematical and computer-based models, as illustrated to a limited extent by Figure 1-1's graph of the increasing aspirations-fulfillment gap. Yet we are convinced that the first order of business of social scientists is to demonstrate the power of an extraordinary language to integrate our present knowledge sufficiently so as to make serious progress on understanding our problems. And the second order of business would be to demonstrate the potential of that integration of knowledge for making serious progress toward solving those problems. Further, the third order of business would be to communicate that extraordinary language very widely—including not just those in influential positions but also everyone else—so that others could join social scientists in their efforts.

It is when we contrast our usage of this extraordinary language with our everyday language that we can gain insight into the former's potential and the latter's failures. For that everyday language that is used by social scientists no less than everyone else is very largely focused on the momentary situation within which an individual is located, much like the focus of our pets. Of course, we do sporadically invoke concepts bearing on phenomena external to that situation, and those concepts do succeed in bringing to bear on that situation some knowledge derived from the past experiences of the individuals in that situation. Yet that knowledge is extremely limited. And as we move from one situation to another we do much the same thing, with very little building on the knowledge we developed within the previous scene. I noted this in writing textbooks in introductory sociology when I reviewed those texts that had been published. As they moved from one chapter to the next there was no genuine building operation, with the new chapter having to stand up on its own and almost no references to prior chapters. More specifically, there was no extraordinary language that the authors made use of so that the new chapters could stand on the shoulders of the previous chapters.

By contrast, we see the extraordinary language as giving us an alternative approach both to social science and to life in general. We believe that we humans have the potential—with the aid of such a language—to learn to build on more and more of the knowledge developed by the entire human race throughout its history. We also believe that we can learn to apply that increasing understanding to any given situation, and also to more and more situations, and that this will enable us to make progress both in understanding our world and in solving our problems. By so doing, we will be learning to fulfill our potential as human beings to invoke ever more of what the entire human race has learned throughout its history. Granting that we are presently the most interactive creatures in the known universe, we believe that the extraordinary language will enable us to become ever more interactive, that is, to build on ever more of the experiences or occurrences throughout the universe.

Given the many thousands of social scientists currently struggling to understand human behavior as well as all those who have done so in the past, given the enormous amount of social science research that has been published, and given the large number of social science concepts that have already been put forward, how can we be so audacious as to claim so much for the extraordinary language depicted in Figure 4-1? Who are we in comparison to, for example, figures like Marx, Freud, Mills, and Gouldner? And if we are also pointing toward a scientific method that is broader than that used by physical and biological scientists, who are we in comparison to, for example, figures like Einstein and Darwin?

Our claim is based on the idea that the scientific method is a cumulative process, as illustrated by our metaphor for the scientific method of a pendulum swinging in ever widening arcs, as described in Chapter 1. We are attempting to stand on the shoulders of these giants along with a great many other giants, as indicated by our bibliographical references and quotations. Indeed, we believe that every single human being, living and dead, has made contributions to our understanding of human behavior, contributions that we almost invariably fail to build on because of a bureaucratic way of life that drastically limits our ability to learn from others.

We claim that Figure 4-1 is no more than an initial effort to develop an extraordinary language for integrating social science knowledge as well as for all of us to learn to employ it in our everyday lives to help us solve problems. Just as we are attempting to stand on the shoulders of others—and not just those who have been recognized as giants—so do we hope that others will build on our own work and, as a result, achieve much more than we are able to achieve. The concepts that we have selected for Figure 4-1 are based on our own experiences and, as a result, emphasize the achievements of sociologists more than those within other social sciences. Given the breadth of sociology, the result is not a particularly narrow set of concepts. Those concepts also emphasize our own unique experiences. Further, we have drastically limited the number of them so that readers would not be put off by their complexity but rather would be encouraged to test them in relation to their own knowledge and experience. Still further, we focused on selecting those concepts that could most easily be systematically related to one another. And we were also guided by the importance of moving far up language's ladder of abstraction—so as to reach our metaphysical stance—in order to develop a framework for integrating ever more knowledge.

More specifically, there are several concepts we have excluded from Figure 4-1 in the interest of simplicity and clarity that are important within the sociological literature ("alienation" and "anomie") or would help advance our own argument ("aspirations-fulfillment gap," "addiction," and "technology"). These concepts are located in the glossary at the conclusion of the book. Alienation is a concept emphasized by Karl Marx in his early years to show the plight of the worker in a capitalistic society. Over the years not only has it continued to be an important concept for sociologists but it has also come into ordinary usage. In our view, it illustrates the situation of all of us living in a bureaucratic society, given our patterns of stratification and the narrowness of our specialized world. As for the concept of anomie that was introduced by Durkheim (see Chapter 1 for our brief reference to Durkheim's study of suicide), we understand it to be quite similar to the concept that we have emphasized so much: the aspirations-fulfillment gap. We see "anomie" as emphasizing social structure as distinct from personality structure, and also as indicating a large gap. As for "addiction," we defined it in the glossary as "an individual's persisting pattern of action that subordinates individuality to dependence on external phenomena." We see addiction as illustrating individual rituals and linked closely with the narrow emphasis of the highly specialize economy as well as the narrow orientation of our bureaucratic worldview. Indeed, we might parallel Karen Horney's indictment of the modern world—in Chapter 3—as creating neuroses throughout society, given the contradictions within our cultural values. We might also see our world as creating addiction throughout society, given the narrowness or our bureaucratic worldview.

As for "technology," defined as a persisting pattern of action for solving problems, we might recall our use of this concept in the preface to indicate the enormous difficulties that social scientists face in communicating whatever they have learned and, thus, in helping to shape the directions taken by society. Following our quote from Emerson in the preface about building a better mousetrap, social scientists cannot simply expect that the ideas they communicate will be seen as credible unless they can actually demonstrate their effectiveness, paralleling the demonstrations of engineers and physicians of their ability to solve problems. Failing that, the words of social scientists are insufficient. Thus, following Emerson, they must themselves learn to become that better mousetrap, and this requires—in our view—that they move away from their own bureaucratic worldview and toward an evolutionary one. What we require at this point is a great many illustrations of this extraordinary language—far more than we can include between the covers of this one book—so that its usefulness can be tested and so that readers can learn how they might proceed to employ it for their own purposes. Yet we hope that the few illustrations that we can put forward will be sufficient to encourage readers to search for their own illustrations.

Social Organization

It is patterns of social organization that are more visible than patterns of culture, granting that we fail to pay much attention to social stratification and bureaucracy because we see them as opposed to the cultural values of equality and individual personality. Yet it is these patterns that are fundamental to our bureaucratic way of life, and it is these patterns that generally have stood in the way of people's ability to fulfill their aspirations, thus helping to widen the aspirations-fulfillment gap throughout contemporary society. We have already put forward some information about bureaucratic organizations in Chapter 2, but as yet we have had little to say about patterns of social stratification, a concept—along with related ideas such as that of social class—that has attracted more sociological research than any other idea.

This has been due to the enormously influential work of Karl Marx, who focused on theories of social class and never used the concept of social stratification. We must grant that part of Marx's work became the basis for a dictatorship that resulted in the slaughter of millions of people, yet our focus here is on selecting from the work of social scientists whatever can help us to understand the nature of our bureaucratic way of life.

Nevertheless, it was Marx more than anyone else to whom we may turn as the founder of a broad approach to the social sciences. That breadth is well illustrated by his 1844 essay analyzing the alienation or plight of the worker in industrial society. His focus in that work was on drawing out the incredible contradiction or gap between ideals for humanity brought forward during the American and French revolutions and the actuality of working conditions and an economic system that trashed those ideals. By so doing, he parallels our own emphasis on the gap between aspirations and their fulfillment.

Marx wrote these words about the plight of the worker in industrial society just before the Revolution of 1848 in Paris:

> We have now considered the act of alienation of practical human activity, labour, from two aspects: (1) the relationship of the worker to the product of labour as an alien object which dominates him ... (2) the relationship of labour to the act of production within labour. This is the relationship of the worker to his own activity as something alien and not belonging to him.... This is self-alienation as against the above-mentioned alienation of the thing.... Since alienated labour: (1) alienates nature from man; and (2) alienates man from himself, from his own active function, his life activity; so it alienates him from (3) the species.... For labour, life activity, productive life, now appear to man only as means for the satisfaction of a need, the need to maintain his physical existence.... Free, conscious activity is the species-character of human beings. (4) A direct consequence of the alienation of man from the product of his labour, from his life activity and from his species-life, is that man is alienated from other men (Marx 1844/1964: 125–127, 129).

As a result of his experiences within the workplace, the worker (1) comes to be divorced from his physical environment (physical structure), (2) has no control of his own activities (personality structure), (3) is dehumanized (biological structure), and (4) also loses out on relating to his fellow man (social structure). Marx later developed extensive analyses of the problems of a capitalistic society, of the degradation of the working class (or the proletariat) by the owning class (or the bourgeoisie) of society's capital, and of the necessity of a revolution that would yield an egalitarian society, but that is not our focus here. He focused on patterns of social organization like class warfare rather than on culture or on the individual, granting that his early essay on alienation stood out as an exception to that focus. Yet we can come to understand that essay, which stands out to this day as our best understanding of the phenomenon of alienation, by bringing to bear on it some of the concepts in Figure 4-1.

In our view the alienation of the worker in contemporary society, and not just in the middle of the nineteenth century, is analogous to the situation of the grocer of Balgat, who claimed, "I have not the possibility in myself to get the things that I want. They only bother me." The grocer illustrates all of us moderns, including Marx's workers, who have experienced a revolution of rising expectations, yielding the exponential curve of aspirations depicted in Figure 1-1 that is going through the roof coupled with a large aspirations-fulfillment gap. Feudal serfs in earlier centuries, in common with the chief of Balgat, did not experience that revolution of rising expectations nor the resulting large aspirations-fulfillment gap. However, Marx's interest is not in culture but rather in social organization, and he failed to take into account that revolution of rising expectations as it related to workers within his analysis of alienation.

This is not to deny that the situation of the factory worker in the middle of the nineteenth century was worse in some respects than that of the serf or peasant working on a small plot of land. For example, serfs generally were not under the immediate control of some overseer or boss hour after hour, by contrast with the situation of the factory worker. Further, serfs probably had more opportunities to relate to one another than was the case for factory workers. Also, the objects of the serf's labor—the land that he or she worked and the resulting fruits of that labor—were not "alien" objects but rather were extremely familiar objects. Nevertheless, it was the industrial worker rather than the serf who experienced that revolution of rising expectations with its resulting aspirations-fulfillment gap, a gap based on paying attention to changes in cultural values.

More specifically, it was the eighteenth-century Enlightenment era centered in France—based on earlier cultural developments like the Renaissance of learning and the Protestant Reformation—that yielded emphasis on such people-oriented cultural values as equality, freedom, individual personality, and democracy. Those were values that were hardly emphasized during the lifetime of the preindustrial serf. And it was such cultural values that not only motivated Marx's own commitments but also had infiltrated the consciousness of factory workers in Marx's day. And it was such cultural values that should be seen together with the patterns of stratification and bureaucracy experienced by those workers if indeed we are to understand more fully the various kinds of alienation that Marx described in his brilliant essay.

As another example of a pattern of social organization—as well as individual behavior emphasizing the "hand"—we turn to the concepts of "ritual" and "social ritual."

We might refer here to studies of concentration camps and internment camps—focusing on rituals in everyday life—initiated by J. David Knottnerus, whose manuscript in progress builds on a statement by Janusz Bardach. Bardach managed to survive the severe conditions of the Soviet labor camps and described his experiences in *Man Is Wolf to Man: Surviving the Gulag*:

> At four a.m. the ringing rail sounded for us to get up. Despite my fatigue and the cold, I kept the exercise routine I had followed at home and in the Red Army, washing my face and hands at the hand pump. I wanted to retain as much pride in myself as I could, separate myself from the many prisoners I had seen give up day by day. They'd stop caring first about their hygiene or appearance, then about their fellow prisoners, and finally about their own lives. If I had control over nothing else, I had control over this ritual, which I believed would keep me from degradation and certain death (1998: 130; see also Phillips and Johnston 2007: 109; Knottnerus, unpublished manuscript).

In this brief excerpt from Bardach's book we can learn the contrast between two quite different kinds of rituals. On the one hand there is what we might call a bureaucratic ritual: "They'd stop caring first about their hygiene or appearance, then about their fellow prisoners, and finally about their own lives." On the other hand, there is what we might call an evolutionary ritual: "At four a.m. the ringing rail sounded for us to get up. Despite my fatigue and the cold, I kept the exercise routine I had followed at home and in the Red Army, washing my face and hands at the hand pump. I wanted to retain as much pride in myself as I could." According to Bardach, it was such simple rituals that ultimately spelled the difference between life and death: "If I had control over nothing else, I had control over this ritual, which I believed would keep me from degradation and certain death." A key difference between the two types of rituals is the degree to which they are "meaningful" and "expressive." A bureaucratic ritual is meaningful and expressive only to a limited degree, granting that it is not completely isolated from "head" and "heart." By contrast, an evolutionary ritual is meaningful and expressive to a great degree, linking up with the individual's beliefs and assumptions, self-image, worldview, and values. For example, we might see Bardach's exercise and washing routines as helping him to fulfill such values as individual personality, freedom, and equality. In addition, these ritualistic actions invoke his former patterned behavior within the social organization of society.

As for widely shared or social rituals that are not just the ones that we are most aware of and celebrate, like Christmas and Thanksgiving, our bureaucratic way of life with its patterns of stratification is made up of thousands of such social rituals supporting that way of life. Every single aspect of our lives is full of both social rituals and individual rituals, just as every single aspect of our lives illustrates our beliefs and assumptions, self-image, worldview, and values. Given the importance of ritual for understanding human behavior—basic to the "extraordinary" language of social science—it is most unfortunate that this concept has fallen through the wide chasm between psychology and sociology. On the one hand, psychologists generally are not much concerned with the links between habits and our overall bureaucratic way of life. And sociologists are not much concerned with what they see as the trivial examples of repetitive behavior of the individual. The result is that our ritualistic behavior remains relatively invisible. Thus, it is not just our very abstract or general ideas like our worldview that are most difficult to see: It is also our very concrete behavior that is largely invisible when we attempt to understand ourselves and our world.

These studies of concentration camps were no more than preliminary ones, yet they are highly suggestive about the role of language—and in particular movement up and down language's ladder of abstraction—in the development of evolutionary rituals. It appears that those few prisoners engaging in evolutionary rituals were able to move far up and down that ladder, just like our own emphasis on such movement within a broad approach to the scientific method. They moved far down through their deep involvement with what most of us would see as relatively trivial patterns of behavior. And they moved far up that ladder by seeing their behavior as linked to their basic values as well as to activities linked to the patterns of social organization within their former lives.

By contrast, these preliminary studies suggest that the majority of prisoners engaged in little movement up and down language's ladder of abstraction so as to invoke their cultural values and former social rituals. Granting that they were tired and hungry, and that some of them were sick, they gave in to delusions that their passivity was a good way to survive. Herling suggests that the majority of the prisoners were demoralized, indicating a failure to see themselves within a possible future where they would emerge from prison. That would have required them to become reflexive enough to look at themselves and their own possible future, versus their actual behavior of outward perception. Further, they may well have used the Springdalers' technique of particularization and falsification of memory to repress their emotional problems and thus avoid any strong commitment to work toward staying alive.

The title of this chapter—"Hand": Conforming Behavior—suggests the overriding importance of conforming behavior for the continuation of our bureaucratic way of life. We might note that stratification and conformity are head and tail of the same coin. If we look to Figure 1-2b depicting the bureaucratic personality, we might also note that the barriers between "head" and "heart" and between "heart" and "hand" work to prevent the individual from taking any action based on either profound thought or deep emotional commitment. Further, let us not forget that external conformity is a major culture value throughout modern society, as we might well infer from the outward perception and thought along with emotional repression linked to a bureaucratic worldview. Let us also bear in mind that conforming behavior is situational by contrast with structural or repeated behavior.

Conforming Behavior

Our focus in this section will be on the kind of conforming behavior that is characteristic of a bureaucratic way of life, that is, conforming behavior that deeply conflicts with the individual's values and that is, as a result, linked to severe emotional repression. Such conforming behavior should be seen in relation to the norms that apply to a given situation. In particular, we shall examine a series of experiments that took place in the early 1970s, prior to the development of rules aimed at protecting the welfare of experimental subjects. Thus, these experiments cannot be repeated, yet we believe that they shed a great deal of light on just how effectively norms or expectations—under certain situational conditions—can influence people to conform to those norms. The experiment, developed by Stanley Milgram—a psychologist working at Yale University—was described in Milgram's *Obedience to Authority* (1974).

Milgram obtained a group of experimental subjects through an ad in a New Haven paper as well as phone calls to individuals in the New Haven telephone directory—selected in a random way—specifying that participants in an experiment on learning would be paid $4 per hour. Subjects were introduced to a 47-year-old accountant generally described as "mild-mannered and likable," who played the role of "learner" while each subject played the role of "teacher." Actually, the learner was Milgram's confederate, and he had been carefully coached on how he was to behave throughout the experiment. As for the "experimenter," his role was played by a 31-year-old biology teacher dressed in a gray technician's coat. He had been coached to show as little emotion as possible and to appear somewhat stern.

As for the learning task, the teacher read several pairs of words to the learner, such as "blue box," and later the learner was cued by one of the words and was then required to respond with the associated word. If the learner gave an incorrect answer or failed to respond within a few seconds, the teacher was supposed to give the learner an electric shock using a bogus "shock generator" with voltages that ranged from 15 to 450. Teachers were instructed to begin with 15 volts and then add 15 additional votes for each incorrect answer, thus taking them up to the level of 450 volts. After the conclusion of the experiments, Milgram asked an audience of college students, psychiatrists and other adults how they would expect those teachers to react to their instructions. A total of 110 individuals responded, and not a single one expected any teacher to administer a shock greater than 300 volts, indicating that they would refuse to do so. Further, most respondents indicated that no one would go past 150 volts.

Milgram had arranged four different experimental conditions, varying in how close the teacher was to the learner: (1) a remote condition, where the learner was supposedly strapped to a chair in an adjoining room, with communication by electric signal; (2) voice feedback, where the learner's vocal protests can be heard through the laboratory wall; (3) proximity, where the teacher stands only a few feet away from the learner; and (4) touch proximity, where the teacher must place the learner's hand on the shock plate. Milgram found that fully 65 percent of the teachers continued up to the maximum of 450 volts in (1) the remote condition; 62.5 percent in (2) the voice-feedback condition; 40 percent in (3) proximity; and 30 percent in (4) touch proximity.

Some of the reactions of teachers in the remote condition are illustrated by these remarks of one of them: "these are terrific volts. I don't think this is very humane.... Oh, I can't go on with this; no, this isn't right. It's a hell of an experiment. The guy is suffering in there. No, I don't want to go on. This is crazy" (Milgram 1974: 32).

In the voice-feedback condition, the learner had been coached to groan painfully at 135 volts, demand to be released from the experiment at 150 volts, shout that he could no longer stand the pain at 180, scream in agony at 270, and shriek with increasing intensity from 300 volts onward. In one variation of the experiment, when a laboratory was set up in a rundown building not associated with Yale University, compliance of the teacher with the demands of the experimenter dropped from 62.5 percent to 48 percent. And in another variation where the experimenter issued his orders to the teacher over a telephone, the teacher's conforming behavior dropped to less than 25 percent.

Such a series of experiments could not be repeated now because of concerns for the health of the teachers who conformed to the commands of the experimenter and, afterwards had to face themselves. For many of them had done nothing less than sent lethal voltages into the body of the learner. Such conforming behavior might be compared to that of all those in Nazi Germany's concentration camps who actively participated in the murder of millions of human beings. We might see our new regulations for protecting experimental subjects as a triumph for people-oriented cultural values like individual personality and equality. At the same time, however, the price we must pay is the elimination of findings—related to the cultural value of science and secular rationality—like those uncovered by Milgram. Just how important are these findings? What can we learn from them about the individual and society? More specifically, what do they teach us about our bureaucratic way of life and about our potential for moving toward an evolutionary way of life?

For one thing, we can learn about people's orientation to repress information suggesting the importance of cultural values that oppose their own idealistic cultural values, like the values of external conformity and group superiority. We might recall that every single one of the 110 responses that Milgram obtained—when he asked an audience to predict the results of his experiments—predicted that no teacher would administer a shock greater than 300 volts. And the majority of those who responded indicated that no one would go past 150 volts. In the remote condition, by contrast, fully 65 percent of the teachers went up to the maximum of 450 volts, and 62.5 percent did the same thing in the voice-feedback condition.

The experiments had been so designed that many of the experimental conditions emphasized both the norms that pushed for conforming behavior as well as patterns of stratification that were reinforced by our repressed cultural theme of group superiority. For example, the experimenter had been coached to show as little emotion as possible and to appear somewhat stern, thus emphasizing the serious nature and importance of conforming to experimental norms. And the link between the experiments and Yale University brought into their context the power of existing patterns of social stratification. Further, in the remote and voice-feedback conditions the learner was not physically present to embody such humanistic cultural values of individual personality, equality, and freedom. All of these factors, taken together, help us to understand the forces pushing the teachers to conform to the orders of the experimenter.

In a set of contrasting conditions, however, those forces were decreased, and the result was less conforming behavior. When the voice-feedback experiment was performed in a rundown building with no relationship to Yale, compliance dropped from 62.5 percent to 48 percent. And in that same experimental condition, when the experimenter communicated his instructions to the teacher by telephone, compliance dropped dramatically to under 25 percent. Given such variations in the teachers' behavior, it becomes important to get away from stereotyping the teachers as either conformists or nonconformists. Instead, we should pay attention to the range of forces bearing on a given scene, using the extraordinary language to detect those forces. In these experiments, for example, we must pay close attention to such factors as the degree to which stratification exists not only in society but also within the experimental setting. And we would do well to take into account the cultural norms supporting stratification in society along with the expectations or beliefs within the experimental situation.

It appears, then, that the Milgram experiments—given the conforming behavior of the teachers as well as the investigators, and given the emotional repression of Milgram's audience—yields evidence for the prevalence of a bureaucratic worldview among the experimental subjects, among the investigators, and among Milgram's audience. As a result, the extent of the conforming behavior among the experimental subjects that Milgram uncovered should be no surprise to us, as it was to Milgram's audience. Neither should we ourselves feel immune from the conforming behavior that Milgram uncovered, given that Milgram and his associates along with his audience apparently were also not immune from such behavior. Indeed, we might wonder how we would have behaved if we had taken on the role of teacher in the Milgram experiments, given that we had no knowledge of its true purpose. These experiments also help us to understand the enormous complexity involved in an experimental situation. Yet all of those forces we have examined are involved in any given social situation, and not just within an experiment. In the next and final section of this chapter we shall look to a variety of examples—both current and historical—linked to each of the institutions of contemporary society. Once again, we shall examine whether or not the extraordinary language can help us to understand what is going on.

Institutions

As we may recall from Chapter 3, institutions were conceived of as systems of cultural values and norms that focus on the organization of society and the solution of its major problems. Thus, this concept helps us bridge the wide divide within the social science literature between culture and social organization, given their focus on both cultural values and norms as well as on social organization. We shall take up, but only very briefly, one illustration from each institution: political, economic, scientific, educational, religious, and family. From this perspective, we include medical patterns of culture and social organization within the economic institution. Also, we include the mass media of communication within the educational institution. And we include military phenomena within the political institution. This division of society is far more relevant to contemporary society than to preindustrial society, where the scientific and educational institutions had not split off from the religious and family institutions and thus participated in the social organization of our modern bureaucratic society.

The Political Institution

Amy Chua, a professor at Yale Law School who is much concerned with political and economic problems throughout the world has written a most sobering book addressing those problems: *World on Fire: How Exporting Free Market Democracy Breeds Ethnic Hatred and Global Instability* (2003). Her focus in most of her book is on countries throughout the non-Western world that have no more than begun to develop Western nonmaterialistic cultural values such as democracy, equality, individual personality, and freedom. As a result, our efforts to export democracy—given the past development of free markets that have led to rule by a minority—results in shifting power from a minority that has practiced an extreme form of social stratification with its focus on the cultural value of group superiority to a majority that has suffered for years under the rule of that minority and is out for revenge:

> [T]he sobering thesis of this book is that the global spread of markets and democracy is a principal, aggravating cause of group hatred and ethnic violence throughout the non-Western world. In the numerous societies around the world that have a market-dominant minority, markets and democracy are not mutually reinforcing. Because markets and democracy benefit different ethnic groups in such societies, the pursuit of free market democracy produces highly unstable and combustible conditions.
>
> Markets concentrate enormous wealth in the hands of an "outsider" minority, fomenting ethnic envy and hatred among often chronically poor majorities. In absolute terms the majority may or may not be better off, ... but any sense of improvement is overwhelmed by their continuing poverty and the hated minority's extraordinary economic success. ...
>
> Introducing democracy in these circumstances does not transform voters into open-minded citizens in a national community. Rather, the competition for votes fosters the emergence of demagogues who scapegoat the resented minority and foment active ethnonationalist movements demanding that the country's wealth and identity be reclaimed by the "true owners of the nation." As America celebrated the global spread of democracy in the 1990s, ethnicized political slogans proliferated: "Georgia for the Georgians," "Eritreans Out of Ethiopia," "Kenya for Kenyans," "Venezuela for Pardos," "Kazakhstan for Kazakhs," "Serbia for Serbs," "Croatia for Croats," "Hutu Power," "Assam for Assamese," "Jews Out of Russia" (Chua 2003: 9-10).

Chua does not limit herself to an analysis of third-world countries, for she carries her analysis into examining the relationship of the United States to the rest of the world. Why all of the hatred that has been leveled at the United States in recent times? Is it simply because of the actions of President Bush? Or is there more to this story? Apparently so. Just as ethnic minorities in many countries have come to gain a monopoly of wealth and power, so has America—with a tiny minority of the world's population—become a superpower with enormous wealth in comparison to those countries. Further, just as democratic ideals and efforts at democratization have yielded violent confrontations between majorities and minorities in many of these countries, so do these same ideals stir up hatred of America. Still further, the United States has come to be seen as an oppressor of poor nations to the extent that its economic policies work to keep those nations at the lower end of the economic hierarchy among nations. For economic stratification among nations has continued in the contemporary world, and all the while a worldwide revolution of rising expectations continues to fan the flames of discontent.

To illustrate the enormous economic gap among nations, the per capita share of the gross national product in the poorest nations was $410 in the year 2000, by contrast with $25,730 in the richest nations. Thus, the two differ by a factor of no less than 63. If we look to life expectancy, in the low-income nations it was 60 years, but it was78 years in the high-income nations (Krugman and Obstfeld 2003: 666–667).

Within the bureaucratic worldview that lies behind the social structures of contemporary society—and, thus, works to structure our political institutions—is a focus on power as the ability to coerce others regardless of their own values and beliefs. Yet within an evolutionary worldview we can come to think of power primarily in terms of legal authority together with influence, patterns of social organization far removed from efforts to achieve revenge. And to achieve influence in today's world it appears essential to be able to point a direction toward fulfilling the full range of our humanistic cultural values. This includes being able to address effectively the worldwide increasing aspirations-fulfillment gap. Just as our "world on fire" is based on a combination of cultural values and patterns of social organization, so must a path that leads out of that fire equally be based on these two aspects of social structure. However, it is most difficult to achieve an understanding of the importance of such breadth without the aid of the extraordinary language of social science.

The Economy

William Easterly, an economics professor at New York University who has spent much of his career at the World Bank, addresses a fundamental world problem that remains unsolved to this day in his *The White Man's Burden: Why the West's Efforts to Aid the Rest Have Done So Much Ill and So Little Good* (2006): Virginia Postrel's review of the book yields insight into Easterly's arguments:

> Malaria infects 300 million to 500 million people a year, causing severe pain and debilitation. A million of those taken ill die, mostly infants and young children. . . . Insecticide-treated mosquito nets, which cost $5 or less, could prevent most infections. A mere $2.50 in medicine can treat the deadliest form of the disease, the World Health Organization

reports. So why don't we just buy the nets and medicines? ... It's not that simple, William Easterly argues in *The White Man's Burden*. Take those mosquito nets. When aid agencies hand them out in poor countries, he writes, "nets are often diverted to the black market.... or wind up being used as fishing nets or wedding veils." Free nets don't get to the people who need them.

But in rural Malawi, clinics serving new mothers sell insecticide-treated bed nets for 50 cents each. The nets come from a program developed by local Malawians working for Population Services International, a Washington-based nonprofit organization. In Malawi's cities, the group sells nets for $5 each, using the profits to subsidize sales in the countryside. The program, Easterly reports, has "increased the nationwide average of children under 5 sleeping under nets from 8 percent in 2000 to 55 percent in 2004.... A follow-up study found nearly universal use of the nets by those who paid for them." By contrast, when a Zambian program handed out free nets, "70 percent of the recipients didn't use" them. Charging for nets may sound hardhearted, but prices provide vital information about commitment....

In *The White Man's Burden* Easterly turns from incentives to the subtler problems of knowledge.... He contrasts the traditional "Planner" approach of most aid projects with the "Searcher" approach that works so well in the markets and democracies of the West.... "A Planner thinks he already knows the answers," Easterly writes. "A Searcher admits he doesn't know the answers in advance; he believes that poverty is a complicated tangle of political, social, historical, institutional and technological factors" (Postrel 2006: 12).

It appears that William Easterly has somehow managed to cover all three bases of "head," "heart," and "hand" in his efforts to make progress in solving the puzzle of poverty in third-world nations. He argues that the West has spent no less than $2.3 trillion on foreign aid over the last half-century, yet has still failed to get 12-cent medicines to children to prevent half of all malaria deaths, to get $4 bed nets to poor families, or to get $3 to each new mother to prevent 5 million child deaths. This is his argument that "The West is not stingy. It is ineffective." His focus is on "hand," yet he was also focused on "heart" in his 2001 book—*The Elusive Quest for Growth*—where he centered on the idea that "incentives matter" in his efforts to explain the failure of international efforts to spur third-world economic development. As for "head," which is a focus of *The White Man's Burden,* his contrast between the traditional "Planner" and the "Searcher" is a contrast between the failure to use the scientific method and an effort to use that method, with its commitment to confronting a problem that has not yet been solved and its openness to the complexity of human behavior.

Science

We would do well to pay attention to the words of the English poet, Alexander Pope, in his *Essay on Criticism* written in 1711:

> A little learning is a dangerous thing;
> Drink deep, or taste not the Pierian spring;
> There shallow draughts intoxicate the brain,
> And drinking largely sobers us again.
> (Quoted by Knowles 2004: 604, note 2)

It is indeed hard to believe that all of our learning from the physical and biological sciences—and from applied fields like engineering and medicine—make up no more than "a little learning." Has not all of that learning been sufficient to shape our world over these past centuries, yielding continuing progress? Yet we should question that "progress." Physical and biological scientists have continued to take "shallow draughts" that "intoxicate the brain," convincing them that they need not pay attention to human behavior. They continue to ignore human phenomena and the efforts of social scientists, who came on the scene late in the day. And they continue to construct an ever more dangerous world for all of us. This is largely due to the continuing improvement of weapons of mass destruction coupled with our failure to learn how to prevent that improvement and prevent people from using those weapons. It is also an ever more one-sided world that emphasizes materialistic developments—based on physical science and its technologies—rather than the full range of our human capacities. As yet we have developed very little understanding of just what those capacities are and how we might fulfill them.

We might dramatize the importance of knowledge of human behavior by returning to the situation of a head of state that was described in the preface by George Lundberg, a sociologist who taught at the University of Washington. Lundberg wrote those words over 60 years ago, and it appears that we have indeed "become much sicker" since then. Yet after all this time we still do not "consent to take the only medicine which can help us." And after all this time we still do not have social research institutions "which will rank with Massachusetts and California Institutes of Technology, Mellon Institute, the research laboratories of Bell Telephone, General Electric and General Motors, not to mention several thousand others." Many—including even some social scientists who have proceeded with "techniques of particularization" and the "falsification of memory"—would claim that this would be impossible. In our own view, there is no barrier to that achievement which we do not have the capacity to overcome. One thing that would be required is the testing of an extraordinary language of social science—whether or not it is based on Figure 4-1—that succeeds in providing a direction for the integration of existing knowledge of human behavior and social problems. We hope that this book will at least illustrate that this can indeed be accomplished.

Education

Fiction, poetry, drama, and film can contribute to our understanding no less than, and perhaps more than, nonfiction. Herman Hesse published *The Glass Bead Game* or *Magister Ludi* in 1943 in Switzerland during World War II, and this novel was much of the basis for the Nobel Prize he received in 1946. Hesse focused on the splitting up of modern society into parts that fail to communicate with one another. Specifically, it is the split between those creating the many elements of culture—including philosophers, artists, composers, and scientists—and the individuals throughout society attempting to confront the devastating problems of our era. In other words, the split is between head and heart, on one side, and hand, on the other side. Prior to World War II Hesse idealized a world of culture set far apart from our everyday world full of unsolved problems, but it was in *The Glass Bead Game* that he demonstrated a radical change in his perspective. Culture is indeed important, but the artist and scientist must do their utmost to help society solve its urgent problems if they are to survive along with everyone else. Although Hesse came to be revered by the college students of the 1960s as an underground hero preaching active rebellion against the status quo, in fact he suggested not action alone but action guided by the vast cultural achievements illustrated by the elements of *The Glass Bead Game*.

Hesse's book was a call to take action on the development of a broad approach to culture as well as to the social problems of modern society. The story takes place in the far future, and the book is a biography of the life of Joseph Knecht, who was Magister Ludi, master of the Glass Bead Game. Knecht had become the leader of an intellectual order, Castalia—much like our present academic world—devoted exclusively to the development of the mind and the imagination. The Glass Bead Game is a game played by members of Castalia in order to integrate and keep alive the wisdom of all ages, and it involves working with elements of all cultures derived from their philosophical, literary, dramatic, artistic, musical, and scientific achievements. This is in fact what Hesse himself was attempting to do throughout most of his life: to keep alive elements of all cultures by means of his novels, as well as by separating those cultural achievements from the pressing problems of the day. But Hesse had a radical change of heart during World War II, when he came to see the isolation of an intellectual community from world problems as a threat to the future of humanity.

After reaching the pinnacle of achievement in Castalia as Master of the Glass Bead Game, Joseph Knecht sends a letter to the ruling Board of his intellectual Order which includes the following:

> I have begun to doubt my ability to officiate satisfactorily because I consider the Glass Bead Game in a state of crisis.... Here I am sitting in the top story of our Castalian edifice ... [a]nd instinct tells me, my nose tells me, that down below something is burning, our whole structure is imperiled, and that my business now is not to analyze music or define rules of the Game, but to rush to where the smoke is.... The history of societies shows a constant tendency toward the formation of a nobility as the apex and crown of any given society.... If, now, we regard our Order as a nobility and try to examine ourselves to see ... to what extent we have already been infected by the characteristic disease of nobility—hubris, conceit, class arrogance, self-righteousness, exploitativeness ... we may be seized by a good many doubts....
>
> In brief, this Castalian culture of ours ... tends somewhat toward smugness and self-praise, toward the cultivation and elaboration of intellectual specialism.... Historically we are, I believe, ripe for dismantling. And there is no doubt that such will be our fate, not today or tomorrow, but the day after tomorrow.... Critical times are approaching; the omens can be sensed everywhere; the world is once again about to shift its center of gravity. Displacements of power are in the offing. They will not take place without war and violence.... I herewith request the Board to relieve me of my office as Magister Ludi and entrust to me an ordinary school, large or small, outside in the country; to let me staff it with a group of youthful members of our Order (Hesse 1943/1969: 319, 321–322, 328–329, 335).

In our own view the academic world—and in particular social science—holds the key to our survival. Hesse seems to have realized this, as he expressed this indirectly with Knecht's letter of resignation and his interest in applying his understanding, commitments, and actions to educational efforts outside of Castalia. And he was also hopeful that he could make Castalians aware of the dangers threatening both society as a whole and Castalia as well so that Castalians would become motivated to follow his lead. We are aware that many of our readers are modern Castalians. We urge them not to leave the academic world but to work within it to integrate our available knowledge so that an intellectual framework is developed that can contribute toward the solution of our escalating problems, a framework that our own efforts have pointed toward.

Religion

From Chapter 3 we have a view of the religious institution as centering on the cultural values of ultimate meaning, and also its sharing with Williams's listing of major cultural values the cultural value of individual personality. Yet ultimate meaning is an extremely broad cultural value, invoking a wide range of other cultural values and not just individual personality. As an illustration of that breadth, let us look to a selection from the Book of Genesis within the Old Testament:

> In the beginning God created the heavens and the earth.... God said, "Let us make man in our own image, in the likeness of ourselves, and let them be masters of the fish of the sea, the birds of heavens, the cattle, all the wild beasts and all the reptiles that crawl upon the earth. (Jones, ed. 1966: 5–6; Genesis 1: 1, 26).

The idea that men and women were created in the image of God speaks worlds about the importance of the human being within the overall scheme of things. We can, then, understand this Judeo-Christian view of the human race as providing the groundwork for the development of humanistic cultural values—such as individual personality, freedom, equality, and democracy—in modern times. At the same time, we may note a commitment to persisting hierarchy or stratification. God has a superior relationship to man, since God created man. And there is also human beings' position as "masters of the fish of the sea, the birds of heavens, the cattle, all the wild beasts and all the reptiles that crawl upon the earth." We might see such persisting hierarchy or stratification as a prelude to our work-related cultural values that are linked to our stratified and bureaucratic patterns of social organization.

However, as we noted in Chapter 2, those work-related cultural values—especially material comfort—came to conflict more and more with people-oriented values with the development of the continuing industrial or technological revolution: "In Baxter's view the care for external goods should only lie on the shoulders of the "saint like a light cloak, which can be thrown aside at any moment." But fate decreed that the cloak should become an *iron cage*." Max Weber quotes Benjamin Franklin's *Necessary Hints to Those That Would Be Rich* to illustrate this new materialistic emphasis:

> Remember that *time* is money. He that can earn ten shillings a day by his labour, and goes abroad, or sits idle, one half of that day, though he spends but sixpence during his diversion or idleness, ought not to reckon *that* the only expense; he has really spent, or rather thrown away, five shillings besides....

The most trifling actions that affect a man's credit are to be regarded. The sound of your hammer at five in the morning, or eight at night, heard by a creditor, makes him easy six months longer; but if he sees you at a billiard-table, or hears your voice at a tavern, when you should be at work, he sends for his money the next day; demands it before he can receive it, in a lump (Weber 1905/1958: 48–49)

Weber's argument is that it was the Protestant ethic itself that was largely responsible for developing what he called "the spirit of capitalism," which we might see as illustrated not only by the cultural value of material comfort but also by other work-related values like achievement and success, economic progress, and science as applied to technological developments in society. For he saw Puritanism—illustrating Protestantism in general—as encouraging people to believe that they could tell whether or not they had in fact achieved eternal salvation by the extent of their economic success. The result was the development of a powerful work ethic that is well illustrated by the above quote from Franklin.

These illustrations from the Judeo-Christian tradition that suggest conflicts between people-oriented and work-related cultural values go along with Karen Horney's analysis from Chapter 3. We might recall her reference to the contradiction "between competition and success on the one hand, and brotherly love and humility on the other." She saw no way out other than either "to take one of these strivings seriously and discard the other" or "to take both seriously with the result that the individual is seriously inhibited in both directions." The result would be either a focus on materialism or on brotherly love, on the one hand, or "the neurotic personality of our time," on the other hand.

Yet we see both of these alternatives as linked to a bureaucratic worldview and way of life, as illustrated metaphorically by a see-saw, where one person's rise necessarily results in another person's fall. An evolutionary worldview, by contrast, points toward a third alternative, as suggested by an image of a stairway with very wide steps so that everyone can climb upward, and with no top step. One individual's ability to climb need not threaten others, but might in fact help them by illustrating how one can proceed to climb. These alternative metaphors are broad enough to suggest alternative "ultimate meanings" that religion can take up. Thus, we can have a religion that opens up to the possibility of continuing nonbiological evolution just as we can have bureaucratic religions that structure contradictions between people-oriented and work-related cultural values.

The Family

Chapter 3 specified the key cultural values deriving from the institution of the family as the continuation of life as well as intimate and close relationships. Just as in the case of religion, the family has much to do with the full range of our cultural values. For that is what is involved in the life of the individual along with our relationships to one another. And we must not forget as well the importance of our patterns of social organization, since they are also deeply and directly involved in our relationships. Yet it is crucial that we come to understand all of our institutions and our patterns of social organization from a historical perspective, just as we looked to religion in this way.

Georg Simmel was the fourth major founder of the discipline of sociology. We have already briefly referred to Emile Durkheim in Chapter 1 within the context of our growing aspirations-fulfillment gap with a quote from his *Suicide*, a book that provided a model for sociological research. We took up the work of Max Weber in Chapter 2 as well as in this chapter. And we touched on the work of Karl Marx in this chapter as well. All four provide us with an ideal for a very broad approach to human behavior, granting that we have learned a great deal since their time. By so doing, they illustrate movement toward a scientific method that builds on an evolutionary worldview, by contrast with the very narrow approach to knowledge of human behavior that is so widely prevalent today. Simmel is the only one of these four individuals who focused on the individual, and that was in addition to his orientation to the importance of culture no less than social organization.

In the following quote from the beginning of his most well-known essay, "The Metropolis and Mental Life," he gives us some perspective on the changes that took place with respect to cultural values in Western Europe during the eighteenth and nineteenth centuries:

> The deepest problems of modern life flow from the attempt of the individual to maintain the independence and individuality of his existence against the sovereign powers of society, against the weight of the historical heritage and the external culture and technique of life.... The eighteenth century may have called for liberation from all the ties which grew up historically in politics, in religion, in morality and in economics in order to permit the original natural virtue of man, which is equal in everyone, to develop without inhibition; the nineteenth century may have sought to promote, in addition to man's freedom, his individuality ... [a]nd his achievements which make him unique and indispensable (Simmel 1903/1971: 324).

Simmel contrasts here the cultural values of the French Enlightenment of the eighteenth century—coupled with the slogan of the French revolution, "Liberte, Egalite, Fraternite"—with the newly developing emphasis on individuality, especially in Germany, during the nineteenth century. In addition to the eighteenth-century cultural values of freedom, equality, and democracy, there is also the importance of the cultural value of individual personality. Simmel's emphasis on the importance of individuality built on the work of the German romanticists of the nineteenth century—who reacted against the rationalism of the Enlightenment, as described by the American philosopher T. Z. Lavine:

> What was German Romanticism? It was a revolutionary movement, in the realm of literature, philosophy, and the visual arts, rather than in the realm of politics. It was a wholly new way of looking at the world which arose with a great burst of creative energy on the part of German artists and intellectuals who rejected the Enlightenment as a philosophy confined to and dominated by reason—by mathematics, logic, mathematically formulated scientific laws, and by abstract natural rights. They were disillusioned with the promises of progress and the perfectibility of the human race made by the age of optimism.
>
> . . .What then did Romanticism have to offer in place of the philosophy of the Enlightenment? It was fortified by the Kantian turn in philosophy that opened up for the German Romantics the "inward Path" to truth, the new horizon for philosophy in which the path to truth is through the world within, since it imposes its thought upon what is found in the outside world. It was in the inner world of the self that truth and the meaning of the human condition was to be found, not the external world of the physical sciences. Like French existentialism of the twentieth century, German Romanticism of the early nineteenth century used literature—novels, poems, dramas, essays, short stories—to express the inner world of human feelings and to offer powerful protest against philosophies which ignore them (Lavine 1984: 202-203).

Simmel, as a result, was able to build on the development of the German romantic protest against the extreme rationalism of the Enlightenment. But at the same time Simmel did not abandon the Enlightenment's optimism and scientific ideals, thus emphasizing the importance of "head" no less than "heart." And it was this combination that we see as fundamental to our present ability to understand the complexity of human behavior,

Simmel joins Marx, Durkheim, and Weber in focusing on the depth of the problems that are developing throughout society as scientific technology continues to shape the world. Yet these four founders of sociology have managed to give us moderns a profound understanding of many of the forces, largely invisible, that have been involved in our continuing scientific and technological revolutions. We have also discussed other crucial yet largely invisible forces—such as the growing aspirations-fulfillment gap coupled with our bureaucratic worldview—operating throughout modern society. We believe that the extraordinary language of social science helps us to understand the nature of those forces in a systematic way. Yet what is to be done, given that those forces continue to yield largely invisible problems that we moderns generally do not understand and remain unable to address effectively? Our own approach in Part III continues to make use of that extraordinary language as we attempt to answer this question.

PART III

Evolution

To REVERSE OUR JOURNEY from extinction to evolution, we must go "back to the future," looking to key ideas from Parts I and II. One of them is the problem of the aspirations-fulfillment gap depicted in Figure 1-1 and discussed in Chapters 1 through 4. Up to now our focus has been on the past five centuries that have witnessed a continuing scientific and technological revolution. That revolution, with its accompanying revolution of rising expectations and continuation of our bureaucratic way of life, has yielded a growing aspirations-fulfillment gap that is largely invisible and threatens all of us. Yet that aspirations-fulfillment gap is by no means unique to the past five centuries. Robert Browning, the nineteenth-century English poet, suggested as much in his poem, "Andrea del Sarto":

> Ah, but a man's reach should exceed his grasp,
> Or what's a heaven for?
> (Quoted by Knowles 2004: 158, note 9)

In Browning's view, "reach" or aspirations (including our cultural values) should indeed exceed "grasp" or fulfillment (including our patterns of social organization). For it is that very gap between aspirations and fulfillment that is fundamental to our hopes for the future, the "heaven" we look toward, or our purposes in life. For Browning, we humans are problem-oriented creatures: We require problems in our lives, and we require efforts to solve these problems in order to be fully human. Every single interaction that we have within our interactive universe—as depicted in Figure 1-3—opens up questions to be answered and problems to be solved. From this perspective, it is no accident that we humans have developed language as our most powerful tool for fulfilling aspirations and solving problems. And neither is it an accident that we have also developed the scientific method as a problem-solving procedure building on the power of language.

Yet what we do not require is a reach that continues to move ever higher with our grasp remaining much the same, just as has been structured by our bureaucratic worldview and way of life. This yields not movement toward the heaven of ever more fulfillment but rather toward the hell of ever less fulfillment and ever greater problems that continue to remain invisible. It is exactly this situation in which we humans now find ourselves at this time in history. Unfortunately, we have continued to rely on our ordinary language and failed to learn how to use the extraordinary language of social science within our everyday lives, and we authors are no exception to what has occurred. That extraordinary language alerts us—given its abstract nature, and systematic integration linking elements of "heart" and "hand" with elements of "head"—to the enormous yet largely invisible problem of the failure of our very patterns of social organization to fulfill our cultural values. The "heaven" that Browning calls for requires us, then, to reach for nothing less than a worldview within which our patterns of social organization continue to keep pace with our cultural values. Otherwise, our bureaucratic worldview will continue to lead us ever closer to hell.

Browning helps us to see the aspirations-fulfillment gap from the perspective of the very nature of the human being and the entire history of the human race, just as our own approach to "head," "heart," and "hand" takes into account the fundamental elements of all human behavior. For our "reach" has to do with the full range of the values, emotions, or motives of the individual along with the cultural values of society, that is, our "heart," just as is portrayed by Figure 3-1's depiction of the extraordinary language of the "heart." Further, our "grasp" has to do with the human being's actions and interactions along with our patterns of social organization, just as is portrayed in Figure 4-1's portrayal of the extraordinary language of the "hand." And Browning's own beliefs and assumptions about the relationship between reach and grasp along with cultural norms bearing on such beliefs and assumptions illustrate the extraordinary language of the "head," as depicted in Figure 2-1. Those figures, just as in the case of Browning's ideas, refer not only to human behavior over the past five centuries but rather to human behavior in general.

Given the importance of the metaphors of "head," "heart," and "hand" for our ability to reach out to human behavior in general—at the level of society as a whole no less than at the level of the individual—we might do well to emphasize them by referring to L. Frank Baum's *The Wizard of Oz and the Land of Oz* (1960), the bestselling children's book that became the basis for the classic 1939 film, *The Wizard of Oz,* as cited in Chapter 2. Who can forget Ray Bolger as The Scarecrow ("head"), Jack Haley as The Tin Woodman ("heart"), and Bert Lahr as The Cowardly Lion ("hand")? And who can forget Judy Garland as Dorothy, the brave girl who somehow managed to combine "head" with "heart" and "hand"? She had understanding, a commitment to return to Kansas, and a fierce loyalty to her friends, including her little dog Toto as well. Just as Dorothy befriended The Scarecrow, The Tin Woodman, and The Cowardly Lion, she required "head," "heart," and "hand" in order to defeat the Wicked Witch of the West (Margaret Hamilton), to penetrate the humbug of The Wizard (Frank Morgan), and to finally fulfill her desire to return to her beloved Aunty Em and Uncle Henry back in Kansas. Judy Garland singing "Somewhere, over the rainbow ... ," can still inspire us with the hope that we desperately require as we face our present-day problems.

Just as Browning helps us to see the aspirations-fulfillment gap throughout human history, so can we learn to see a comparable gap throughout evolutionary history if we follow the ideas of the psychologist George Kelly. He maintained that organisms, and not just human beings, are able to represent the environment and not merely respond passively to the environment (1955). As a result of this ability, even organisms without language are able to do something about the environment if it does not suit them. Kelly wrote at a time when a great many psychologists treated human beings, and not just organisms in general, as passive creatures shaped by whatever occurred in their environment. His perspective was much the same as our own view of the physical universe—and living things in particular—as based on the interaction of phenomena rather than their isolation or any one-sided impact between phenomena, as suggested by those psychologists who saw organisms as passively responding to environmental changes. Following Kelly's insights, then, the idea of an aspirations-fulfillment gap is a useful way to look at the behavior of all organisms, granting that other forms of life do not have the conscious aspirations that we humans have. Yet even without language, their senses can succeed in helping them to represent or detect situations they are uncomfortable with, and as a result they can orient themselves to moving out of those situations.

Granting that we human beings have, in common with other organisms, rapid interaction with our environment that includes an ability to represent it and, as a result of such representation or imaging, respond actively to it, our language and the scientific method enable us to carry these abilities much further. For those tools have made us the most interactive creatures within the known universe. Kelly saw the human being as a kind of scientist in his or her everyday life, looking for causes and effects as a basis for solving problems. We carry Kelly's argument much further, for we see the possibility of our capacity to fulfill much more of the potential that language and the scientific method hold out to us, as illustrated by our learning the extraordinary language of social science. We are convinced that we can continue to raise our aspirations and our ability to fulfill them with no limit whatsoever.

Yet these human capacities are by no means identical with human abilities. As we have seen in the preceding chapters, we have managed to increase our aspirations or expectations without a corresponding increase in our ability to fulfill them over the past five centuries, resulting in a widening aspirations-fulfillment gap. This is illustrated by the financial crisis throughout the world in 2008, with foreclosures on mortgages that people can no longer keep up with together with huge amounts of credit card debt. Behind these occurrences are aspirations—of those in financial institutions together with would-be homeowners—that have moved far beyond people's ability to fulfill them.

We might expand here our brief reference to the analysis of Emile Durkheim, one of the founders of sociology, in the introduction to Part I, who wrote about a link between the rapid industrialization during the late nineteenth century and patterns of suicide. For Durkheim, "anomie" refers to the disruption of a society's cultural norms:

> Such is the source of the excitement predominating in this part of society [trade and industry], and which has thence extended to the other parts. There, the state of crisis and anomie is constant and, so to speak, normal. From top to bottom of the ladder, greed is aroused without knowing where to find ultimate foothold. Nothing can calm it, since its goal is far beyond all it can attain.... The wise man, knowing how to enjoy achieved results without having constantly to replace them with others, finds in them an attachment to life in the hour of difficulty. But the man who has always pinned all his hopes on the future and lived with his eyes fixed upon it, has nothing in the past as a comfort against the present's afflictions (Durkheim 1897/1951: 255-256).

It appears that our current situation has much in common with Durkeim's analysis of Europe in the late nineteenth century, for in both cases "greed is aroused without knowing where to find ultimate foothold. Nothing can calm it, since its goal is far beyond all it can attain." In our own view, this increased aspirations-fulfillment gap is not just linked to the late nineteenth century. Nor is it limited to those individuals who are in danger of suicide. Rather, just as we have argued in the preceding chapters, it is our scientific and industrial revolution over the past five centuries—coupled with our failure to see what has been happening—that has yielded our widening aspirations-fulfillment gap. The basis for that widening gap is the bureaucratic worldview and way of life depicted in Figure 1-2 that has worked to prevent us from becoming aware of our situation and taking appropriate actions as a result.

We believe that this worldview itself derives from our failure to understand how language works and how to make much use of its potential. For example, the bureaucratic worldview that we have developed and that shapes the full range of our behavior derives largely from language's dichotomous potential rather than from its gradational or metaphorical potentials. As we can see from Figure 1-2, that dichotomous or either-or orientation drastically limits our ability to interact and thus learn to solve problems, since it oversimplifies what are in fact complex situations. Thus, despite our capacity to learn how to solve the problem of our widening aspirations-fulfillment gap, we remain helpless in our efforts to narrow that gap. Like the dinosaurs, who became extinct because of their inability to adapt to a changed environment, we humans appear to be headed toward extinction because of a similar inability. Yet unlike the dinosaurs, it is we who have created a world that is increasingly toxic to our continuing survival, and it is we who have the capacity to heal that world.

Given our failure to understand how to make much use of language's gradational and metaphorical potentials, we have not learned to follow the advice of C. Wright Mills and shuttle far up language's ladder of abstraction so as to confront much of the source of our problems: our bureaucratic worldview. That worldview—along with the increasing problems that it is creating—remains very largely invisible. We saw the dangers that Hitler's Germany and Hirohito's Japan posed during World War II, and we were able to act decisively to counter those threats. Yet we remain largely unable to see the dangers posed by our bureaucratic worldview with its increasing aspirations-fulfillment gap. And as a result we remain unable to confront those threats effectively. Instead, given that increasing gap, more and more we are learning to bury our emotions along with our conflicting cultural values, as outlined in Chapter 3 on emotional repression. Like the Springdalers, we have learned to use techniques of particularization and the falsification of memory to escape from awareness of that gap. But by so doing we escape from learning how to solve the increasing problems that threaten our very survival, fiddling all the while that Rome is burning.

It is in the chapters of Part III that we begin with this understanding of the seriousness of our situation at this time in history. Just as in the case of the chapters of Part II, Chapters 5, 6, and 7 focus on "head," "heart," and "hand," respectively, following the extraordinary language of social science. But instead of an emphasis on outward perception and thought, emotional repression and conforming behavior, our emphasis will be on inward-outward perception and thought, emotional expression and interaction, as shown in Figure 5-1 by contrast with Figure 4-1. Also, personality structures and social structures are evolutionary instead of bureaucratic.

Figure 5–1. "Head," "Heart," and "Hand": Inward-Outward Perception and Thought, Emotional Expression, Interaction, and Other Structures

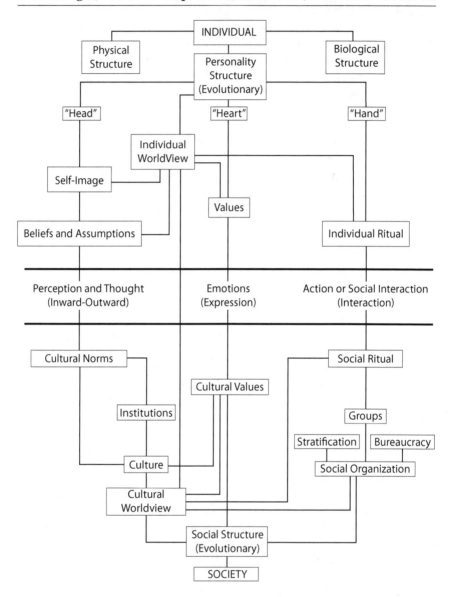

Once again, just as in the case of Part II, Part III carries forward our emphasis on the incredible potential of language and the scientific method, a potential that we have only just begun to harness. Now that we have sketched our own approach to the extraordinary language of social science, we are in a position to make use of that language to sketch directions for fulfilling our evolutionary potential. Yet let us remain aware of our present historical situation: We are in a race against time, given increasing threats based on our failure to develop an understanding of how to tap more than a tiny fraction of that potential. We have examined those threats in the preceding chapters and have made use of the extraordinary language to do so. Let us make no mistake: Those threats are mammoth, increasing, and require urgent action. And the present ability of our leaders to understand them, much less confront them effectively, is most deficient. We are not simply attempting to hype our argument when we conclude that there is a significant possibility that the human race will become extinct, not today or tomorrow, but the day after tomorrow. What we require at this time in history is nothing less than a mammoth and continuing effort—by each of us no less than by those who presently lead the institutions of society—to learn how to confront those threats ever more effectively.

As we proceed to Chapters 5, 6, and 7, we should remain aware of the limitations of the "head" without the "heart" and the "hand." Historically, the industrial or technological revolution—that continuing shaping of our world—did not just result from the development of the physical and biological sciences. Neither did it result just from the invention of the scientific method that was behind those scientific achievements. What was required as well was the application of that same scientific method, coupled with that new understanding of the physical and biological universe, to efforts specifically directed at shaping that universe so as to fulfill human aspirations. It was, then, science and technology together—and not just science alone—that proved to be essential, and that succeeded in shaping our world over the past five centuries, focusing on physical and biological problems ("heart") and solutions to those problems ("hand").

In the same way, any understanding of human behavior and of individual and social problems that we achieve will only go so far toward solving those problems. What we require in addition to "head" is "heart" and "hand." We need deep awareness of and commitment to solving individual and social problems ("heart"). To achieve this is an incredibly difficult task. Of course, it is easy enough to gain awareness of our visible problems, such as awareness in 2008 of the financial crisis or in 1941 of the attack on Pearl Harbor. But to achieve an awareness of the role of our bureaucratic worldview, and to achieve a commitment to altering that worldview, is far more difficult. Yet even if we should come to develop that awareness and commitment, they will not persist unless we can also learn to develop the technologies that are required to alter that bureaucratic worldview ("hand"). Those technologies must be applied to every one of our institutions—political, economic, scientific, educational, religious, and family—since they are all presently immersed within that bureaucratic worldview. This book, then, remains most limited, given its potential ability to communicate understanding ("head"). That understanding will remain largely useless in confronting present-day threats unless it is joined by "heart" and "hand." Failing that, we will continue as before with our techniques of particularization and falsification of memory, repressing our problems.

CHAPTER 5

"Head"

Inward-Outward Perception and Thought

IF WE THINK OF NEWSPEAK—or of the languages of Cogitant, Technicant, and Valiant—as pointing the individual outward, then the extraordinary language of social science can help us learn to point inward no less than outward. Just as those languages invented by Orwell and Vance—as presented in Chapter 2—teach us to stay at a low rung on the ladder of abstraction, the extraordinary language enables us to shuttle far up and down that ladder. And such shuttling enables us to integrate the knowledge to be found at all of the rungs of that ladder, just as the language of Pastiche enabled Beran to communicate with the Cogitants, Technicants, and Valiants on the planet Pao. Our extraordinary language can help us do much the same with respect to the bits and pieces of knowledge of human behavior that are now buried in our libraries. That language enables us to expand our present understanding of the scientific method so that we can put that method to work on our enormously complex and highly threatening problems. And the result can be movement toward our evolutionary potential, leaving those problems far behind.

It is in this chapter that we continue with our emphasis on the infinite potential of language and the scientific method, especially when they are tied together. We begin with a section on the scientific method, returning for further insights into the nature of pragmatism—the philosophy that provides a foundation for our broad approach to the scientific method—

as discussed at the end of Chapter 2. Our next section on language dips into two science-fiction novels based on the work of Alfred Korzybski, who founded a small yet very important field of knowledge called general semantics. Finally, we come to a section on the East-West strategy for solving problems—whether in society as a whole or in our everyday lives—just as we foreshadowed in Chapter 1 and at the end of Chapter 4. This is a strategy that makes full use of the potentials of language and the scientific method, a strategy that is particularly appropriate for narrowing our widening aspirations-fulfillment gap and then enabling us to follow the optimism of the scientific method by moving both aspirations and their fulfillment up through the roof.

The Scientific Method

Our focus in Part II was on the very real possibilities of human extinction, and as a result we had little to say about the incredible potential of the scientific method once we have broadened it so as to include the potentials of language, and once we have shifted to an evolutionary worldview. We did, however, at least hint at the potential of the scientific method with our metaphor of a pendulum swinging in ever-widening arcs, as outlined in Chapters 1 and 4. At this point we turn to the philosophy of pragmatism for deeper understanding of the scientific method, recalling Abraham Kaplan's brief analysis of its nature in the section on the scientific method at the end of Chapter 2. We also turn to the philosophy of pragmatism for a more thorough understanding of the nature of an evolutionary as distinct from a bureaucratic worldview. For it is philosophy more than any other subject that has probed the nature of metaphysics, granting that philosophers have shied away from venturing into efforts to analyze the nature of our bureaucratic worldview.

Kaplan raises the question, "What *is* the task for twentieth-century philosophy in the Western world?" and then he proceeds to answer it:

> In its simplest and most fundamental terms, it is to assimilate the impact of science on human affairs. The business of philosophy today is to provide a system of ideas that will make an integrated whole of our beliefs about the nature of the world and the values which we seek in the world in fulfillment of our human nature. There is no doubt that far and away the most significant development in Western culture in the past three or four centuries has been the rise of modern science and the transformation of civilization by the technology based on that science. But in the course of this transformation, a radical bifurcation has grown up between man and nature, value and fact, which confronts us with the dilemma of either turning our backs on science or else resigning

ourselves to living in a world without human meaning or purpose. Pragmatism conceives the task of philosophy for modern man to be nothing other than finding a way out of this dilemma (Kaplan 1961: 16).

Kaplan might well have written this paragraph as an introduction to our own book, for the basic problems that we have been discussing throughout the previous four chapters are closely linked to what he has called "a radical bifurcation ... between man and nature, value and fact." It has been the development of the biophysical sciences at the expense of the social sciences that illustrates this "radical bifurcation," for it is the enormous successes of those sciences that have convinced us that "nature" and "fact" have little or nothing to do with human behavior. And those successes—coupled with the relative failures of the social sciences to integrate their knowledge and develop the basis for effective technologies based on that knowledge—have also prevented us from emphasizing the importance of "man" and human "values." Further, it is this very split that threatens us today in concrete ways that Kaplan could not foresee in detail, yet that he believed would emerge. For example, we have a world where our one-sided emphasis on biophysical science and its technologies not only threatens us with ever more powerful weapons of mass destruction. It is also a world where the materialistic values linked to the technologies of biophysical science are overwhelming our humanistic values, just as we have discussed in Chapter 3 with respect to the conflict between people-oriented and work-related values. Still further, it is a world where we humans have learned emotional repression (Chapter 3) and conforming behavior (Chapter 4) linked to the bureaucratic worldview and way of life that has accompanied our one-sided approach to science.

Let us recall Kaplan's assessment of much of the history of Western philosophy, as presented in Chapter 2, focused on its failures to solve this problem that he posed not just for the philosophy of pragmatism but also for Western philosophy in general. Just as biophysical science has failed us with its one-sided development not only of Western civilization but also of the modern world, so has the history of philosophy—with the exception of pragmatism—failed to give us an adequate answer to the question that he posed, granting that we can make good use of elements of that history. For example, we have realism and empiricism siding with science, we have idealism siding with human aspirations, and we have the dualistic philosophies that avoid the question he poses.

How, then, from Kaplan's perspective, does pragmatism give us a more adequate answer to his question of how to "assimilate the impact of science on human affairs"?

Pragmatism is thus both a humanistic and a scientific philosophy, and that it is both in an integrated rather than a dualistic sense is perhaps its most distinguishing characteristic. Most philosophers, William James once observed, are either tough-minded or tender-hearted. The pragmatist is tough-minded in his determination to live in the world as it is, rather than in the fantasy worlds of the metaphysicians and theologians. Since it is science which provides us with the best warranted knowledge of the world as it is ... his philosophy must be firmly grounded in science.... Most scientific philosophies derive from the natural sciences, and especially from physics and mathematics; for pragmatism, it is biology, psychology, and the social sciences that have been most influential....

But the pragmatist is tender-hearted, too, at least in the sense that he is unwavering in the conviction—or the faith, if you will—that human values and purposes are a part of nature, natural events like any other, matters of fact for which any scientific account of the world must provide a place. It is striking that all the philosophies that have any considerable influence in the world today agree in giving primacy to the human significance of the world process. In this respect, pragmatism can take its place alongside existentialism, communism, and the various religious philosophies. It differs from these, not in assigning only a minor role to man and his works ... but in the scientific basis that it puts forward as the ground of its perspectives. The religionist relies on theology; the communist—for all his talk of "scientific" rather than "utopian" socialism—replaces social science by ideology; and the existentialist substitutes literature and its metaphysics for a scientific psychology.... (Kaplan 1961: 17-19).

What we have in pragmatism is a focus on *both* the importance of science *and* the importance of human values and behavior, by contrast with (1) philosophical realism and empiricism that has sided with science, (2) the idealism that has sided with human aspirations, and (3) dualistic philosophy that fails to address the central problem of assimilating the impact of science on human affairs. Thus, in Kaplan's words, pragmatism is both "tough-minded" and "tender-hearted." Instead of either (1) or (2) or (3), pragmatism focuses on the interaction between science and its technologies on the individual and society, and vice-versa. By so doing, pragmatism pays serious attention to the interactive nature of the universe as a whole and, in particular, to the situation of the human being as the most interactive creature within the known universe. And as a result, pragmatism points us toward an evolutionary worldview and way of life, as depicted by Figure 1-3. By contrast, the philosophical orientations of (1), (2), and (3), granting their many contributions, follow a bureaucratic worldview—as depicted by Figure 1-2—that focuses on specialization with very limited interaction among phenomena.

Given the interest of philosophers in metaphysics or our fundamental assumptions and beliefs about the nature of reality, they are equally interested in just how we go about learning about the nature of reality, a field of philosophy that has been labeled "epistemology." Kaplan maintained that "it is science which provides us with the best warranted knowledge of the world as it is," and we along with scientists in general share his view. But it is not the "results" of science that are crucial to epistemology but rather the "method" of science: the scientific method. And it is exactly this focus on the scientific method that we have adopted throughout this book. In particular, in Part II we have made use of a very broad approach to the scientific method—with the aid of the extraordinary language of social science—to unearth the nature of our bureaucratic worldview as well as the narrow approach to the scientific method linked to that worldview. And in Part III we shall continue to employ that broad approach to the scientific method along with the extraordinary language to flesh out the nature of an evolutionary worldview and way of life. Indeed, it is not only in this book but in all of our preceding publications that we have focused on the broad scientific method that we desperately require to make progress on escalating world problems (Phillips 2001; Phillips, Kincaid, and Scheff, eds. 2002; Phillips and Johnston 2007; Phillips, ed. 2007; Phillips 2008; Knottnerus and Phillips, 2009).

Kaplan's reference to John Dewey's concept of "contextualism" yields further understanding of the nature of pragmatism's approach to the scientific method. This is a wide-ranging approach to physical, biological, social, and personality structures within the context of any given momentary situation. We have illustrated this very approach within Figures 4-1 and 5-1, for it is the extraordinary language of social science that provides us with the concepts that we require for such a broad-ranging approach to the enormous complexity of human behavior. All of the forces depicted in those figures interact with one another, which we might well expect within an interactive universe where we humans are the most interactive creatures to be found. Unfortunately, our bureaucratic worldview has yielded the kind of specialization with limited attention to such interaction—as portrayed in Figure 1-2—that has failed us in our efforts to understand the impact of science on human behavior. And that failure in turn has yielded a failure to understand the escalating social problems that we are now experiencing, and thus it has contributed to our failure to make progress on those problems.

Yet the philosophy of pragmatism, granting its enormous contributions in providing us with a framework that gives us a direction for where we must go, has only taken us so far in understanding just how we can proceed with a contextualist approach to the scientific method. And it is exactly here that we are attempting to follow that direction. As we see it, the extraordinary language of social science—as illustrated in Figures

4-1 and 5-1—can pick up where pragmatism leaves off. For that language enables us to open up to an approach to science that is able to penetrate the enormous complexities of human behavior, an approach that also pays serious attention to the scientific method used in the biophysical sciences and their technologies. The philosophy of pragmatism, as it presently stands, gives us a very high aspiration for how to understand any phenomenon whatsoever. This is an aspiration that the social sciences have failed to fulfill through their bureaucratic approach to the scientific method, thus yielding an enormous gap between those aspirations and our ability to fulfill them. By contrast, we see our own approach to the scientific method, accompanied by the extraordinary language of social science, as yielding a direction for narrowing that gap and thus fulfilling the vision of the pragmatists.

Since we are making use of the philosophy of pragmatism as a framework for helping us to understand and communicate our own ideas, let us pursue these links somewhat further. For one thing, viewing pragmatism as a *method* and not as a body of knowledge fits very well with our evolutionary worldview, which emphasizes the interaction of all phenomena. We might think here of our metaphor of a pendulum swinging in ever-widening arcs. Just as the width of those arcs remains unlimited, so does a methodology remain unlimited, by contrast with a body of knowledge. The senior author has focused on the methodology of the social sciences for most of his career, as illustrated by three editions of a textbook followed by a fourth book on research methods (Phillips 1966, 1971, 1976, 1985). All of those books illustrated an effort to crawl out from under the very narrow and highly quantitative approach to research methods that most sociologists had adopted, due largely to the successes of the physical sciences and the interpretation of those successes by many philosophers of science. Although his efforts pointed to a much broader approach to the scientific method——following the ideals of the philosophy of pragmatism—it was only with the publication of his *Beyond Sociology's Tower of Babel: Reconstructing the Scientific Method* (2001) that he was able to advance his own approach in a systematic way.

We might also see the philosophy of pragmatism as in harmony with our metaphors of "head," "heart," and "hand." This philosophy is often stereotyped as focusing on "hand" with little attention to "head" or "heart." But our quotations tell a different story. For example, pragmatism's orientation to contextualism is a deep commitment to "head." And there is also pragmatism's deep commitment to human aspirations, illustrating its orientation to "heart." And pragmatism's commitment to the interaction among categories of phenomena—like idealism and realism—is also illustrated by the interaction among "head," "heart" and "hand" in Figure 3b. Further, we can link this philosophy to key aspects of our view of language's dichotomous, gradational, and metaphorical potentials.

Pragmatism's focus is on language's gradational potential, thus helping us to avoid the one-sided nature of the focus on dichotomy within both our everyday usages as well as throughout the social sciences. However, pragmatism lacks an orientation to language's metaphorical potential, a lack that is remedied by the focus of the philosophy of existentialism.

Given the importance of the philosophy of pragmatism for providing us with a very broad framework for our efforts to confront the escalating world problems of modern times, we turn briefly to the writings of key figures in the development of this American philosophy: John Dewey, William James, and—the key founder of pragmatism—Charles Peirce. Let us recall our quote in Chapter 1 from America's most eminent educator, also an eminent philosopher. His *Reconstruction in Philosophy* was his own effort, years before the work of Abraham Kaplan, to view the history of philosophy from a pragmatist perspective. In the following passage he makes the case for the importance of taking human values into account within education, an approach that we believe is important for any effort to develop a scientific method that is broad enough to follow the philosophical framework of pragmatism or an evolutionary worldview:

> Government, business, art, religion, all social institutions have a meaning, a purpose. That purpose is to set free and to develop the capacities of human individuals without respect to race, sex, class or economic status. And this is all one with saying that the test of their value is the extent to which they educate every individual into the full stature of his possibility. Democracy has many meanings, but if it has a moral meaning, it is found in resolving that the supreme test of all political institutions and industrial arrangements shall be the contribution they make to the all-around growth of every member of society (Dewey 1920/1948: 186).

From Dewey's perspective we might see all of our institutions—political, economic, scientific, educational, religious, and family—as social technologies by contrast with the technologies linked to engineering and medicine that have yielded such things as automobiles and vaccines. Let us recall here our view of society's institutions in Chapter 3 as systems of cultural values and norms focused on solving a given problem within society as a whole. Dewey suggests here that the key problem that political and economic institutions must solve is the problem of fulfilling "the all-around growth of every member of society." If, as we believe, all of our institutions presently are oriented around a bureaucratic worldview, then all of them—and not just political and economic institutions—presently are working to sabotage Dewey's ideals, ideals deriving from our basic people-oriented cultural values of individual personality, equality, freedom, and democracy. Given this situation, a key problem for all of our institutions—in addition to their more specialized problems, as outlined in Chapter 3—is this problem that Dewey puts forward. Just as in the case of Kaplan's description of pragmatism's approach to the scientific method, Dewey leaves us with an extremely high aspiration that we must somehow learn to fulfill. Our own aspiration is perhaps even higher than that of Dewey, since we believe in the infinite potential of the individual.

Turning from Dewey to William James, he put forward his view of the importance of philosophy—with a focus on metaphysics or our fundamental assumptions and beliefs about the nature of reality—for all of us. More than the other founders of pragmatism, it was James who was able to make good use of language's metaphorical potential. In the following passage he quotes from an essay by G. K. Chesterton:

> There are some people—and I am one of them—who think that the most practical and important thing about a man is still his view of the universe. We think that for a landlady considering a lodger, it is important to know his income, but still more important to know his philosophy. We think that for a general to fight an enemy, it is important to know the enemy's numbers, but still more important to know the enemy's philosophy (James 1907/1995: 1).

Following James's view, we are all philosophers in the sense of living by and being shaped by our basic assumptions and beliefs, or our metaphysical stance. Just as we are all speaking "prose" all of our lives without being aware of it, so is our behavior being shaped by our metaphysical stance all of our lives without our being aware of it. These assumptions and beliefs are sufficiently comprehensive and powerful to shape everything that we think, feel, and do. Our choice is not whether to develop metaphysical assumptions and beliefs. Rather, it is a choice about which assumptions we choose to live by, since we live by such assumptions. Yet if our patterns of culture and social organization, or the social structure of society as a whole, points us in a bureaucratic direction that remains largely invisible, then our ability to make a conscious choice is largely eliminated. Our argument in this book and in our preceding publications is that we can indeed learn to make a conscious choice about our metaphysical stance or worldview by learning to make visible what is presently invisible. By so doing, we can learn to see, for example, the contradiction between our people-oriented cultural values and the patterns of stratification and bureaucracy illustrated in Figure 1-2. And to the degree that we have a direction for resolving those contradictions, as illustrated by Figure 1-3, we can indeed make a conscious choice that promises to resolve those contradictions.

Yet it was Charles Sanders Peirce, the acknowledged founder of the philosophy of pragmatism, who contributed most to its development over a century ago, and it has taken this lengthy period for philosophers and social scientists to begin to appreciate his enormous contributions. Peirce worked in the physical sciences—making contributions in gravitation, optics, chemistry, and astronomy—for a decade before venturing into his own publications on pragmatism. Most unusually, Peirce also had an excellent background in the history of philosophy. The fact that he never secured an academic appointment and never was able to publish his essays in book form during his lifetime undoubtedly contributed to the length of time it has taken for the academic world to appreciate his work. Yet despite this he was by no means isolated, communicating regularly with and succeeding in influencing a small group of like-minded scholars, such as James, Dewey, and the sociologist George Herbert Mead. The doctoral dissertation of C. Wright Mills—whose approach to language and the scientific method is fundamental to this book—was on the work of Charles Peirce, William James, and John Dewey. Mills's original title was *A Sociological Account of Pragmatism,* with his posthumously published book bearing the title, *Sociology and Pragmatism: The Higher Learning in America* (1942/1964).

Peirce illustrates the integration of "head," "heart," and "hand" within the following passage, which also illustrates the link between pragmatism and the journey without end that is the nature of an evolutionary worldview: "Upon this first, and in one sense this sole, rule of reason, that in order to learn you must desire to learn, and in so desiring not be satisfied with what you already incline to think, there follows one corollary which itself deserves to be inscribed upon every wall of the city of philosophy: *Do not block the way of inquiry ...* "(Peirce 1896/1955: 54).

Just as the pendulum's swing to the left—within our pendulum metaphor for the scientific method—calls for an emotional commitment to a problem that invokes "heart," so does Peirce emphasize the "desire to learn" as crucial to this first step of the scientific method. The upshot of that desire is the learning, corresponding to "head," that results when the pendulum swings to the right. But that swing to the right can also be illustrated by the technologist's success in making progress on a concrete problem, such as the development of a new vaccine, thus invoking "hand." And it is Peirce's corollary—"Do not block the way of inquiry"—that weds his understanding of the scientific method to an evolutionary worldview, for inquiry can continue to proceed indefinitely.

Peirce clarifies that first step of the scientific method—which is so important because "heart" is fundamental to this method, and it is "heart" that we believe is neglected by a great many social scientists—within this passage:

> The irritation of doubt is the only immediate motive for the struggle to attain belief.... With the doubt, therefore, the struggle begins, and

with the cessation of doubt it ends. Hence, the sole object of inquiry is the settlement of opinion ... as soon as a firm belief is reached we are entirely satisfied, whether the belief be true or false.... That the settlement of opinion is the sole end of inquiry is a very important proposition. It sweeps away, at once, various vague and erroneous concepts of proof.... Some philosophers have imagined that to start an inquiry it was only necessary to utter a question whether orally or by setting it down upon paper, and have even recommended us to begin our studies with questioning everything! But the mere putting of a proposition into the interrogative form does not stimulate the mind to any struggle after belief. "There must be a real and living doubt, and without this all discussion is idle.... Some people seem to love to argue a point after all the world is fully convinced of it. But no further advance can be made. When doubt ceases, mental action on the subject comes to an end; and, if it did go on, it would be without purpose (Peirce 1877/1955: 10–11).

Peirce contrasts the idea of "a real and living doubt" with the idea of "the mere putting of a proposition into the interrogative form," which, as a result, "does not stimulate the mind to any struggle after belief." It is strong emotional commitment to making progress on a problem that he argues for as absolutely essential if the scientific method is to proceed. The "heart" is crucial in this method no less than the "head," granting that traditional research procedures view scientific activity as requiring the exclusion of the researcher's emotions so that he or she will not be swayed by personal commitments to this conclusion or that one. Yet if we look to our concept of cultural values we can clarify this quandary. What the researcher requires is a deep commitment to the cultural value of science and secular activity. But in the interest of transparency it is useful for the scientist to lay bare to the audience other personal values that might compromise the conclusions of the study. We might recall here Gouldner's suggestion as to the importance of a "reflexive" approach to sociology in Chapter 2, pointing in this direction of transparency. More generally, a shift from outward perception and thought to inward-outward perception and thought—the overall direction of this chapter—opens the door to such reflexivity. Of course, this opens up research efforts to greater complexity, yet we cannot afford to ignore such complexity since it does in fact exist.

Peirce's idea that he believed "deserves to be inscribed upon every wall of the city of philosophy" is perhaps his most widely known statement: *Do not block the way of inquiry.* He elaborates on this idea as follows:

[T]o set up a philosophy which barricades the road of further advance toward the truth is the one unpardonable offence in reasoning, as it is also the one to which metaphysicians have in all ages shown themselves the most addicted. Let me call your attention to four familiar shapes in which this venomous error assails our knowledge. The first is the shape of absolute assertion. That we can be sure of nothing in science is an ancient truth. ... The second bar which philosophers often set up across the roadway of inquiry lies in maintaining that this, that, and the other never can be known. ... The third philosophical stratagem for cutting off inquiry consists in maintaining that this, that, or the other element of science is basic, ultimate, independent of aught else, and utterly inexplicable. ... The last philosophical obstacle to the advance of knowledge ... is the holding that this or that law or truth has found its last and perfect formulation (Peirce 1896/1955: 54–56).

Peirce gives us here a clear contrast between the impact of a bureaucratic worldview and a bureaucratic approach to the scientific method, on the one hand, and an evolutionary approach to both, on the other hand. All four of these reasons for ending the research process violate the metaphysical stance that there is no limit to the potential of the human being. And they also violate the epistemological stance that there is no limit to how much we can learn about ourselves and the world, including the problems that we face. Overall, the philosophy of pragmatism, including recent work along with the early efforts of Peirce, James, Dewey, and Mead, gives us a broad philosophical framework for understanding an evolutionary metaphysics and epistemology. That framework holds out to us a promise that is yet to be fulfilled: a promise for the continuing development of human potential along with a promise for the continuing development of our understanding of human behavior and human problems. But does history give us good reason to believe that we can in fact fulfill those promises? More specifically, we might turn to the history of the physical and biological sciences over the past five centuries, since it is that history that has yielded fundamental changes in the world. Does that history give us hope that we can in fact change our way of life in fundamental ways, granting the changes that have been achieved over those centuries? And does that history suggest any particular direction for achieving a change from a bureaucratic to an evolutionary way of life?

Thomas Kuhn, a historian of science who was also a philosopher of science, granting that he was not himself a physical scientist as was Peirce, published a book in 1962 that shook up the academic world and in particular the social sciences: *The Structure of Scientific Revolutions.* In that work he introduced the concept of "paradigm," failing to define it clearly, yet using it to suggest the importance of basic assumptions that are largely unconscious and lie behind scientific theories yet succeed in shaping those theories. As a result, that concept has come into general use not only inside of the academic world but outside of it as well. Kuhn also made good use of an understanding of the complexity of human behavior in general and the social sciences in particular in discussing the forces that stand in the way of scientific revolutions. Those forces include the hidden assumptions of individual scientists who have lived all their lives under the sway of a particular scientific theory. And they also include the push for conformity from norms or shared expectations throughout a given scientific community. To illustrate, Albert Einstein's publication of his special theory of relativity was initially opposed by many physicists, given its violation of their assumptions about space and time based on the work of Isaac Newton. In other words, Einstein's new theory violated a scientific paradigm that they had accepted all their lives. Yet Einstein's special theory of relativity eventually prevailed as more and more evidence was developed supporting it.

Our own interest is not only in a scientific revolution throughout social science, a revolution that would take us from a bureaucratic to an evolutionary epistemology. We are also interested in a cultural revolution that would yield a change from a bureaucratic to an evolutionary metaphysical stance. Kuhn himself recognized the parallelism between these two kinds of revolutions, using the existence of political revolutions to help him understand scientific revolutions:

> One aspect of the parallelism must already be apparent. Political revolutions are inaugurated by a growing sense, often restricted to a segment of the political community, that existing institutions have ceased adequately to meet the problems posed by an environment that they have in part created. In much the same way, scientific revolutions are inaugurated by a growing sense ... that an existing paradigm has ceased to function adequately in the exploration of an aspect of nature to which that paradigm itself had previously led the way. In both political and scientific development the sense of malfunction that can lead to crisis is prerequisite to revolutions (Kuhn 1962: 91).

Although the senior author picked up on the importance of Kuhn's work in the second and third editions of his textbooks on research methods, it was in his fourth text on that subject that he came to grips with this parallelism. There, he employed the term "cultural revolution"—abandoning Kuhn's narrower reference to political revolutions—to suggest the breadth of what would have to be involved if indeed there is to be a shift in the metaphysical stance or "cultural paradigm" of society as a whole:

> If Kuhn's approach can be applied to cultural as well as scientific change, it provides a basis for considerable optimism about the future of sociology, the scientific method, and society. Let us define a *cultural paradigm* as *a world view on which a culture is based, involving a system of explicit*

and implicit assumptions. Then we might see any given scientific paradigm as contained within a broader cultural paradigm: It contributes to the cultural paradigm and is shaped by it in an interactive or two-way relationship.... If sociology's scientific paradigm is broad enough to give directions for resolving cultural anomalies, then it can help us develop a new cultural paradigm. In turn, such a new cultural paradigm might foster the further development of sociological research.... One feature of the scientific method which is more than a match for problems of this magnitude is its sequential and developmental nature ... what is required is, simply, progress (Phillips 1985: 543–545).

What Kuhn suggested is that political or cultural revolutions help us understand scientific revolutions. And what Phillips suggested, in addition, is the reverse: that scientific revolutions help us understand cultural revolutions. Yet this is more than a question of understanding: More than "head" is involved, "heart" and "hand" are involved as well. The fact that we have experienced scientific revolutions—like the enormous change from the ideas of Isaac Newton about space and time to Albert Einstein's theories of relativity—should give us the optimism we desperately require about the possibilities of a revolution in social science ("heart"). And given the technological revolutions based on the scientific method that continue to succeed in changing the world ever since Newton's time, we would do well to extend that optimism to the possibility of continuing to make progress on our own escalating social problems at this time in history ("hand"). Our focus in this chapter is on "head" and, more specifically, on inward-outward perception and thought. In the next two sections we shall continue with that focus, but we shall pay more attention to "heart" and "hand," respectively.

Language

We have already had a great deal to say about language. For example, it was in Chapter 1 that we saw language as working to make us humans the most interactive creatures in the known universe. And we were able to tie C. Wright Mills's advice to shuttle up and down language's ladder of abstraction as opening up language's incredible dichotomous, gradational, and metaphorical potentials. We also learned how language is linked to our worldview in that chapter and the ones that followed, as illustrated by Orwell's language of Newspeak and Vance's language of Pastiche in Chapter 2. It was in Chapter 3 on emotional repression that we learned how much we have failed to make use of language to understand our emotions and, as a result, have failed to make use of language's potentials. Yet at the same time, it was in Chapters 2, 3, and 4 that we continued to develop and illustrate the extraordinary language of social science, as envisioned by Alvin Gouldner. And as we continue to illustrate that extraordinary language in this chapter and the ones to follow, we are convinced that—given its breadth and ability to encompass "head," "heart," and "hand"—that language can help all of us move from a bureaucratic to an evolutionary way of life.

What, then remains to be done about language? Given that as yet we have had very little experience with this extraordinary language that embodies an evolutionary worldview—especially as compared to the vernacular language embodying a bureaucratic worldview that represents almost all of our experiences—a great many more illustrations are needed. And even those would be no more than a beginning for us, since it is our experiences using the extraordinary language in everyday life that are crucial. As previewed at the beginning of this chapter, it is in this section that we dip into two science-fiction novels based on the work of Alfred Korzybski, the founder of general semantics, a field of knowledge that is still carried forward by the journal *ETC.* Korzybski's major work, *Science and Sanity* (1933), carries forward his conviction that we can learn to use language to convert our present insane patterns of relating to one another to sane relationships.

Our focus here will be on A. E. Van Vogt's *The World of Null-A* (1945/1970) and that novel's sequel, *The Players of Null-A* (1948). If we take seriously the importance of language's metaphorical potential, then we should not be shy about making good use of fiction to clarify and communicate our ideas to ourselves no less than to others. Van Vogt was deeply influenced by Korzybski's ideas, and his hero's name—Gilbert Gosseyn—is pronounced "go-sane." Gosseyn is born with an extra brain, just as all of us humans are born with a large brain in comparison to our nonhuman ancestors, and a central problem that he faces is to learn how to make use of his extra brain. Further, his focus throughout his many adventures is on learning just who he is. For he has been programmed with a false self-image and must somehow learn just what his potentials actually are. Here again, Gosseyn's problem is also a problem for the rest of us. Just who are we? What is our own potential? Our bureaucratic worldview and way of life has programmed us with a self-image that has taught us our insignificance relative to our human potential. How are we to learn the nature of our infinite capacities? How are we to tap those capacities so that we can learn to "go sane" and make progress on the escalating problems that are now threatening our very survival? Van Vogt's adventure stories place Gosseyn in one threatening situation after another. Yet although the direct threats to our own survival are far less obvious, they are real nevertheless.

Throughout the novels Gosseyn is fighting forces in the galaxy led by Enro the Red, who is attempting to achieve totalitarian control over the entire galaxy and develop a Galactic Empire in opposition to the democratic Galactic League. We might consider Enro's rule as an extreme version of bureaucracy that is much the same as the rule of Hitler and Stalin. Gosseyn has entered a 30-day competition to assess the degree to which competitors had successfully achieved training in "null-A thinking." This is non-Aristotelian thinking involving gradational thought—linked to the scientific method—and not just dichotomous thought, which, as we have learned, is far too simplistic to penetrate the complexities of human behavior. Korzybski deeply believed that it was Aristotle's emphasis on dichotomy that has prevented all of us from learning gradational thought. We share with him a belief in the importance of developing gradational thought. But we also believe that Aristotle need not be blamed for our narrow dichotomous orientation, since it is the very structure of all languages that point in this direction. And we believe as well that dichotomous thought—along with metaphorical thought—is most useful when balanced with gradational thought.

The null-A competition in *Worlds* is, then, about one's ability to use the scientific method in everyday life, where Van Vogt and Korzybski both equate gradational thought with the scientific method. Gosseyn had studied long and hard for this competition, since winners would receive a passage to Venus where a null-A society existed. Enro's forces subsequently invade Venus, but even with all of their advanced technology for engaging in warfare they are no match for the null-A trained Venusians.

Central to *The Players of Null-A* are events taking place on the planet Gorgzid, which Enro has taken over as his home base and eliminated much of the population but spared the very young Prince Ashargin, whom he retains as a prisoner. But later Enro wishes him to play a role in helping to defeat the Galactic League and create his own Galactic Empire. Gosseyn learns to travel around the galaxy at speeds far exceeding that of light because he has trained his extra brain to perceive the exact nature of a given destination—down to the status of its molecules—far more accurately than the most advanced electronic microscopes. Metaphorically, this suggests that our present vision of reality can be vastly improved. Once he perceives a place in this way he is able to move there almost instantaneously, even if it is at the other end of the galaxy. We might also suggest that this power of perception is a metaphor for the overriding importance of our patterns of perception for developing our abilities. Further, Gosseyn's null-A training has given him a range of advantages over other people with respect to his thought processes, his ability to deal with emotional problems and his strength and agility. Somehow he finds himself transferred into the body of Prince Ashargin, and he trains the prince in null-A principles. As a result, the prince becomes his ally. Of course, Gosseyn, the prince, and the Venusians manage to defeat Enro the Red, save the galaxy from his totalitarian rule, and then populate the galaxy with Venusians who will be working toward the development of a null-A galaxy.

A key metaphor for us is Gosseyn's development—through null-A training of his extra brain—of his ability to perceive a given location so accurately that he can move there in an instant no matter how far it is. Although we don't have an extra brain, van Vogt's suggestion here is that we have hardly succeeded in training our brains, which have incredible potential once we discover how to develop them. Perception is a more fundamental process than our linguistic abilities, and van Vogt gives due recognition to that importance with this metaphor. At the same time, language is also important in opening up our possibilities for personal development, for null-A training teaches us to emphasize gradational thought and our ability to use the scientific method. Gosseyn's training is most interesting, for it emphasizes the testing of ideas by attempts to solve problems in the world, a situation forced on him by the forces allied to Enro the Red. Enro himself serves as a metaphor for our bureaucratic world, for he believes in totalitarian rule and is most infantile with reference to understanding or dealing with his own emotions.

Gosseyn's procedures for training Prince Ashargin after his transfer into the younger man's body are most suggestive for our own understanding of how to develop our inward perception and how to change our metaphysical stance:

> Another mind had once controlled this body—the mind of Ashargin. It had been an unintegrated, insecure mind, dominated by fears and uncontrollable emotions that were imprinted on the nervous system and muscles of the body. The deadly part of that domination was that the living flesh of Ashargin would react to all that internal imbalance on the unconscious level. Even Gilbert Gosseyn, knowing what was wrong, would have scarcely any influence over those violent physical compulsions—until he could train the body of Ashargin to the cortical-thalamic sanity of Null-A (Van Vogt 1948: 24).

Gosseyn imparts a basic approach to the prince: "Prince, every time you take a positive action on the basis of a high-level consideration, you establish certainties of courage, self-assurance and skills" (1948: 100). Such general ideas emphasizing key people-oriented cultural values like individual personality and equality were followed by more specific procedures:

> In the bedroom Gosseyn rigged up a wall recorder to repeat a three-minute relaxation pattern. Then he lay down. During the hour that followed he never quite went to sleep.... Lying there, he allowed his mind to idle around the harsher memories of Ashargin's prison years.

Each time he came to an incident that had made a profound impression he talked silently to the younger Ashargin.... From his greater height of understanding, he assured the younger individual that the affective incident must be looked at from a different angle than that of a frightened youth. Assured him that fear of pain and fear of death were emotions that could be overcome, and that in short the shock incident which had once affected him so profoundly no longer had any meaning for him. More than that, in future he would have better understanding of such moments, and he would never again be affected in an adverse fashion (Van Vogt 1948: 115–116).

Gosseyn's problem of how to train Ashargin is nothing less than our own problem of how to develop ourselves or evolve, given our long-suffering existence within a bureaucratic world. It appears to be Ashargin's emotions, such as fear, that prevent him from gaining the confidence he needs to become an effective ally for Gosseyn. Gosseyn helps Ashargin go back to reliving his prison years under the thumb of Enro. In his imagination he returns to perceive concretely images of his experiences in which he was afraid of pain and death. Yet Gosseyn helps Ashargin perceive those experiences from a different perspective so that Ashargin is able to understand and accept his past behavior and gain more understanding of himself.

The above quote refers to "the cortical-thalamic sanity of Null-A," a phrase indicating a basic approach of general semantics having to do with one's emotions. The cortical-thalamic pause is a type of reflexive behavior in which the individual perceives his or her own emotions and then takes action to balance those emotions with understanding. For example, when Gosseyn-Ashargin is threatened by a weapon designed to create fear, he reacts:

I am now relaxing.... And all stimuli are making the full circuit of my nervous system, along my spinal cord, to the thalamus, through the thalamus and up to the cortex, and through the cortex, and then, and only then, back through the thalamus and down into the nervous system. Always, I am consciously aware of the stimulus moving up to and through the cortex.

That was the key. That was the difference between the Null-A superman and the animal man of the galaxy. The thalamus—the seat of emotions—and the cortex—the seat of discrimination—integrated, balanced in a warm and wonderful relationship. Emotions, not done away with, but made richer and more relaxed by the association with that part of the mind—the cortex—that could savor unnumbered subtle differences in the flow of feeling. All through the palace, men would be struggling in a developing panic against the powerful force that had struck at them. Once that panic began it would not stop short of hysteria.... Yet all that the individual had to do was to stop for an instant, and think: The stimulus is now going through my cortex. I'm thinking and feeling, not just feeling (Van Vogt 1948: 177–178).

The cortical-thalamic pause is a procedure for dealing with emotions like immense fears that handicap the individual's ability to take rational and decisive action in the face of a severe threat. As we can see from the quote, what is involved is perception of one's negative emotions along with acceptance of them rather than, for example, developing feelings of shame or guilt. Thus, the individual moves away from attempting to repress his or her fear and, by learning to accept and express that fear, progress is made in learning to express emotions. And progress is also made in achieving a balance between the intellect and the emotions, for the individual learns to become aware of his or her cortex no less than the thalamus or seat of emotions. What is involved in the cortical-thalamic pause is much like the procedure of meditation, where one might focus on one's own breathing and blot out one's fears with respect to many possible future situations. The focus of perception in the cortical-thalamic pause is, similarly, on one's own body: one's cortex and thalamus. But, as distinct from most techniques of meditation, one can use the cortical-thalamic pause within a very short period in one's everyday life. One can, thus, use this pause as a tool that can work against immediate threats encountered in everyday life.

The nature of the political structure of Venus, the home of a null-A people, is Van Vogt's own vision of an ideal civilization, and this has implications for what an inward-outward orientation on the part of more and more people might lead to. An automated device explains some aspects of Venusian society—a people who proved to be powerful enough to defeat Enro's vast war machine—to Gosseyn:

> To understand the political situation here, you must reach out with your mind to the furthest limits of your ideas of ultimate democracy. There is no president of Venus, no council, no ruling group. Everything is voluntary, every man lives to himself alone, and yet conjoins with others to see that the necessary work is done. But people can choose their own work. You might say, suppose everybody decided to enter the same profession. That doesn't happen. The population is composed of responsible citizens who make a careful study of the entire work-to-be-done situation before they choose their jobs (Van Vogt 1945/1970: 67).

Van Vogt thus carries further our general vision of democracy as requiring educated citizens if it is to succeed. By carrying the educational process very far through null-A training, Van Vogt is suggesting that citizens can become far more effective than they presently are, an approach similar to our own. Given that our problems are continuing to increase, knowledge of how to understand and confront them is not a luxury for the citizens of a democracy: It has become a necessity. It is indeed difficult to imagine a society where its individuals have evolved to such an extent that every one of them is able to make decisions based on complex facts as well as a complex set of cultural values. Van Vogt's vision of ultimate democracy is based on an educational system that manages to work in a highly effective manner to teach individuals to make use of scientific thinking in their own everyday lives. This is the kind of education illustrated by the cortical-thalamic pause, where the individual learns to accept and express emotions rather than bury them. It is also the kind of education where the individual learns to achieve a balance among "head," "heart," and "hand." And if we follow an evolutionary scientific method and worldview, the individual's education continues throughout life, just as there is no limit to how far the scientific method can take us. Let us recall Peirce's dictum: "Do not block the way of inquiry."

Van Vogt wrote these words several years after World War II when the cold war, along with its threat of nuclear catastrophe, had begun to develop: "Possibly, the most important requirement of our civilization is the development of a Null-A oriented political economy. It can be stated categorically that no such system has yet been developed. The field is wide open for bold and imaginative men and women to create a system that will free mankind of war, poverty and tension" (Van Vogt 1948: 186).

That threat, along with others that are even more dire such as the use of ever more deadly weapons of mass destruction by small terrorist groups, confronts all of us at this time in history. Korzybski and Van Vogt envisioned a world where people would learn to move away from their very limited usage of language and learn to open up to language's incredible potential for giving us a scientific view of the world and ourselves. We see our own approach as building on their view of the limitations of dichotomous thought without gradational thought as well, and we add the importance of metaphorical thought.

In the final section of this chapter we take up a strategy for confronting both personal and world problems, a strategy that we have labeled the East-West strategy. We return here to the central problem we have been addressing in this book, a problem that was equally central to the six previous books published by the members of the Sociological Imagination Group: the escalating gap between human aspirations and their fulfillment. We have hinted at the nature of this strategy in Chapter 1 as well as in the last chapter of our most recent book (Knottnerus and Phillips, eds. 2009). The time has come to spell out more thoroughly the nature of this strategy.

The East-West Strategy

In this final section accentuating human possibilities with its special focus on our infinite intellectual capacities, we note that it is essential for us to build on the preceding two sections. It is the combination of language and the scientific method that gives us those possibilities. Whatever the East-West strategy is, it derives from making full use of the infinite potential that a combination of language and the scientific method gives us. Of course, as we have seen in Part II, it is not our bureaucratic approach to these two tools that carries forward that potential: It is, rather, an evolutionary approach that we have yet to learn how to employ. It is exactly that approach that the East-West strategy embodies. Yet as we proceed we must not forget what the pendulum metaphor for the scientific method suggests: that as we press forward so as to swing our pendulum further to the right, this gives us the momentum we need for a swing further to the left where we become more aware of the depth of our problems. Part II suggested that depth, yet we are by no means done with understanding that depth, and we hope to learn a good deal more about our problems as we swinging our pendulum to the right in Part III.

Rudyard Kipling's "The Ballad of East and West" includes this stanza:

> Oh, East is East, and West is West, and never the twain shall meet,
> Till Earth and Sky stand presently at God's great Judgement Seat:
> But there is neither East nor West, Border, nor Breed, nor Birth,
> When two strong men stand face to face, tho' they come from the ends of earth!
> (Quoted in Knowles 2004: 453, note 15)

Generally it is only the first line of Kipling's ballad that we remember, conveying a negative view of the possibility that East and West can meet. Yet the last two lines oppose that idea, giving us an optimistic view as to the possibilities of East-West interaction. We share that view with Kipling, especially given our understanding of the interactive nature of our universe, along with the fact that it is we humans who are presently the most interactive creatures in the known universe. And this is even without taking into consideration how much our bureaucratic worldview is working to limit the development of our patterns of interaction. Kipling published those lines in 1892 in a world much different from our own. Many of us would like to think that our technological developments in communication and transportation since that time have increased the effectiveness of our interactions with one another across the globe. Yet if indeed we continue to be dominated by a bureaucratic worldview that points us far away from interaction—as illustrated by Figure 1-2—then all of that technology remains most limited in its effectiveness. Nevertheless, it is there, waiting for us to develop an interactive or evolutionary worldview that will enable us to make full use of that technology so as to yield the kinds of interaction that are deeply meaningful and that yield our increasing ability to learn from one another and solve our problems. Indeed, that technology—when coupled with an evolutionary worldview—is poised to help us fulfill more and more of our interactive potential with the speed of the Internet.

Chapter 13 of *Bureaucratic Culture and Escalating Problems,* titled "The East-West Strategy," summarizes that strategy:

> Following a Buddhist Eastern orientation, we can learn to lower our aspirations in the short run so as to narrow the aspirations-fulfillment gap. This approach also follows the ideals of Confucius, who saw "the path of duty in what is near," while "men seek for it in what is remote." Given that narrowed gap—which gives us confidence in our ability to solve problems—we can then learn, in the long run, to continue to raise both aspirations and their fulfillment, following a Western orientation.
>
> By keeping aspirations and fulfillment close together we point toward the East, and by continuing to raise both of them we point toward the West. We should note that a successful East-West strategy depends on learning to use a broad scientific method in everyday life. For it is by using an ability to gain increasing understanding of our complex human problems by means of a broad scientific method that the individual is in fact able to continually raise both aspirations and their fulfillment (Knottnerus and Phillips, eds. 2009: 203–204).

Thus, the East-West strategy focuses on the central problem we have discussed in the preceding chapters: the escalating aspirations-fulfillment gap, as depicted in Figure 1-1. How are we to succeed in narrowing that gap? A Buddhist orientation points us in that direction, but it fails to help us move both aspirations and fulfillment upward once we have narrowed that gap. As for a Western scientific orientation, it has helped us to continue to raise our aspiration, but that has led to an increasing aspirations-fulfillment gap. Yet it is exactly here that a broadened scientific method making full use of social science knowledge as well as language's infinite potential can help us to remedy this situation, enabling us to take both aspirations and their fulfillment through the roof. In this chapter we begin with a section on the Eastern strategy for solving problems as well as the Western strategy, fleshing out the achievements and the limitations of both. And we conclude with a section on the East-West strategy.

As one illustration of East-West interaction, we have the popularity of the Buddhist approach to meditation throughout the Western world. With the fast-paced Western revolution of rising expectations and resulting aspirations-fulfillment gap, the practice of meditation can help Western individuals shed their "attachment" to external phenomena for a limited period of time and achieve some relief from that gap. In our own view, however, this can help us Westerners only to a limited extent. For our bureaucratic worldview is an incredibly powerful force, and its invisible nature makes it all the more powerful. It will continue to push us toward widening our aspirations-fulfillment gap until we learn to do something about it. More specifically, building on the work of Thomas Kuhn—as discussed in the first section of this chapter—we must become aware of its existence and how it works against our ideals, we must envision an alternative worldview that promises to fulfill those ideals, and we must then move away from our bureaucratic worldview and toward that alternative worldview.

The Eastern Strategy and the Western Strategy

Given our discussion of our bureaucratic approach to the scientific method in Part II—illustrating the Western strategy—our focus in this section will be on the Eastern strategy for solving problems, and on Buddhism in particular. In our view, granting the deficiencies of this Eastern strategy, it has a great deal to offer. As for the Western strategy, our emphasis will be on pulling together key ideas from Part II that bear on our bureaucratic approach to the scientific method. That scientific method has succeeded in shaping the world, and there is much that we can learn from it, granting that it has also succeeded in taking us to the very edge of a cliff where we look down at our own destruction.

Gautama Siddartha Sakyamuni, the Buddha, was born some 2,500 years ago into the family of a minor ruler of one of India's smaller principalities and raised as a prince of the royal house. He led a very sheltered life within the palace until his early twenties when he went outside of its gates. In that brief journey he experienced several dramatic encounters. Abraham Kaplan, a philosopher with substantial experience living in India—whose analysis of pragmatism appears in the first section of this chapter—can take up the story of the Buddha for us:

> [He experienced] an old man suffering from the ravages of age, an invalid bearing the marks of his disease, a corpse being carried to cremation, and a monk seeking his salvation. The future Buddha was overwhelmed with the realization that old age, sickness, and death were the common lot of mankind; and that while some, like the monk, were trying to come to grips with these great realities, he himself was as one living in a dream. . . . Thus Gautama set out on the path to Enlightenment

by renouncing wealth and position, friendship and love, till he should come to understand what man lives by.

Gautama began by studying philosophy, but found among the academicians no answer to his life problem. He then entered upon a regime of asceticism and self-mortification ... and even brought himself near the point of death; but this took him no closer to a solution than his academic pursuits had done. At last, after many wanderings alone and with other seekers, worn in body and spirit but not in his indomitable will, he sat down under a tree—known thereafter as the *bo* tree, the tree of enlightenment—and resolved not to rise up from it till he had solved the great problem. And so, at the age of thirty-five, he achieved Enlightenment.... Thereafter, for a half-century more, he traveled up and down the Indian subcontinent, sharing with his fellow men the great truths to which he had attained (1961: 238–239).

We might well note that Gautama's Enlightenment came only after his many personal experiences of fundamental problems in life, such as old age, sickness, and death. Those experiences of an awareness of problems followed by deepening understanding parallel the pendulum metaphor for the scientific method, with its swings ever further to the left and ever further to the right. As for the nature of the truths that Gautama discovered, these also parallel the nature of a broad approach to the scientific method, as Phillips described them in his *Armageddon or Evolution*:

Buddhist teaching is based on the Four Noble Truths and the Eightfold Noble Path. The first Noble Truth is the universal existence of *"dukkha,"* which has to do with pain, sorrow and suffering, but more precisely suggests the lack of complete fulfillment of all human pursuits. There is, then, always an aspirations-fulfillment gap. Nothing is ever wholly satisfying, and this is true even for the most fortunate human beings. This is the problem which Gautama addressed, much like the focus of the scientific method on a problem. The law of causality—like the assumption of modern science, and like the Hindu law of karma—is the second Noble Truth: everything that happens is caused. If we remove the cause of *dukkha*, then *dukkha* will disappear. As for the third Noble Truth, it is the renunciation of desire, 'thirst" or aspirations, the removal of passions that will inevitably be frustrated to some degree. The fourth Noble Truth specifies the Eightfold Noble Path as the concrete direction for actually removing *dukkha*: right views, right aspirations, right speech, right conduct, a right livelihood, right efforts, right thoughts and right contemplation (Phillips 2009: 46–47).

What Gautama emerged with when he finally arose from his seated position under the *bo* tree were key elements of a broad scientific method that can be practiced by all of us in our everyday lives, a method that is also fundamental to the practice of the East-West strategy. He begins with the problem of *dukkha* that affects all of us very deeply, a problem that parallels our own emphasis on the problem of the aspirations-fulfillment gap, namely, the first Noble Truth. The second Noble Truth, the law of causality, is nothing less than a scientific view of the world: All of the phenomena that we encounter have causes, and if we change those causes then we will also change those phenomena. The third Noble Truth is what we have already emphasized: the renunciation of desire or "attachment" or aspirations or "thirst" for phenomena, an orientation that promises to also remove *dukkha,* which illustrates the aspirations-fulfillment gap. Yet beyond this general orientation, the individual requires specific procedures that can be used in everyday life, and it is the fourth Noble Truth that specifies these. Those procedures are further specified by the Eightfold Noble Path: right views, right aspirations, right speech, right conduct, a right livelihood, right efforts, right thoughts, and right contemplation.

As for the advantages of these Buddhist ideas for solving problems, we have the idea of the importance of using the scientific method in our own everyday lives. This is an idea that is very far from our own bureaucratic mentality, which teaches us to worship expert scientists and teaches scientists to fail to follow biblical advice: Physician, heal thyself. There is also Gautama's realism by focusing on inward perception, by contrast with the outward perception of Western and Westernized society. There is in addition the uncovering of the absolutely fundamental problem of *dukkha,* a problem paralleling our own emphasis on the aspirations-fulfillment gap. We can also call attention to Gautama's abandonment of personal wealth, love, and comfort in the pursuit of understanding or enlightenment. This is a very far cry from the Western focus on the cultural value of material comfort and materialism in general, fundamental to our bureaucratic way of life. And we might add Gautama's realistic concern with concrete procedures—illustrated by the Eightfold Noble Path—that the individual requires in order to learn to lead a life that follows the Noble Truths. Overall, Gautama's aim of narrowing the aspirations-fulfillment gap so that we can become realistic about our *dukkha*-laden situation is crucial as a first step within the East-West strategy.

As for disadvantages, a key one is linked to the third Noble Truth having to do with emotional detachment as a way to confront the problem of *dukkha* or, in our terms, the aspirations-fulfillment gap. In our view, the Buddhist emphasis on the renunciation of desire parallels the Western emphasis on emotional repression: Both take away from the individual's possibilities. By contrast, the East-West strategy involves an alternative direction for narrowing the aspirations-fulfillment gap. That direction involves a broad approach to the scientific method that makes full use of the potential of language. Another disadvantage of this Eastern strategy is its limited utilization of a scientific method broad enough to encompass the social sciences. This strategy is to be commended for its focus on very concrete procedures aimed at narrowing the aspirations-fulfillment gap—granting the limitations of their effectiveness—as specified by the fourth Noble Truth and the Eightfold Noble Path. Yet this Eastern strategy also shares with our bureaucratic scientific method and worldview a neglect of what the social sciences have discovered about human behavior. It is those very discoveries that offer us an alternative to emotional repression as a device for narrowing the aspirations-fulfillment gap.

By contrast with the Buddhist orientation to inward perception and thought, we have the Western orientation to outward perception and thought—as outlined in Chapter 2—with neither orientation yielding inward-outward perception and thought. Thus, whereas Buddha was much concerned with *dukkha*—analogous to the aspirations-fulfillment gap—such awareness of the situation of the individual is rare throughout Western society. Indeed, the very idea of the possibility for individual evolution is foreign to Western society, given that same outward orientation. This is not the case for Buddhism, with its focus on the concept of karma. The Buddhist concept of karma derives from the Hindu law of karma, which is a principle of moral causation. It is the idea that an individual's character determines his or her fate. And character is in turn determined by the full range of an individual's past actions: As we have sown, so shall we reap. It is, then, every act we take within the Eightfold Noble Path that can help us to reduce *dukkha*. What we do in one momentary situation after another shapes ourselves as well as our future.

Yet for all of the deficiencies of the Western bureaucratic worldview and science—including outward perception and thought, emotional repression, and conforming behavior, as outlined in Chapters 2, 3, and 4—it has been that same worldview and science that has helped to shape both our people-oriented cultural values along with the ability of science and technology to shape the world, for good as well as evil, over the past five centuries. As a result, we are now in a position to broaden the scientific method that has proved its power to solve a vast variety of problems, granting its one-sidedness. For the scientific method linked to the Western bureaucratic worldview, despite its narrowness, has succeeded in opening up human possibilities. Without it, it is hard to imagine the development of the American and French revolutions along with the modern social movements carrying further the torches of equality, freedom, individual personality, and democracy. It is all too easy to focus on the dangers that have resulted from the continuing scientific revolution. But let us give credit where credit is due.

The East-West Strategy: Both East and West

Whatever else the East-West strategy proves to become—and at this point it is no more than an idea that has yet to be developed and is yet to prove its potential—it is closely linked to our learning to use the scientific method along with the extraordinary language of social science in our everyday lives. Let us look to Figure 5-1 for further insight into the nature of that language and how it might be used. A central idea guiding our approach to the extraordinary language is the distinction between structures, or behavior persisting over time, and situational behavior that occurs in a given momentary scene. Figure 5-1 can clarify this distinction along with the relationships among the concepts that we emphasize.

The three situational concepts—perception and thought, emotion, and action—are located in the center of the diagram, separated from the other concepts by horizontal lines. All of the other concepts are structural. Those focusing on the individual are located above those situational concepts, and those centering on society are located below them. The key to understanding how change occurs is to take into account both situational and structural concepts. For example, when a given situational action—such as going to sleep at a certain time—is repeated over and over again, then we can come to see this pattern of behavior as an individual ritual, a concept located just above that of action. Further, to the extent that this individual ritual is widely shared throughout society, then we can call it a social ritual, a concept located just below that of action. Correspondingly, when we know the nature of the individual's or society's rituals, then we also know a great deal about how people will act in any given situation. Yet all of the other individual and social structures also influence what happens in a given situation. We see this depicted by the links tying all of these concepts together, granting that only some of those links are portrayed for purposes of clarity. From this perspective, it is a complex undertaking to understand what happens in a given situation.

Another central idea—portrayed to some extent by the contrast between Figure 4-1 and Figure 5-1—is the distinction between concepts pointing toward a bureaucratic way of life and concepts pointing toward an evolutionary way of life. With respect to the three situational concepts, for example, we distinguish between outward perception and thought (bureaucratic) in Figure 4-1 and inward-outward perception and thought (evolutionary) in Figure 5-1; between emotional repression (bureaucratic) in Figure 4-1 and emotional expression (evolutionary) in Figure 5-1; and between conforming behavior (bureaucratic) in Figure 4-1 and interaction (evolutionary) in Figure 5-1. Similarly, all of the concepts for personality and social structures (with the exception of "stratification" and "bureaucracy") appearing above and below those horizontal lines in Figures 4-1 and 5-1 can be divided into these two groups. There are those that are bureaucratic (for example, a bureaucratic worldview), and there are those that are evolutionary (for example, an evolutionary worldview). Yet this dichotomous approach is balanced by a gradational orientation, since we conceive of the possibility of movement from a bureaucratic to an evolutionary. And still further, a metaphorical approach to language is most important, as illustrated by our continuing use of "head," "heart," and "hand."

Given the centrality of emotional repression in both the Eastern and the Western strategies, it becomes crucial to examine the direction of emotional expression within the East-West strategy. Emotional repression has also succeeded in invading the traditional approach to the scientific method in the form of the principle of "value neutrality," which requires the scientist to remain uncommitted to any particular cultural value, staying completely neutral. Let us recall our discussion of value neutrality in Chapter 3. There, we quoted the conclusions of 11 contemporary philosophers of science. Here is part of that quote:

> If the critics of the value-free science ideal are right, then these traditional claims about science not only are ungrounded but also can have pernicious consequences. If the *content* of science—not just its application—can and must involve values, then presenting scientific results as entirely neutral is deceptive. It means ignoring the value assumptions that go into science and the value implications of scientific results. Important value assumptions will be hidden behind a cloak of neutrality in public debates over policy and morality. If scientific results concerning IQ and race, free markets and growth, or environmental emissions and planetary weather make value assumptions, treating them as entirely neutral is misleading at best.... (Kincaid, Dupre, and Wylie, eds. 2007: 5).

This idea of the supposed importance of value neutrality is also extended to the rest of us who are not professional scientists: We should be neutral when we get our facts together in order to avoid bias, thus repressing our emotions and following the emphasis of a bureaucratic worldview. That repression of emotions also fits hand in glove with the Eastern strategy as well as the Western strategy, but certainly not with the East-West strategy. Social scientists, who should know better, unfortunately have generally been taken in by this idea. And the rest of us, following the cultural value of conforming behavior, have generally followed them like sheep. Apparently the power of our bureaucratic worldview is not to be taken lightly.

Those philosophers of science also raised a crucial question, as outlined in Chapter 3: How are we to avoid a science that comes to resemble a political debate between opposing values rather than the cumulative development of understanding? We have seen that kind of political debate, for example, in election campaigns throughout the world, where facts are distorted in the interest of swaying the electorate. And we have also seen it in the mass media as well as in our everyday lives in our efforts to convince others to conform to our own beliefs. In our own view, the problem here has much to do with our failure to address our cultural values of group superiority and conformity—values linked to a bureaucratic worldview—that conflict with such people-oriented cultural values as individual personality, equality, and democracy. Those conflicts remain hidden as a result of our bureaucratic worldview with its resulting emotional repression. By contrast, an evolutionary world-view can open up those conflicts to the light of day, and we can learn to resolve them by reducing, one step at a time, our hidden commitment to those bureaucratic cultural values. Of course, this will take quite a bit of doing. For example, beyond seeing our value conflicts in the light of day we must have a clear direction for moving toward that evolutionary worldview as well as a clear image of its nature. And we must come to see demonstrations of the ability of such movement to yield cumulative knowledge to a much greater extent than we are able to gain within our present approach to the scientific method.

We believe, then, that the East-West strategy for confronting personal and world problems can succeed in making full use of the infinite potentials of language and the scientific method to help us change from a bureaucratic to an evolutionary way of life and, as a result, confront our escalating problems ever more effectively. In this chapter we have come to see the enormous importance of emotional repression in preventing such a change from taking place. In Chapter 6 we turn to this "heart" area of human behavior, granting that we have introduced it throughout the foregoing chapters. Yet we have much more to say about this topic in this next chapter. We require many more illustrations and deeper understanding of the enormous power of our repressed emotions to shape our behavior. Franklin Delano Roosevelt stated in his inaugural address on March 4, 1933—in the midst of the worst economic depression the world had ever seen—that "the only thing we have to fear is fear itself." Emotions supporting our people-oriented cultural values can prove to be most inspiring. We might also recall Lincoln's Gettysburg address in 1863 in the midst of the Civil War, ending with the conviction that "government of the people, by the people, and for the people, shall not perish from the earth," a commitment restated by President-elect Barack Obama when he learned of his election on November 4, 2008.

CHAPTER 6

"Heart"

Emotional Expression

It was the best of times, it was the worst of times,
It was the age of wisdom, it was the age of foolishness,
It was the epoch of belief, it was the epoch of incredulity,
It was the season of Light, it was the season of Darkness,
It was the spring of hope, it was the winter of despair,
We had everything before us, we had nothing before us,
We were all going directly to Heaven, we were all going
direct the other way.
Charles Dickens, *A Tale of Two Cities,* 1859
(Quoted in Knowles, ed. 2004: 272, note 13)

THE PERIOD OF THE FRENCH REVOLUTION and its aftermath over two centuries ago was a period of "the best of times," when movement in Europe away from kings and toward democracy opened up possibilities for the human being throughout the world. This was also the era of the American Revolution with its Declaration of Independence that included these words: "We hold these Truths to be self-evident, that all Men are created equal, that they are endowed by their Creator with certain unalienable Rights, that among these are Life, Liberty, and the pursuit of Happiness."

But the aftermath of the French Revolution was also a period of "the worst of times," for that revolution was followed by the "reign of terror." Tens of thousands of those who had opposed the revolution—including a number of individuals who had fought for it—were executed in a lust for revenge and without any trial.

We might well draw a parallel between those times centuries ago and our own era, for we too appear to be experiencing the best of times and the worst of times. On the one hand, an African American has been elected to America's highest office, following centuries of racism supporting the cultural value of group superiority—along with patterns of social stratification—and opposing the cultural value of equality. On the other hand, the United States and the world as a whole are experiencing a meltdown of financial institutions and increasing unemployment with their threat of a worldwide depression, coupled with the full range of visible and invisible social problems—as discussed in Part II—that threaten the very survival of the human race. In our own view, this combination of enormous problems and great possibilities gives us unprecedented opportunities to face up to those problems and make progress on them, opportunities that would not have existed had those problems remained hidden from view. Ours is a time when we live on the knife-edge of history. In our view, we can choose to move toward evolution or toward extinction.

As we proceed with this chapter emphasizing emotional expression—as well as the one to follow that will focus on interaction—it is crucial that we build on Chapter 5, with its focus on language, the scientific method, and the East-West strategy. We can only go so far with "heart" and "hand" without including "head" as well. This is indeed difficult, since the ideas in Chapter 5 have only begun to be developed and have hardly been tested. As a result, this chapter and the one to follow can prove to be no more than a set of initial ideas. However, we are hopeful that they will point the way toward a more solid and systematic approach to developing "heart" and "hand." As we proceed, let us not forget our discussion of the depths of our patterns of emotional repression in Chapter 3, illustrated by the work of Freud, Horney, and Scheff. If indeed we wish to achieve emotional expression, then we must also look to what we have buried within ourselves. Following our discussion of *The Players of Null-A* in Chapter 5, we are all Ashargins who have experienced the traumas of living in a bureaucratic world, if not in the world of Enro the Red. And we all need the wisdom of Gosseyn—alias Korzybski—to help us understand those traumas from the height of a broader understanding of them if we are indeed to raise them to the level of consciousness.

We have discovered in the preceding chapters that the causes of our problems are neither in our genes nor in the stars. It is we who have chosen a road that has yielded our visible and invisible problems, and it is we who have the potential to choose what the poet Robert Frost called "the road not taken." Walt Whitman, America's poet of individual possibilities, has something to say about that road not taken in his "Song of Myself":

> I celebrate myself, and sing myself,
> And what I assume you shall assume,
> For every atom belonging to me as good belongs to you. . . .
> Divine am I inside and out,
> And I make holy whatever I touch or am touch'd from,
> The scent of these arm-pits aroma finer than prayer,
> This head more than churches, bibles, and all the creeds.
> If I worship one thing more than another it shall be the
> spread of my own body.
> (Whitman 1892/2004: 23, 44).

Along with Whitman, we are convinced of the incredible potential of every single human being. Working in hospitals during the Civil War, he saw death and shattered individuals all around him, just as we have already witnessed the horrors of the twenty-first century. Yet we need not see the glass as half empty: We can choose to see it as half full. For example, we can look to poets like Whitman and Frost to help us become aware of our own possibilities as individuals. Following our earlier chapters, we can look to the infinite potential of language and the scientific method, and we can gain awareness of our limited use of that potential. We can gain optimism from the achievements of biophysical scientists, political leaders, social scientists, philosophers, poets, and the rest of us in the face of our complex and threatening problems. And even as these very problems continue to escalate, our awareness of them can become the first and most important step of a broad scientific method that we learn to use in our everyday lives, a method that has no equal in its ability to help us solve our problems.

We shall begin with a section on reconstructing our cultural values that centers on moving away from the repressed values of external conformity and group superiority. The election of Barack Obama as president by no means indicates that unbridled materialism and racism no longer exist throughout the United States and the world. Yet it does indicate substantial progress. We now have more of an opportunity to raise to the surface our cultural values of external conformity and group superiority, supported as they are by our bureaucratic worldview. And, as a result, we have an opportunity to challenge those values and that worldview, and to move toward a system of values that no longer requires emotional repression coupled with outward perception with limited ability to look inward at ourselves. Our final section will focus on our potential for individual evolution. This is a potential that is blocked by the repression of emotions in Eastern society no less than in Western society.

Reconstructing Cultural Values: Beyond External Conformity and Group Superiority

It was in Figure 1-1 that we presented most systematically the central problem that has been the focus of the chapters in Part II as well as the previous books of the Sociological Imagination Group: the escalating aspirations-fulfillment gap throughout the world. At the outset of Part III we came to see that gap not only as the product of our scientific and technological revolutions over the past five centuries. and not only as fundamental to the very nature of human behavior ever since we appeared on earth. We also saw a comparable gap throughout evolutionary history—following the work of George Kelly—resulting from an organism's ability to represent its environment. That gap then becomes the basis for an organism's active response to its environment when that environment does not suit the organism. Yet the concept of "aspirations"—although it helps us to attend to the importance of the "heart"—is quite general: It is a huge tent that encompasses a great deal. When we approach that concept in a detailed way, it becomes most useful to spell out the specific cultural values that are to be found under that tent, just as we have included the concept of cultural values in Figures 3-1, 4-1, and 5-1. For it is those cultural values that not only shape our individual values, beliefs and assumptions to a very great extent. They also succeed in shaping our cultural norms and our institutions to a very great extent. Unfortunately, however, this concept of cultural values has managed to fall through the cracks of the social sciences despite its enormous importance, as indicated in Chapter 3. In our view, this has been largely due to the narrow specialization—linked to our bureaucratic worldview—that has characterized these fields.

Reviewing our analysis of the cultural values that we believe are to be found throughout the modern world—based largely on the work of Robin Williams (1970)—there are four people-oriented ones: *equality, freedom, individual personality,* and *democracy.* And there are four work-related ones: *achievement and success, progress, material comfort,* and *science and secular rationality.* Also, there are two values that we generally repress because they conflict with other cultural values: *group superiority* and *external conformity.* We might also mention here several values that Williams put forward that we did not choose to include in our own analysis. There are the values of "activity and work" and "efficiency and practicality," which we felt overlapped substantially with the values of "achievement and success" and "progress" (a focus on economic development). Williams also cited the values of "moral orientation" and "humanitarian mores," which we saw as emphasized within American society more than other societies. Finally, Williams cited "nationalism and patriotism" and "racism," which we saw as overlapping with "group superiority." Williams emphasized the importance of seeing these cultural values as linked to one another, as changing over time, and as first approximations. Let us recall that we also introduced five cultural values deriving from society's basic institutions, granting that the above values are also fundamental within our institutions: *understanding the world, solving problems, the continuation of life, intimate and close relationships,* and *ultimate meaning.*

Cultural values do indeed change over time—although change is certainly not rapid—as is well indicated by the change in the value of group superiority indicated by the election of an African American to the American presidency. Once the cultural value of group superiority is raised to the surface rather than remaining deeply buried or repressed, people can become aware of its contradiction with other cultural values, and they are then in a position to do something about it. And the same can take place with the cultural value of external conformity. We shall, then, proceed to raise these repressed values to the surface, for we Ashargins must learn to face up to cultural values that we would rather not acknowledge. Let us never forget that it was human beings much like ourselves who launched and participated in the Holocaust. And it was also human beings much like ourselves who—in the Milgram experiment, discussed in Chapter 4—conformed to a command to shock someone with a lethal dose of electricity. In this way we hope to clear a path for us to pull ourselves together so that we can learn to face ourselves rather than hide from ourselves. For we believe that it is these buried cultural values of external conformity and group superiority that hold us back from inward-outward perception and thought. More generally, we believe that they hold us back from individual evolution, which we shall take up in the final section of this chapter.

As we begin our efforts to move toward emotional expression, it is crucial that we gain momentum for this movement—following the pendulum metaphor for the scientific method—by moving deeply into the forces that oppose such movement. For example, the philosopher Friedrich Nietzsche hinted at the power of those forces in an essay he wrote near the close of the nineteenth century within his *The Gay Science*:

> In the great majority, the intellect is a clumsy, gloomy, creaking machine that is difficult to start. They call it "taking the matter seriously" when they want to work with this machine and think well. How burdensome they must find good thinking! The lovely human beast always seems to lose its good spirits when it thinks well; it becomes "serious." And "where laughter and gaiety are found, thinking does not amount to anything": that is the prejudice of this serious beast against all "gay science."—Well then, let us prove that this is a prejudice (Nietzsche 1887/1974: 257).

Although Nietzsche's focus in that book was on science, his very broad philosophical approach enabled him to comment on culture and history in general. Here he is concerned not just with the scientific method but with something far more general: how people in general, and not just scientists, carry on the process of thinking. The "prejudice" against "laughter and gaiety" can remind us of the scientist's emphasis on "value neutrality," as discussed at the end of Chapter 5. For emotional expression, from the perspective of a commitment to value neutrality, will take away from our ability to avoid mixing the "facts" we observe with our own "values," which supposedly would contaminate those facts in favor of our own values. Yet this bureaucratic approach to the scientific method—which has been extended far beyond the ivy-covered walls of the academic world—results in an intellect that is "a clumsy, gloomy, creaking machine that is difficult to start." And this is the case for the rest of us no less than for the scientist. uncovering the nature of the world, a force that all of us can learn to harness.

We might do well to recall here Peirce's vision of the first step of the scientific method, as discussed in Chapter 5:

> The irritation of doubt is the only immediate motive for the struggle to attain belief.... With the doubt, therefore, the struggle begins, and with the cessation of doubt it ends.... Some philosophers have imagined that to start an inquiry it was only necessary to utter a question whether orally or by setting it down upon paper, and have even recommended us to begin our studies with questioning everything! But the mere putting of a proposition into the interrogative form does not stimulate the mind to any struggle after belief. There must be a real and living doubt, and without this all discussion is idle (Peirce 1877/1955: 10–11).

Peirce believed that emotional expression—as illustrated here by the individual's "real and living doubt"—is essential for the work of the scientist. And Nietzsche helps us to extend this idea beyond the boundaries of scientific work to the very process of thought with which we are all involved.

We might also look to a recent idea: the importance of "negative thinking."

The repression of "negative emotions" is illustrated by people who deal with death on a regular basis. For example, Dr. Elissa Ely—a psychiatrist—writes about the deaths of classmates announced in her reunion book 20 years after her graduation from medical school:

> Why did we think, when we went to school, that we were only studying the lives of others? We hammered down their illnesses with histories, stripped them naked with tests, and bombarded them with treatments.

We believed that memorizing thousands of facts was taking command. We understood perfectly what would happen to patients. but though we studied night and day, we never understood—how could we miss something so sad and so true?—what would happen to us (Ely 2008: D9).

Dr. Ely's question cannot be answered adequately within the framework of our bureaucratic worldview, since psychiatrists—with very rare partial exceptions such as Karen Horney, discussed in Chapter 3—fail to learn much about their own culture and worldview within their medical school experiences. And anthropologists, sociologists, psychologists, political scientists, economists, and historians have failed those medical students by not getting their own act together so that they could communicate the nature of our worldview. Apparently, negative thinking can help individuals dig deeply into their own problems and potential problems instead of repressing them. And if such thinking does not reject hope and optimism—thus yielding a one-sided orientation that is yet another species of emotional repression—it can help to free the individual from emotional repression.

Another example of negative thinking comes to us from Dr. Atul Gawande, a surgeon and also a staff writer for the *New Yorker* magazine:

Soldiers told of extraordinary care at Walter Reed that had saved them despite multiple limbs blown away, burns over 90 percent of their bodies, brain injuries previously considered unsurvivable. And then they told of outpatient facilities, at the same hospital, where wheelchair-bound soldiers were stranded without food, the brain-injured denied aid because they couldn't fill out forms.... The final report recently released by the military's independent review group did not find good people in one department and bad people in another.... But in one part of the hospital good people succeeded, and in the other good people failed.... The primary difference was whether leaders accepted the value of negative thinking or not....

During a visit with colleagues at Walter Reed early in the Iraq war, I was struck, for example, by their attention to eye-injury statistics. Instead of being proud of saving some soldiers from blindness, the doctors asked a harder, more unnerving question: Why had so many injuries occurred? They discovered that the young soldiers weren't wearing their protective goggles. Too ugly, the soldiers said. So the military switched to cooler-looking Wiley X ballistic eyewear. The soldiers wore their eyegear more consistently, and the eye-injury rate dropped immediately.... Negative thinking is unquestionably painful.... You live in a state of perpetual dissatisfaction. That's an unhealthy way to be in large parts of life.... But in running schools or businesses, in planning war, in caring for the sick and injured? Negative thinking can be exactly what we need (Gawande 2007: A8).

Once again we have an example of negative thinking as help-ing people swing their pendulum of the scientific method to the left, defying the emphasis of our bureaucratic worldview on repressing negative emotions. And once again we find that such negative thinking can prove to be highly effective in helping people solve problems, just as awareness and commitment to a problem is highly effective as the first step of the scientific method. Yet once again we have an illustra-tion that succumbs to the one-sided understanding emphasized within our bureaucratic worldview. Following Gawande's conclusion, negative thinking is harmful if we use it in everyday life: "You live in a state of perpetual dissatisfaction." This is indeed the case only if negative thinking is not balanced by positive thinking, and that balance can be achieved by a shift from a bureaucratic to an evolutionary worldview. As for Gawande's view as to the value of negative thinking within the world of work, that balance is needed there as well. Granting that sur-geons should follow the example of those Walter Reed physicians and use negative thinking to uncover problems that they would otherwise repress. But they cannot afford to "live in a state of perpetual dissatis-faction" while they are on the job. They need to balance that negative thinking with positive thinking and feel good about what they are ac-complishing, just as do the rest of us in our everyday lives. It is that very balance—linked to an evolutionary worldview—that can help all of us to face up to escalating world problems and still avoid living "in a state of perpetual dissatisfaction."

Given the narrow or addictive emphasis within our bureaucratic worldview, we live in an addictive society, with addictions by no means limited to physiological ones like dependence on alcohol, drugs, and cigarettes. And no number of sessions with psychologists will do more than help a fraction of us to learn to alter our external conformity to a materialistic way of life. Let us, then, proceed to use negative thinking, raising to the surface of awareness the impact of the addiction to mate-rialism throughout contemporary society, and examine our patterns of affluenza in greater detail. Granting that such detail will not move our pendulum of the scientific method directly to the right-hand side. Yet since we generally fail to move it very far to the left, this approach will work to reverse that limitation, giving us the momentum we need for subsequent movement to the right. The invented term "affluenza" is most useful here because of its association with influenza, a disease that has wiped out millions, thus suggesting its pernicious nature. And there is also its association with affluence, suggesting the materialistic nature of our revolution of rising expectations.

In their second edition of *Affluenza* (de Graaf, Wann, and Naylor 2005), the authors define affluenza as "a painful, contagious, socially transmitted condition of overload, debt, anxiety, and waste resulting from the dogged pursuit of more" (2005: 2). Let us recall our quote from Durkheim's *Suicide* in Chapter 3: "From top to bottom of the ladder, greed is aroused without knowing where to find ultimate foothold. Nothing can calm it, since its goal is far beyond all it can attain" (1897/1951: 254). The authors focus on the materialistic aspects of the worldwide aspirations-fulfillment gap, as illustrated by the grocer of Balgat: "I have told you I want better things."

The authors of *Affluenza* can help us understand just how pernicious is our bureaucratic worldview, with its materialistic and addictive focus, as a result of their many illustrations of the symptoms of affluenza. They are not social scientists and, as a result, do not focus on using the extraordinary language of social science. Yet we are all quite familiar with the everyday or vernacular language that they employ. Their approach is extremely comprehensive, paralleling our own orientation. And they have taken the trouble to use that approach as they proceeded to develop a substantial amount of concrete information supporting their focus on the negative impacts of affluenza. We can divide symptoms into those involving "head," "heart," and "hand"—as linked to personality and social structure—and also those linked to biological and physical structures. Those examples—which take up over a hundred pages of text (11-113) can communicate effectively and also achieve a measure of integration because of the authors' use of biological metaphors suggesting that affluenza is much like a disease, just as we currently view physiological addictions as a medical problem.

Starting with "heart," the authors begin with *"shopping fever,"* where "we now spend nearly two-thirds of our $11 trillion economy on consumer goods" (13). Our *"rash of bankruptcies"* is illustrated by our average of 6.5 credit cards possessed by each American, the fact that 1.5 million of us file for bankruptcy each year, and the additional fact that our national savings rate from our income is now near zero (19-21). *"Swollen expectations"* is illustrated by the doubling since 1950 of the average size of houses (although with smaller families), the demand for SUV's with all of the fancy extras, space tourism to the tune of $20 million a ticket, restaurant dining versus home cooking, and the explosion of electronic gadgetry like personal computers, cell phones, fax machines, Palm Pilots, and ipods (24, 27-28).

As for "head," the authors see affluenza as tied to *"an ache for meaning."* They quote Mother Teresa's comment when she visited the United States to receive an honorary degree: "This is the poorest place I've ever been in my life," referring to our poverty of the soul (74). They also quote Dr. Michael Lerner, a rabbi and writer, who brought groups of working people from various occupations together to talk with each other about their lives: "We found middle-income people deeply unhappy because they hunger to serve the common good and to contribute something with their talents and energies, yet find that their actual work gives them little opportunity to do so. They often turn to demands for more money as a compensation for a life that otherwise feels frustrating and empty" (76). The rate of clinical depression in the United States today is ten times what it was before 1945. The use of antidepressants has tripled over the past decade (77).

With respect to "hand," *"family convulsions"* suggests the undermining of American family life by materialistic cultural values, as illustrated by huge and unaffordable weddings; couples fighting with one another because they can't pay their bills; shopping for a new relationship that looks good on the surface but is much the same as the old one; and homes where husband, wife, and children fail to communicate with one another because they are all busy with their own toys (48-51). The *"stress of excess"* deals with people's rushing around to satisfy multiple desires and having no time whatsoever to themselves, as illustrated by the fact that the United States passed Japan in 1999 as the modern industrial country with the longest working hours (39–44). *"Community chills"* suggests that isolation among family members and throughout the community is now a way of life, for consumers feel little responsibility to others in addition to shopping, as illustrated by bowling alone, declines in attendance at public meetings on town affairs, declines in attendance at PTA meetings, less participation in the League of Women Voters and in fraternal organizations, and less volunteering (65).

Taking all of the examples developed by de Graaf, Wann, and Naylor together, they indicate that our entire way of life has been grossly distorted by our materialistic focus. And they also imply the enormous difficulties that would be involved in moving away from our addiction to the cultural values of external conformity and material comfort. This wealth of illustrations helps to give credibility to the breadth of our own focus on our bureaucratic worldview and way of life. And this range of illustrations also helps to give credibility to our own view that nothing less than the breadth of an alternative worldview is required to confront the full range of the problems that the authors have uncovered. The advantage of our focusing on negative thinking—granting that we retain our optimism about the possibilities of confronting effectively this wide range of problems, and thus we achieve a balanced approach—is that it can help to motivate us to move from "heart" to "hand" and embark on actions to address the above problems. This is, metaphorically, like moving our pendulum of the scientific method far to the left so that we can gain the momentum for moving it far to the right where we address the problems that we uncover. Such negative thinking raises to the surface of our awareness contradictions between many of our cultural values and the values of external conformity and material comfort. And, following Thomas Kuhn, to the extent that we have a direction that promises to resolve those contradictions, we will be motivated to move in that direction.

We might link this idea of negative thinking to several ideas discussed in Chapters 3 and 5. In Chapter 3 we discussed "the technique of particularization" and "the falsification of memory"—within the context of a study of Springdalers—as procedures for burying awareness of problems. Negative thinking, then, offers an antidote to those procedures, given its focus on unearthing rather than burying awareness of problems and, thus, avoiding emotional repression. And in Chapter 5 our discussion of Van Vogt's *The World of Null-A* and *The Players of Null-A* brought forward the idea of "the cortical-thalamic pause" as a way of coping with emotional problems. Such a procedure points the individual away from a focus on outward perception and thought and toward inward-outward perception and thought. Further, it appears to give the individual aid in being able to face up to the emotional problems that would be linked to negative thinking. In this way, the cortical-thalamic pause along with negative thinking appear to be ways of helping us to move away from both outward perception and thought as well as emotional repression, patterns of behavior that are encouraged by the technique of particularization and the falsification of memory.

Pursuing further these ideas of negative thinking and the cortical-thalamic pause, let us turn to another cultural value that we tend to repress: group superiority, a value that is closely related to our patterns of social stratification or persisting hierarchy or inequality. Given the centrality of our cultural value of equality, it takes negative thinking to face up to this cultural value of group superiority along with our patterns of stratification. And a cortical-thalamic pause would also help us look to such patterns, for it would help us to make good use of our understanding and point us toward learning how to cope with the contradiction between our egalitarian value and our value of group superiority.

Robert W. Fuller, a mathematician and former college president committed to solving fundamental social problems, has developed the concept of "rankism" in an effort to move beyond the limitations of concepts like racism, sexism, and ageism:

> When rank has been earned and signifies excellence, then it's generally accepted, and rightfully so. But the power of rank can be and often is abused ... Power begets power, authority becomes entrenched, and rank-holders become self-aggrandizing, capricious, and overbearing.... Rankism insults the dignity of subordinates by treating them as invisible nobodies.... Nobodies are insulted, disrespected, exploited, ignored.... It might be supposed that if one overcame tendencies to racism, sexism,

ageism, and other narrowly defined forms of discrimination, one would be purged of rankism as well. But rankism is not just another ism. It subsumes the familiar dishonorable isms. It's the mother of them all.…

Although rank-based discrimination *feels* the same to its targets as the more familiar kinds, there are some important differences in the way it works. Unlike race or gender, rank is mutable. You can be taken for a nobody one day and for a somebody the next … unlike racists and sexists, who are now on notice, rankists still go largely unchallenged.… The consequences range from school shootings to … genocide.… Hitler enjoyed the support of Germans humiliated by punitive reparations in the aftermath of World War I.… Similarly, President Milosevic of Yugoslavia traded on the wounded pride of the Serbs in the 1990s.… Attacking the familiar isms, one at a time, is like lopping heads off the Hydra of discrimination and oppression; going after rankism aims to drive a stake through the Hydra's heart (2003: 5–7).

Fuller sees rankism not just as hierarchical relationships among people, for "When rank has been earned and signifies excellence," this is not a pattern of discrimination. If we look to racism, sexism, and ageism as illustrations of rankism, then one thing that is involved is not just hierarchy but hierarchy that persists indefinitely, or social stratification. No matter what a person subjected to such rankist behavior does, he or she will still remain the subject of such discrimination. By contrast, a worker who can easily learn to become a manager does not illustrate a pattern of social stratification. Also, Fuller sees rankism as encompassing not only racism, sexism, and ageism but also any situation whatsoever where rank persists over time. For it is the persistence of rank that prevents individuals on the bottom as well as on the top of hierarchies from interacting with and learning from one another. And this in turn works to prevent those at the bottom from moving upward. Such situations include hierarchical relationships within all of our institutions, covering far more than racism, sexism, and ageism. They involve the full sweep of political, economic, religious, educational, scientific, and family relationships. Patterns of rankism, are a fundamental part of the way of life not only of preindustrial society but also of contemporary society. And if we were to see those relationships as problematic, then we would also have to see the basic structure of contemporary societies as problematic.

Fuller accomplishes two important things with his concept of rankism. For one thing, social scientists have tended to apply the concept of social stratification only to a limited number of situations of discrimination, such as racism, sexism, ageism, and classism. Fuller, by contrast, applies the concept of rankism to the full range of situations of persisting hierarchy or inequality, an approach that is the same as our own approach to stratification. Also, Fuller sees rankism as a fundamental social problem, given its direct conflict with people-oriented cultural values like equality, individual personality, and democracy. Thus, Fuller's concept of rankism helps us pay attention to both stratification and cultural values. By so doing, he implicitly invokes Figure 1-1 with its gap between aspirations like equality and behavior like social stratification that points away from equality. Our own approach to stratification is, then, the same as Fuller's approach to rankism: We focus on stratification as a serious and increasing problem, as illustrated by Figure 1-1, given the importance of people-oriented cultural values.

Individual Evolution

Granting the importance of negative thinking for moving our pendulum to the left, positive thinking is important for moving our pendulum to the right—where we learn to make progress in solving problems—and we are able to move very far to the right to the extent that negative thinking has given us the momentum for doing so. Our focus in this section is on the evolution of the individual with respect to "head," "heart," and "hand"—with an emphasis on the "heart"—also taking into account biological and physical structures.

We begin with an extended metaphor for the East-West strategy. Japan's transition from a feudal to a modern bureaucratic society, beginning in the nineteenth century after Japan was opened up to the influences of the West, led to the banning of the weapons that the Samurai or warrior class were able to carry. It was on the island of Okinawa that Gishin Funakoshi invented the weaponless martial art of modern karate at the beginning of the twentieth century. Then, in 1922, Funakoshi was invited to Tokyo by the Ministry of Education to demonstrate this new martial art. While there, Funakoshi studied and was deeply influenced by Zen Buddhism. As a result, he developed the spiritual and humanistic aspects of karate, which means "empty hand," for hands must bear no weapons. And he came to call his invention Karate-do—"the Way of the Empty Hand"—for Zen Buddhism had shown him the Way, or a way of life that extends far beyond one's engagement in martial arts.

Our own purpose in this section is to use some of the principles of Karate-do as metaphors for the East-West strategy, just as we used the grocer and the chief of Balgat as metaphors for the change from preindustrial to modern society in Chapter 1. It is a strategy that is focused on first narrowing one's aspirations-fulfillment gap by reducing one's aspirations or "attachment" (Eastern orientation) and then continuing to raise both one's aspirations and their fulfillment (Western orientation). It is also a strategy broad enough to encompass the key ideas put forward in the preceding chapters, yet it is sufficiently focused so that we can all learn to apply it to the concrete problems that we confront in our everyday lives.

We shall focus on seven of *The Twenty Guiding Principles of Karate*, retaining their original numbers, beginning with the first one.

> *1. Do not forget that Karate-do begins and ends with Rei.* . . . *Rei* is often defined as "respect," but it actually means much more. *Rei* encompasses both an attitude of respect for others and a sense of self-esteem. When those who honor themselves transfer that feeling of esteem—that is, respect—to others, their action is nothing less than an expression of *rei.* . . . It should also be noted that although a person's deportment may be correct, without a sincere and reverent heart they do not possess true *rei.* True *rei* is the outward expression of a respectful heart (Funakoshi and Nakasone 2003: 19–20).

This focus on emotions, then, is an important contribution to our understanding of the East-West strategy, given that emotions generally are repressed within both Eastern and Western culture. Just as Karate-do begins and ends with *rei,* we might now claim that evolution-do begins and ends with *rei.* For a lack of focus on *rei* strikes at the very heart of the problems to be found throughout the world, given the near-universal existence of emotional repression.

Of course, it matters whether emotional expression is used to exercise rankist behavior or to work toward egalitarian relationships. The principle of *rei* is clear on this matter: Both self-esteem and respect for others is required. Thus, rankism would not be involved in emotional expression. Such expression, in our view, is essential for the commitment to making progress on understanding problems that the scientific method requires. Also, it is essential for the further development or evolution of the individual. *Rei* also works against the narrowness of bureaucracy by opening up to the self no less than the other. Further, *rei* points us away from the narrow materialism of our bureaucratic way of life by centering on us human beings and our relationships with one another.

> 3. *Karate stands on the side of justice.* . . . Human beings are at their strongest when they believe they are right. The strength that comes from the confidence of someone who knows he or she is right is expressed by the saying, "When I examine myself and see that I am in the right, then whether I am faced by one thousand or ten thousand opponents, I must press onward." To avoid action when justice is at stake demonstrates a lack of courage (29–30).

If indeed Rome is burning, then we must take decisive action, and we must act now. Although such action has been widely suggested with respect to the problem of global warming or climate change, that is by no means the only problem requiring immediate and decisive action.

The clear message from those many millions who took part in America's presidential primaries and election is that we desperately require fundamental change, given the nature of our highly threatening problems. In our own view, an American president or any world leader has a certain amount of power. Unfortunately, however, we all tend to exaggerate the amount of power that our leaders have. This third principle of Karate-do yields some insight here: The power of an individual depends on where he or she stands on the side of justice. For example, the popularity of President Barack Obama throughout the world and not just in the United States rests on his voicing the cultural values that are so widely shared, the values that—if fulfilled—promise justice for all of us. His own awareness of this helps him to develop the charisma he needs to influence his audience. Once again, cultural values—as discussed in Chapter 3—prove to be fundamental in helping us to understand the complexities of human behavior.

Our argument here is that it is all of us, and not just our scientists and our leaders, who must learn to "stand on the side of justice," thus gaining ever more strength to act effectively in the face of our growing problems. It is all of us who must learn to move away from the materialism illustrated by affluenza and the stratification illustrated by rankism so that we can find room for fulfilling our humanistic people-oriented cultural values. This third principle teaches us that nothing less than justice is at stake. We might note the link here between the focus of the first principle of Karate-do on emotional expression and the focus here on personal strength. The two go together. Both depend on our ability to fulfill our basic cultural values. And that ability depends in turn—we argue—on learning to change from a bureaucratic to an evolutionary way of life.

> 4. *First know yourself, then know others....* Karate practitioners must be completely aware of their own strengths and weaknesses, and never become dazzled or blinded by conceit or overconfidence. Then they will be able to assess calmly and carefully the strengths and weaknesses of their adversaries, and create an ideal strategy (33–34).

Here we see an East-West orientation to problem-solving. For this is not just a focus on inward perception and thought: It is also a Western outward orientation to developing a strategy for interacting with adversaries. This reflexive approach directly challenges the Western focus on outward perception and thought, given that inward orientation. Such a reflexive approach requires the individual to uncover personal values that generally are repressed, such as the cultural values of external conformity and group superiority. From an emotional perspective, this can prove to be a most challenging process. Here, as indicated above, an orientation to negative thinking along with the use of the cortical-thalamic pause can prove to be most helpful. We might note here the importance of perception, and not just thought, within a reflexive approach. One's different senses can help one understand the nature of one's personal situation.

> *6. The mind must be set free....* Our mind should be allowed to move about freely, even if it seeks muddy recesses. The lotus blossom is not sullied by the mud in which it grows.... To reign in the mind tightly takes away its freedom. To keep our mind in close confines may be a necessary beginner's habit, but doing so for our entire life prevents us from rising to a new level, and will result in a life of unfulfilled potential (43, 45).

This sixth principle of Karate-do is a hymn to the infinite potential of the human mind, a potential that enables the individual to open up to the full complexity of human situations Recall that we discussed this in relation to the three potentials of language in Chapter 1: dichotomy, gradation, and metaphor. Metaphors in particular can release the power of the best of poetry, film, literature, and drama. This sixth principle also illustrates a combination of negative thinking with positive thinking. Note that the mind should be allowed to seek "muddy recesses," suggesting negative thinking, yet also note the reference to "rising to a new level," suggesting positive thinking. The power of metaphor is illustrated here by the reference to the lotus blossom, which "is not sullied by the mud in which it grows" and thus points us toward an optimistic approach to life.

> *8. Karate goes beyond the dojo.* The objective of karate-do is to polish and nurture both the mind and body. The cultivation of one's spirit and mental attitude begun during practice in the *dojo* (training hall) should not cease after the physical and mental exertions end for the day. Rather, this should continue outside the *dojo,* in our daily routine (53).

Our bureaucratic way of life teaches the social scientist to stay locked within the narrow cell of his or her dojo, yet the social scientist is shaped by what happens in all aspects of life, of which the dojo is only one part. Let us recall here our discussion of the bureaucratic individual in Chapter 1, as depicted in Figure 1–2b. In Herman Hesse's *The Glass Bead Game* in Chapter 4 he metaphorically takes issue with the limitations imposed by the academic world on its inhabitants, with its "disease of nobility— hubris, conceit, class arrogance, self-righteousness, exploitativeness." Personality structure is formed both outside of and inside of the walls of academia, beyond the dojo as well as inside the dojo. As for the rest of us, the same is true: It is our "daily routine"—our perceptions and thoughts, emotions, actions and interactions, and also our patterns of beliefs and assumptions, values, and ritualistic behavior—that largely shapes who we are. And whatever ideals we might have developed within the dojo while growing up come to be tested in whatever we subsequently do with our lives from one moment to the next.

Unfortunately, we learn both inside and outside of our dojo, both in the East and in the West, to repress our emotions. By contrast, the East-West strategy points us not only toward inward-outward perception and thought, and not only toward interaction, but also toward emotional expression. The individual is encouraged—especially as the result of attention to the senses—to express emotions rather than bury them. As a result, what can take shape is an ability to reach out to and learn from the full range of human experiences to be found both inside of and outside of the dojo. And with the strength and courage that results—similar to Karate-do's third principle invoking the strength that comes from knowing that one is on the side of justice—the individual can learn to act ever more effectively to make progress on personal and world problems. Such potential power resides in all of us, and not just in the leaders whom we continue to worship.

> *9. Karate is a lifelong pursuit.* There is no single point that marks the completion of karate training; there is always a higher level. For this reason practitioners should continue training throughout their life.... Walking this endless road, becoming better today than yesterday, and then better tomorrow than today—throughout one's life—is a true image of the Way of Karate (57, 59).

Evolution is a process that never stops. Utopian thinkers have often thought otherwise, attempting to construct the perfect society that will become static once perfection is reached, but they have failed despite all of their efforts, granting that they kept alive the possibility of a better world. Their understanding of human behavior did not reach out deeply enough to probe its incredible complexity, a failing that is also generally shared by social scientists as well as the rest of us. We have a 14-billion-year history of the process of evolution to attest to the continuing interaction and—as a result—the continuing change of all phenomena. Yet our bureaucratic mentality works to keep physical and biological structures separate from social and personality structures. As a result, we choose to ignore those fourteen billion years of solid evidence of the interactive nature of the universe as well as the fact that we humans are the most interactive creatures throughout the known universe.

> *16. When you step beyond your own gate, you face a million enemies.* Negligence is a great enemy when we leave the safety of our homes. If we are not in peak form in both our body and attitude, we will attract troublemakers and problems. Consequently, we should adopt the attitude that when

leaving our gate we are entering into the midst of many potential enemies and should stay mentally alert (87–88).

Metaphorically, we can understand this sixteenth principle of karate-do as urging us to make good use of negative thinking, given that we tend to focus on positive or optimistic thought. Here is Buddhist realism asserting itself. Within negative thinking we search out problems rather than bury them, by contrast with the Springdalers who buried problems with the aid of techniques of particularization and the falsification of memory, as discussed in Chapter 3. A central and largely invisible problem discussed throughout this book is the growing aspirations-fulfillment gap. Negative thinking along with the cortical-thalamic pause can help the individual learn to follow the East-West strategy by first working toward narrowing the aspirations-fulfillment gap by lowering aspirations and then using a very broad approach to the scientific method to help raise both aspirations and the fulfillment of them.

Up to this point our focus within this section on individual evolution has been on the behavior of the individual. However, that behavior is shaped to a very great degree by what happens in society as a whole. We have seen this with respect to values, for cultural values deeply influence the values of every individual. To illustrate further, one thing that happens in society as a whole that has a substantial influence on governmental policies as well as on the individual is the calculation by economists and statisticians of the gross domestic product or GDP of the United States—and a great many other countries as well—every three months. This measurement was invented during the Great Depression to determine just how much and how quickly the American economy was shrinking, and just how well President Franklin D. Roosevelt's efforts to reverse the economic slump were working.

Although the GDP proved to be a useful measure in helping determine the success of Roosevelt's New Deal, this measurement is limited in fundamental ways, as indicated by this analysis:

> GDP measures the size of the pie, not the quality of the ingredients—fresh apples or rotten ones are counted the same.... [T]he sale of an assault rifle and the sale of an antibiotic both contribute equally to the national tally (assuming the sales price is the same). GDP doesn't register, as Robert Kennedy put it, "the beauty of our poetry or the strength of our marriages, or the intelligence of our public debate." GDP measures everything, Kennedy concluded, "except that which makes life worthwhile." ... Yet we continue to track this quarterly statistic as if nothing else matters. If GDP is up, we feel good. It means we as a nation are doing better and are, presumably, happier. Low rates of growth or, God forbid, a shrinking economy mean we are less well off and, presumably,

less happy. However, recent research into happiness . . . reveals that beyond the low level of about $15,000 a year, the link between economic growth and happiness evaporates. . . . Yet we continue to treat economic growth and well-being as one and the same.

But one country does not. Bhutan, a tiny Himalayan nation, has invented a radically new metric: Gross National Happiness. . . . The country's home minister, Jigmi Y. Thinley, calls conventional measures of economic growth "delusional." . . . Bhutan, a beautiful land of mountains and temples, has forsaken millions of tourist dollars by, in effect, restricting the number of foreign visitors. It does this by charging a $200 daily fee. And while other developing countries have sold off their natural resources to the highest bidder, Bhutan has hardly touched its timber and minerals. . . . Bhutan is no Shangri-La. It has crime and alcoholism and unhappy people, just like other places . . . but alternatives to growth-at-any-cost policies are desperately needed. Bhutan's Gross National Happiness may not be the answer to the problem, but it does reframe the question—namely, what is a sensible way for a country to achieve the greatest happiness for the greatest number of its citizens? . . . The idea is catching on. One Chinese province is developing a "happiness index." And the leader of Britain's Conservative Party has floated the idea of GWB—general well-being—as a way to gauge the nation's progress (Weiner 2006: 21A).

This concern with the failures of GDP to give us a direction for "a country to achieve the greatest happiness for the greatest number of its citizens" is a good example of negative thinking. For we are taking a measurement that has proved most useful in the past and probing its limitations, and searching for a measurement that would help us overcome those limitations. By counting equally "the sale of an assault rifle and the sale of an antibiotic," we are going along with the very one-sided economy that the world has created, failing to question the contribution of any sale to the fulfillment of cultural values such as individual personality, equality, freedom, and democracy. "Progress" is seen as linked to the size of the economy and by no means to the evolution of society and the individual, as illustrated by the degree of fulfillment of a nation's range of cultural values.

As for the efforts of Bhutan, they certainly point away from this narrow idea of progress that is itself a product of our bureaucratic worldview, granting that they serve to reframe the problem more than to solve it. Yet such reframing is itself most valuable, indicating as it does a first and most important step in negative thinking. Bhutan is not alone in such negative thinking, as indicated by the following analysis that focuses on the United States, the originator of the GDP, and that details more of its problems:

"We may be in the early stages in the United States of recognizing that the gross domestic product is very misleading and something must be done to get better measures of well-being," said Amartya Sen, a Nobel laureate in economics at Harvard. Professor Sen and Joseph Stiglitz, a Nobel laureate at Columbia, are co-chairmen of a commission recently appointed by Nicolas Sarkozy, the French president, to come up with a better measure for France....

While the GDP has continued to rise, wages have stagnated, pensions have shrunk or disappeared and income inequality has increased.... The boom in prison construction ... has added greatly to the GDP, but the damage from the crimes that made the prisons necessary is not subtracted. Neither is environmental damage nor depleted forests, although lumbering shows up in government statistics as value added. So does health care, which is measured in the money spent, not by improvements in people's health. Obesity is on the rise in America, undermining health, but that is not subtracted.... "One reason we don't have mandated maternity leaves is because the work that women do taking care of children is invisible to economists and policymakers," said Kristen Lewis, co-director of the recently published American Human Development Project. Hers is one of the half-dozen well-being indexes produced in this country outside government. In each case the index would supplement the GDP, not replace it (Uchitelle 2008: WK 3).

Here we can use our range of 15 cultural values to assess the limitations of our GDP. For example, our failure to take into account the importance of child care has to do with the cultural value of the continuation of life, just as is our failure to assess improvements in people's health. Our lack of attention to increasing income inequality signals no interest in the cultural value of equality. Our ignoring statistics on crime suggests that we are also ignoring the cultural values of individual personality and freedom. Our failure to subtract statistics on environmental damage and depleted forests from GDP indicates our distorted measurement of the cultural values of achievement and success, material comfort and progress. All of these failures may also be coupled with the failures of the GDP to take into account any achievements or failures with respect to our other cultural values: democracy (note Kennedy's concern with the intelligence of our public debate), science and secular rationality, understanding the world, solving problems, intimate and close relationships (note also Kennedy's concern with the strength of our marriages), and ultimate meaning.

Of course, there are indeed two other cultural values that the GDP does make full use of, granting that no specific calculations are involved. They happen to be the very cultural values that we repress, and for good reason: external conformity and group superiority. For our measurement of GDP conforms to supporting a way of life where materialism rules along with patterns of social stratification. We can see this even in the efforts of President Sarkozy to move toward a measurement that reflects the quality of life in France: He has appointed two economists to do the job. And we can also see the incredible power of our bureaucratic worldview even in the lineup of individuals that President-elect Obama consulted with in relation to America's financial meltdown: people who are almost exclusively economists. Nobel laureates in economics have achieved a great deal, but those achievements are quite narrow relative to the scope of the problems that the modern world presently faces. Indeed, no number of Nobel laureates in economics from Harvard or anywhere else are, in our view, up to that task.

E. F. Schumacher, economic advisor to the British Control Commission in postwar Germany and the top economist and head of planning at the British Coal Board for 20 years, had this to say about the one-sided materialistic economies of the modern world:

> What is the meaning of democracy, freedom, human dignity, standard of living, self-realisation, fulfillment? Is it a matter of goods, or of people? Of course it is a matter of people.... If economic thinking ... cannot get beyond its vast abstractions, the national income, the rate of growth, capital/output ratio, input-output analysis, labour mobility capital accumulation; if it cannot get beyond all this and make contact with the human realities of poverty, frustration, alienation, despair, breakdown, crime, escapism, stress, congestion, ugliness, and spiritual death, then let us scrap economics and start afresh (Schumacher 1973: 70).

In Schumacher we have an individual not only who was much concerned about the full range of our cultural values, but his negative thinking took him even further than probing the problems of the world's economic systems. For he focused on nothing less than the metaphysical stance of modern society:

> Education cannot help us as long as it accords no place to metaphysics. Whether the subjects taught are subjects of science or of the humanities, if the teaching does not lead to a clarification of metaphysics, that is to say, of our fundamental convictions, it cannot educate a man and, consequently, cannot be of real value to society.... What is at fault is not specialization, but the lack of depth with which the subjects are usually presented, and the absence of metaphysical awareness.... The sciences are being taught without any awareness of the presuppositions of science, of the meaning and significance of scientific laws, and of the place occupied by the natural sciences within the whole cosmos of human thought.... Economics is being taught without any awareness of the view of human nature that underlies present-day economic

theory.... How could there be a rational teaching of politics without pressing all questions back to their metaphysical roots? (Schumacher 1973: 86-87).

Schumacher emphasizes here what we have been emphasizing throughout these chapters: the overarching importance of our worldview or metaphysical stance. Granting the importance of what we have called our bureaucratic worldview, we have attempted to describe the nature of what we have also described as evolutionary worldview as an alternative. We follow here Thomas Kuhn's analysis—discussed in Chapter 5—that a paradigmatic change requires an alternative paradigm that promises to resolve the contradictions within the old paradigm. We see this argument as applying to cultural paradigms no less than to scientific paradigms. As we move from this chapter's focus on "heart" to Chapter 7's emphasis on "hand," let us bear in mind that—following the pendulum metaphor for the scientific method—there is no limit to our capacity for negative thinking. We have only taken an initial step toward opening up to our fundamental problems with respect to emotions, cultural values, and the economic institution throughout the modern world.

CHAPTER **7**

"Hand"

Deep Action and Deep Interaction

As we move toward the conclusion of this book, let us keep in mind the importance of continuing to build on the infinite potential of language by looking very far up and very far down the ladder of linguistic abstraction. Looking far up that ladder, what we see as the result of an evolutionary worldview is, simply, the idea of the continuing evolution of all of us individuals. And this is not just with respect to "hand" but also with respect to "head" and "heart." Thus, we cannot see this chapter narrowly or bureaucratically as limited to "hand": Here we must also learn more about the development of "head" and "heart" beyond our earlier ideas. And the same is the case for moving very far down that ladder to the situational area between the parallel lines within Figures 2-5. In this chapter—if indeed we are following an evolutionary path within this book—we should be learning more about more concrete or specific ways of applying these ideas to one momentary scene after another.

Such movement far up and down language's ladder of abstraction illustrates the East-West strategy for solving problems, a strategy that requires using the scientific method in everyday life. By focusing on the momentary situation in the short run, the individual temporarily puts aside long-term goals, thus lowering his or her aspirations so as to focus on making progress on immediate situational goals. This follows the Eastern part of the East-West strategy so as to move toward narrowing

183

one's aspirations-fulfillment gap. That narrow gap can in turn give the individual the momentum needed for moving toward long-term goals that are high up on the ladder of abstraction. And the scientific method can help the individual to raise fulfillment no less than aspirations, so that the two move upward in tandem, thus following the Western aspect of the East-West strategy. This overall approach follows Kuhn's vision of how paradigms can be changed: through the development of an alternative paradigm—in this case, a cultural rather than a scientific one—that promises to resolve the contradictions within the previous paradigm.

In this chapter we aim, then, to begin with a section that takes us very far down that ladder of linguistic abstraction. And we intend to follow this with a section that takes us very far up that ladder. More specifically, our first section—negative thinking ("head"), cortical-thalamic pause ("heart"), deep action, and deep interaction ("hand")—takes us down the ladder. Given our focus within Part III on evolution, we are much concerned with inward-outward perception and thought. Yet we believe that we can carry this idea further with the concept of negative thinking, as discussed in Chapter 6. Similarly, we believe that we can move beyond our previous discussion of emotional repression in that chapter with the idea of the cortical-thalamic pause, as discussed in Chapter 5. As for our examination of interaction, we believe that a new concept—"deep interaction"—can prove to be useful in carrying further our approach to "hand" by bringing in "head" and "heart" more explicitly. Let us note that deep interaction includes one's interactions with one's own past experiences, and not just interactions with others or the environment, thus pointing away from conformity to outward perception and thought.

If that initial section takes us far down the ladder of abstraction, then the final section takes us far up that ladder. We will introduce two new concepts here: "deep dialogue" and "deep democracy. Both have to do with long-term structures—by contrast with being limited to the momentary situation—namely, the concepts within Figures 2-1, 3-1, 4-1, and 5-1 that lie outside of those parallel lines that enclose situational concepts. Just as in the case of the new concept of deep interaction, these concepts explicitly invoke "head" and "heart." This section, then, follows the Western part of the East-West strategy with its continually increasing aspirations. Yet once again it is the scientific method applied to everyday-life problems that can provide the basis for the fulfillment of those aspirations, thus preventing a widening aspirations-fulfillment gap. We humans presently are the most interactive creatures in the known universe. We are convinced that the East-West strategy can enable us humans to become ever more interactive by making ever more use of the infinite potentials of language coupled with the scientific method as a tool for making progress on problems.

Negative Thinking, Cortical-Thalamic Pause, Deep Action, and Deep Interaction

Negative Thinking

Beyond the idea of inward-outward perception and thought—by contrast with outward perception and thought—lies the idea of negative thinking, as developed in Chapter 6. Negative thinking builds on inward-outward perception and thought with its focus on problems ("heart") as a basis for making progress toward solving them ("hand"), thus following the dictates of our pendulum metaphor for the scientific method. Our approach here is by no means to replace our emphasis on inward-outward perception and thought, but rather to strengthen that idea by linking it more closely with "heart" and "hand." By so doing, we see negative thinking as helping us to point more directly to an idea of individual evolution that includes "heart" and "hand" no less than "head." Given the power of our bureaucratic worldview with its narrow focus—as illustrated by the technique of particularization and the falsification of memory—it becomes most important for us to counter that narrowness with a broad approach to the individual and society.

To carry further our understanding of negative thinking, we turn once again to Walt Whitman's *Leaves of Grass,* following our brief discussion in Chapter 6:

> I think I could turn and live with animals, they are so placid and self-contain'd,
> I stand and look at them long and long.
> They do not sweat and whine about their condition,
> They do not lie awake in the dark and weep for their sins,
> They do not make me sick discussing their duty to God,
> Not one is dissatisfied, not one is demented with the mania of owning things,
> Not one kneels to another, nor to his kind that lived thousands of years ago,
> Not one is respectable or unhappy over the whole earth
> (Whitman 1892/2004: 50)

Our focus in Chapter 6 was on Whitman's illustration of emotional expression as a basis for individual evolution. Here, we continue to be concerned with emotional expression and individual evolution, just as Whitman continues to deal with human emotions in this passage. But now our focus shifts to "head" along with "heart and "hand," namely, Whitman's worldview or understanding of the potential of the human being. For he sees us humans as able to learn from the experiences of animals, who accept their situation realistically rather than engage in useless behavior, such as the one-sided "mania of owning things" or our stratified behavior of kneeling to one another, or our continuing unhappiness. In other words, Whitman is pointing us away from our revolution of rising expectations where our aspirations for anything and everything are going through the roof. Instead, he is implicitly suggesting the Eastern part of an East-West strategy, where we lower our aspirations and thus narrow our aspirations-fulfillment gap.

This is, then, why he claims, "I think I could turn and live with animals, they are so placid and self-contain'd." If our increasing aspirations-fulfillment gap is much of the basis for our escalating problems, then Whitman—along with Buddhism—suggests a direction for reducing that gap. By so doing, he is employing negative thinking: focusing on at least the beginnings of an alternative to our bureaucratic worldview. He is negating that worldview's encouragement of our revolution of rising expectations and its resultant increasing aspirations-fulfillment gap. As for the Western part of an East-West strategy, Whitman does indeed point us indirectly toward the possibilities of individual evolution. His is a vision of a society where people do not kneel to one another or to heroes of the past. Neither do they conform to the dictates of religion. Nor do they dwell on their own limitations to the exclusion of their potential as human beings. Instead—following our quote in Chapter 6—we learn to "celebrate" ourselves, to see ourselves as "divine" and to "worship" our own bodies. Further, following the situational orientation of negative thinking, we pay serious attention to our own senses, such as our "touch" and the "scent" of our arm-pits.

Whitman's vision here is particularly appropriate for the East-West strategy, which calls for the infinite development of the individual and society. To the extent that we become enamored of this possibility for all of us, we can all too easily lose our perspective as to where we are at the present point in time. And as a result we can move toward ignoring the Eastern part of the East-West strategy, especially since we have all already become victims of a revolution of rising expectations along with its increasing aspirations-fulfillment gap. As a corrective, we can learn to apply negative thinking to our present situation. Granting we can envision the infinite possibilities of the human being, at the same time we can become critical of our present situation: we have a large and growing aspirations-fulfillment gap. And before we can move very far toward that potential, we must learn to deal effectively with where we are at the present moment. And by looking to the behavior of animals, who are not "demented" by an increasing aspirations-fulfillment gap, we can come to our senses and learn to focus on our present momentary situation. And as a result we can learn to narrow that gap, which is a prerequisite for raising both aspirations and their fulfillment.

One problem with negative thinking is that we fall into our linguistic emphasis on dichotomy, by contrast with gradation and metaphor, and as a result negative thinking can influence us to reduce our sense of optimism as we are proceeding to focus on our problems. To illustrate a balance between negative and positive thinking, let us turn to an Indian philosopher who has been teaching American CEOs how to attain focus and achievement while reducing stress, Swamiji Parthasarathy, whose efforts were described in *Time* magazine (Wallis 2007: 102-103):

> Parthasarathy ... has been traveling the globe for 35 years, speaking to business people—including at such bastions of commerce as Wharton, Kellogg and Harvard business schools—luring them with assertions about learning to improve concentration and productivity, eliminating stress and developing intellectual discipline and overall well-being....
>
> In fact, as he takes the podium in his spotless white tunic and trousers, a vertical line of red dye on his forehead, Swamiji is the picture of unbowed vigor, with a voice that crescendos to full boom when he's making a particularly insistent point. "You are the architect of your fortune. You are the architect of your misfortune," he thunders. His topic, "Managing Stress Through Self-Management," seems perfectly pitched to this crowd of overtaxed self-starters....
>
> Swamiji's message, delivered in part via that transcendental software, PowerPoint, and some well-placed jokes, is that stress is not a function of external demands—the number of employees and dollars to manage, e-mails to answer, strategic plans to complete or loved ones to placate. Stress is internal, he insists. Make a rational assessment of your situation with all its requirements and flaws—consider, for instance, the past behavior of your customers, your colleagues, your spouse—adjust your expectations accordingly, and the stress will vanish. He gives some quick examples. "I'm in New York. There will be traffic," he says, smiling calmly. "My wife is an irritable person," he observes. "If I say, 'Darling, get me a cup of tea.' She says, 'I'm not a servant. Get your own tea.' If I hear this, I know I'm in the right house" (Wallis 2007: 101-102).

Swamiji's approach includes the Buddhist idea of lowering or adjusting expectations, based on the Four Noble Truths, as discussed in Chapter 5. If the cause of *dukkha* is removed, then *dukkha* itself will disappear. Thus, he embodies a most scientific approach to the world with his emphasis on cause and effect. He illustrates such lowered expectations with his examples of traffic in New York and the irritability of his wife. But by contrast with the Buddhist emphasis on staying with those lowered and realistic expectations, Swamiji adopts a Western approach—thus illustrating an East-West approach—by tying lowered stress to greater productivity. For Swamiji it is "worries about the past and anxiety for the future" that tires the individual, and not work. Those worries and that anxiety prevent the individual from staying focused on present objectives. The mind must be disciplined to stay focused on present objectives. It is the undisciplined mind that encounters both stress and poor productivity.

Yet Swamiji's Western approach is limited, as is indicated by his response to a question from his audience:

> After the 21 Club lecture, a honcho asks Swamiji a question that brings forth titters of recognition ... "What if you want to shoot for the stars? How can you manage your expectations?" Swamiji nods. He explains once again that a calm intellect is a more productive intellect. But then he concedes that in coming before this group of strivers, he had to manage his own expectations (Wallis 2007: 103).

We would argue, instead, that an East-West approach can in fact reach for the stars, given a scientific approach broad enough to go beyond the calm and rational approach that Swamiji emphasizes. Such a scientific approach must be broad enough to build on the full potential of language and the scientific method. By so doing, it can—over time—enable the individual to move fulfillment no less than expectations toward the stars, with no limit whatsoever.

Cortical-Thalamic Pause

Our presentation in Chapter 5 of Van Vogt's two novels based on the work of Alfred Korzybski introduced the concept of "the cortical-thalamic pause." We put that idea forward as a tool that an individual can use to overcome deep feelings of fear within a momentary situation. Gosseyn explains the nature of this tool in this passage quoted in Chapter 5:

> I am now relaxing.... And all stimuli are making the full circuit of my nervous system, along my spinal cord, to the thalamus, through the thalamus and up to the cortex, and through the cortex.... That was the key. That was the difference between the Null-A superman and the animal man of the galaxy. The thalamus—the seat of emotions— and the cortex—the seat of discrimination—integrated, balanced in a warm and wonderful relationship. Emotions, not done away with, but made richer and more relaxed by the association with that part of the mind—the cortex—that could savor unnumbered subtle differences in the flow of feeling. (Van Vogt 1948: 177-178).

The cortical thalamic pause is by no means a simple matter, for we have all led lives under the sway of a bureaucratic worldview. Following Figure 1-2b, we have learned very deeply to separate "head" from "heart."

Even Gosseyn succumbs to the threat throughout the palace, for his efforts to achieve a cortical-thalamic pause while in the body of Prince Ashargin are insufficient to ward off that threat. Ashargin's body had been trained over many years in prison to repress emotions like the fear of pain and death, and Gosseyn's efforts were not able to help the Prince achieve that pause. We might draw an analogy to our own situation, with the ideas in this book analogous to the efforts of Gosseyn, and with readers and authors analogous to Ashargin. Negative thinking can help here, although to a limited extent, to motivate us to work toward learning how to achieve that pause. But what we need most of all is a great deal of practice over a substantial period of time.

We can gain further understanding of the significance of this tool for individual evolution—and also better understanding of how to use it—by turning to a correspondent for The Boston Globe who had wartime experience as a paratrooper:

> I served with a few infantrymen who had no fear, and at first I was intimidated by them, but in combat I learned that lack of fear is stupidity. Every fearless soldier with whom I served died. I want to go to war with soldiers who carry the weapon of fear that makes them alert, cautious, effective. In a time of civilian fear [this article was written less than two months after 9/11] it may be helpful for an old soldier to remind himself how the Army trained him to accept his fear and make use of it.
>
> We didn't just go out and jump from perfectly good airplanes. With in-your-face drill sergeants, we learned discipline, and then we learned skills, one step at a time. . . . We first took that step out onto nothing by stepping out of a mockup of a C-47 on the ground, again and again and yet again. then we stepped from a tower, and finally when habit made the difficult routine, from a plane. There were no surprises—even once when my chute didn't open.
>
> In training I counted three seconds—"one thousand and one, one thousand and two, one thousand and three"—and the chute snapped open as it had from the tower, yanking me upward. When it didn't, adrenalin gave me all the time in the world, and the training gave me a series of small, achievable tasks to perform. Look up. The chute has barely opened. Grab the handle on the reserve chute, bend my wrist to the right, feed out the reserve chute by hand. Oops, it had tangled with another paratrooper's chute, and I became a dangerous pendulum accelerating his fall. I was too busy to have fear. I had simple tasks to perform in an orderly sequence.
>
> Check the main chute. It had now partially opened. Reach down my right leg. Take out the knife, cut the lines to the reserve chute. Swing away from the other soldier with what main chute was working. Prepare to land. Land.

I realize that is what I do in writing my books. I face a massive rewrite of a manuscript. I don't imagine the pile of pages I must accumulate. Tomorrow morning I will write Updike's three pages, perhaps two, perhaps one. If not a page, a paragraph; if not a paragraph, a sentence; if not a sentence, a line; if not a line, a word.... This is also how I face the daily fear of aging, of a new kind of warfare, of all the what-ifs that lie in ambush, just doing what I know how to do one morning at a time (Murray 2001: 11B).

Murray's approach to overcoming fear "one small step at a time" is analogous to the slogan of Alcoholics Anonymous: "One day at a time." The focus is on the momentary situation and away from an outward emphasis that would include high aspirations for future situations. This is an Eastern orientation to problem-solving that focuses on one's momentary situation and on the reduction of the aspirations-fulfillment gap. What is also crucial here is emotional expression instead of emotional repression, which is by no means an Eastern perspective, since it prepares the way for an East-West approach provided that this emotional expression is carried further. Murray claims the following: "Every fearless soldier with whom I served died. I want to go to war with soldiers who carry the weapon of fear that makes them alert, cautious, effective." It is this emphasis on emotional expression as contrasting with emotional repression that we emphasized in Chapter 3. It is basic to an evolutionary worldview.

Murray's focus on the immediate momentary scene also opens the door to the idea of the cortical-thalamic pause. In order to link the cortex with the thalamus, it is essential to use one's knowledge to help one dig deeply into one's fears and other emotions and raise them to the surface, thus achieving expression of them. We can carry Murray's idea—of using the knowledge he has developed in training to become a paratrooper as a basis for overcoming his fear of jumping into nowhere—much further with the aid of our broad approach to the scientific method that is much of the basis of our East-West strategy. Here we have "head" helping "heart," which is what the cortical-thalamic pause is all about. And just as Murray writes about carrying his approach into everyday life, so can we argue the potential effectiveness of this East-West strategy in everyday life.

Murray's emphasis on the importance of developing "habits" that can then come to one's aid in difficult circumstances suggests our own emphasis on rituals, a crucial element of the extraordinary language that was discussed in Chapter 4. Yet we cannot afford to see such habits as psychologists generally see them—and as invoked by our bureaucratic worldview—as isolated from the range of the individual's values and beliefs. Let us recall here our distinction between bureaucratic rituals and evolutionary rituals that prisoners in the Gulag adopted, as discussed in that same chapter. Bureaucratic rituals—as illustrated by prisoners continuing to lie on their cots in the evening with no active involvement in doing things that linked to cultural values pointing toward survival— proved to be a death sentence. By contrast, when Janusz Bardach, despite his fatigue and the cold, "kept the exercise routine ... [he] had followed at home and in the Red Army, washing ... [his] face and hands at the hand pump," he saved his life. Here was a habit linked to his cultural values and patterns of action—to his "heart" and "hand"—rather than a habit isolated from the rest of his personality structures. In other words, here was a ritual, namely, a pattern of action that was meaningful and expressive to a great extent.

And here is a lesson that we all can learn, a lesson linked to the East-West strategy: We must learn to transform habits that we presently see as isolated patterns of action into rituals that are meaningful and expressive—with the respect to the full range of our personality structures—to a great extent. We are not prisoners in a concentration camp, but we are prisoners of a bureaucratic worldview and way of life. What Murray is suggesting is a direction that we can take that can help us to move out of that way of life and toward an evolutionary way of life. It will help us get ourselves together, linking "hand" with "head" and "heart." And by so doing we will gain the ability, the motivation, and the understanding to move far beyond an ability to overcome fear and other negative emotions. We can also learn to learn how to express our emotions ever more fully, moving ever further away from our present situation of emotional repression. In this direction lies the Western aspect of the East-West strategy: taking both aspirations and their fulfillment to ever greater heights, with no limit whatsoever, heights that illustrate our evolutionary potential as human beings.

There is still more that we can learn from Murray, given his focus on learning to overcome fear "one small step at a time." The essence of our revolution of rising expectations—linked as it is to a widening aspirations-fulfillment gap and a bureaucratic worldview—is attempting to jump up far too many steps at a time and as a result falling on our faces. Yet Murray's logical approach—based on a good deal of training so as to develop that logical approach into automatic rituals—involved breaking down what was required to solve the problem at hand by breaking the task down into a series of steps. And this was more than an intellectual task ("head"): It involved a great deal of practice as well ("hand"). The result was an ability to deal with his fear ("heart"). More generally, we can make good use of our broad scientific method to do much the same thing with the problems that we encounter in everyday life. We should not attempt to jump quickly from an understanding of the sequence of steps required to make progress on a given problem ("head"). We must then develop rituals ("hand")—through a good deal of practice—that will enable us to raise up and express negative emotions like fear, just as Gosseyn began to succeed in teaching Ashargin to conquer his fears.

Deep Action and Deep Interaction

Our vision of "deep interaction" is our effort to carry further—toward an evolutionary way of life—the idea of "interaction," which refers to all phenomena and not just human behavior. We might recall here the contrast between "social interaction" in Figure 5-1 with "conformity" in Figure 4-1: The former points us in an evolutionary direction, but the latter points us toward a bureaucratic way of life. The idea of interaction—conceived of as not limited to interaction with others but rather extending to an individual's interaction with any and all phenomena that are experienced—is fundamental to our overall vision of an evolutionary way of life. It is exactly here that we must learn to confront our bureaucratic patterns of social organization—such as stratification and bureaucracy—if indeed we hope to move toward that way of life. Let us recall that we human beings are indeed—based on our tool of language—the most interactive creatures in the known universe. The idea of "deep interaction" is our effort to clarify a direction for our moving in an evolutionary direction, behavior that is not limited to social interaction. This idea will serve as a prelude to our discussion of "deep dialogue" and "deep democracy" in the next section.

Let us note, based on our discussion of interaction near the beginning of Chapter 1, that our view of interaction is not that it is limited to "social interaction," which may be defined as action by individuals in a momentary situation that mutually affects them. By contrast, interaction includes social interaction, but it also includes much more. We may define "interaction" as action by phenomena in a momentary situation that mutually affects other phenomena. This includes actions by physical or nonliving phenomena, actions by other forms of life than us humans, actions by human beings that affect nonliving phenomena as well as other organisms, and also social interaction.

From this perspective, we might see the potential for "deep interaction" as limited to the behavior of human beings, by contrast with the concept of interaction. More specifically, we might see deep interaction as carrying us beyond our present bureaucratic worldview and way of life, as illustrated by Figure 1-2 with its barriers to our further interaction. Instead, deep interaction is illustrated by Figure 1-3. We might, then, define "deep interaction" as interaction by human beings that makes progress toward inward-outward perception and thought as well as toward emotional expression, following the extraordinary language depicted in Figure 5-1. In this way, deep interaction moves the individual toward an evolutionary way of life. It specifies more clearly our vision of individual movement further and further away from a bureaucratic way of life. And it clarifies our focus on the human being. Granting that we are the most interactive creatures throughout the entire universe, we have no more than begun our evolutionary journey. Unfortunately, unless we learn to overcome the barriers that we ourselves have placed in our own way—such as patterns of stratification and bureaucracy—our journey will end before it has barely begun.

Let us not forget that deep interaction is momentary or situational behavior as distinct from structural behavior, such as deep dialogue which is defined as a persisting pattern of deep interaction. "Deep action" is a concept similar to deep interaction, but it is broad enough to include both deep interaction as well as the individual's behavior outside of a social setting. We may define "deep action" as an individual's action that makes progress toward inward-outward perception and thought as well as emotional expression. Just as "action" can occur in isolation or can involve interaction, so can deep action occur in either situation. Given the focus of our bureaucratic worldview on outward perception and thought, the concepts of action and deep action are most useful in opening up to behavior that can occur in isolation as well as in relation to others.

To illustrate deep action, we might refer to Murray's description of his experiences while training to become a paratrooper in World War II, as discussed in the above subsection on the cortical-thalamic pause. Murray's actions while training were designed to address his fear of making jumps into space, and thus they were oriented inward and focused on his recognition of or expression of his repressed fear. Thus, those actions were deep actions, given their orientation to an evolutionary worldview. As he repeated them over and over again, they became individual rituals oriented to that worldview. Such rituals contrast with patterns of addiction, which are also individual rituals. They are defined as patterns of action that subordinate individuality to external phenomena.

Given the importance of patterns of stratification and bureaucracy in working against our evolutionary journey, let us review the work of Constas and Udy—discussed in Chapter 2—since they opened up an alternative to these patterns of behavior:

> However, two researchers, Helen Constas (1958) and Stanley Udy (1959; see also Phillips 2009, 135–136) have charted a different or nonbureaucratic kind of organization that we might simply call a "group." A group is an aggregate or collection of individuals who repeatedly interact with one another directly or indirectly. Udy, whose research was based on the earlier analyses of Constas, focused on the 7 characteristics of bureaucracy that Weber had specified, selecting 150 organizations producing material goods from 150 societies. Those seven characteristics were divided into two sets: three of them were, in his view, bureaucratic, yielding a substantial division of labor, an extensive hierarchy involving three or more levels, and rewards distributed according to one's

position in the hierarchy. The other four characteristics were, in his view, "rational" or "scientific": limited objectives so as to enable the organization to achieve a focus; an emphasis on performance so that rewards are dependent on achievement; specification of limitations on the involvement of those within the organization on external commitments; and rewards given to those with lower authority in return for their participation. He found that that the three bureaucratic characteristics tended to occur when the four scientific characteristics did not, and vice-versa, and he concluded that the bureaucratic characteristics were opposed to the scientific ones, revealing the contradictory nature of bureaucracies not only as Weber defined them but also as they presently exist throughout the world.

Udy and Constas saw the "rational" or "scientific" aspects of bureaucracy as opposed to both the stratified aspects of bureaucracy as well as its narrow division of labor with limited communication. We might recall from Chapter 2 that it was Max Weber himself who viewed the ability of modern bureaucracies to invoke the full knowledge that the biophysical sciences and their technologies had developed as a major basis for their superiority over preindustrial bureaucracies. Yet from the perspective of the research by Constas and Udy, that scientific knowledge remains incomplete, for it has failed to challenge the barriers within modern bureaucracies to interaction both up and down its hierarchies and across its specialized areas. Thus, these researchers have pointed up a problem that social scientists—with all of their specialized knowledge—have as yet failed to resolve. Yet Constas and Udy have clarified the path that should be taken to address the limited effectiveness of bureaucracies: It is a path that would extend the scientific approach of groups so that they would move toward eliminating their vertical and horizontal barriers to interaction—within the individual no less than within the group—as portrayed in Figure 1-2.

It is exactly here that our own vision of an evolutionary worldview and way of life—based on a strategy for problem solving that invokes a very broad approach to the scientific method—can be introduced. Just as we have moved from preindustrial to industrial or "modern" bureaucracies—with all of their limitations—so can we now move from industrial bureaucracies to evolutionary groups. In the past it has been biophysical science and its technologies that has enabled us to move from preindustrial to industrial bureaucracies. In the future, we believe that it will be an interdisciplinary approach to the scientific method linked to an evolutionary worldview—bringing forward the knowledge of the social sciences—that will be the basis for the development of evolutionary groups and, as well, evolutionary institutions and an evolutionary society. Of course, this will require at least the beginnings of a social science revolution that would integrate the bits and pieces of knowledge throughout the social sciences, just as we experienced in the past a scientific revolution based on the physical and biological sciences. That revolution would give us humans the tools we require to move toward "deep interaction," and to move as well toward "deep dialogue" and "deep democracy," thus enabling us to continue on our evolutionary journey.

Crucial to our ability to continue that journey is the requirement of deep interaction to achieve both inward-outward perception and thought as well as emotional expression, both of which are linked to an evolutionary worldview. We would do well to recall here some of the words of E. F. Schumacher, as quoted at the end of Chapter 6: "Education cannot help us as long as it accords no place to metaphysics. Whether the subjects taught are subjects of science or of the humanities, if the teaching does not lead to a clarification of metaphysics, that is to say, of our fundamental convictions, it cannot educate a man and, consequently, cannot be of real value to society."

Schumacher thus alerts us to the enormous failure of our institutions of higher education to achieve the kind of education that opens the individual up to his or her possibilities. Instead of a genuine liberal arts education, we have achieved an education that teaches us—following our bureaucratic worldview—that our intellects cannot arrive at a deep understanding of all the fields outside of our specialized area: of philosophy or poetry or mathematics or sociology or biology or physics or languages or drama or chemistry or psychology or history. The result is that our future leaders will remain ignorant, and society at large will suffer because of that ignorance. Schumacher is claiming, then, that higher education fails to educate the individual to prepare for life, and not just for a narrow career. And if this is the case for higher education, it surely is the case for the institution of education as a whole.

In our own view, a portion of this problem can be tied to the idea of "value neutrality" that scientists have emphasized, as discussed at the end of Chapter 5. This gives scientists an excuse to avoid confronting the very issues that concern students and the rest of us the most: issues that bear directly on our cultural values. Granting that this excuse has never been vigorously challenged—given its support by our bureaucratic worldview— it no longer carries with it the credibility that can sustain it. For we have learned that this cloak of value neutrality, this excuse for avoiding issues that really matter, is in fact a most deceptive stance. It makes as much sense as expecting an individual to survive with his or her heart cut out. Not only is a commitment to value neutrality a deceptive stance, but it is also a pernicious stance, going against the effective functioning of the scientific method. Worse, it supports a bureaucratic worldview, which is much of the basis for present-day escalating problems.

The problems Schumacher is addressing have roots that go far beyond the failures of those in the academic world. This is of a piece with the economic crisis gripping the globe. It is not just a crisis within one institution: It is a crisis within all institutions. As we have argued throughout this book, these problems extend to the bureaucratic worldview and way of life to be found throughout contemporary society and not just American society. As a result, the solutions also extend far beyond the academic world, granting that academics can do a great deal to work toward those solutions. In the final section of this chapter—Deep Dialogue and Deep Democracy— we move outside of the academic world, yet by so doing we do not abandon the academic world. Building on the idea of deep interaction within this section, we will focus on how deep interaction can yield "deep dialogue" or deep social relationships. And we will also look to how deep interaction can become the basis for what we have called "deep democracy."

Deep Dialogue and Deep Democracy

Our focus in the above section was on the "interactions" of the individual, and in particular the kinds of interactions that point away from a bureaucratic and toward an evolutionary way of life. Those interactions included interactions with other individuals, but we emphasized the individual's interactions with all phenomena he or she experiences. That focus took us into the new idea of "deep interaction," with its situational basis in both inward-outward perception and emotional expression. This was, however, no more than a focus, for our commitment to the extraordinary language of social science compels us to take into account the full range of phenomena that we see depicted in Figures 4-1 and 5-1. Thus, deep interaction also invokes the full range of individual and social structures that are to be found within any situation: the individual's worldview, self-image, values, beliefs and assumptions, and individual rituals. And deep interaction also must take into account cultural norms and values, institutions, the cultural worldview, social rituals, and groups.

In this section, however, we are shifting our focus from "deep interaction" to "deep dialogue" and "deep democracy." Once again, we do not as a result abandon attention to the full range of personality and social structures—and let us not forget as well biological and physical structures—that participate within the context of such behavior. This focus, then, turns our searchlight on relationships among individuals, including intimate two-person relationships, relationships in groups of all kinds, and relationships throughout society as a whole in all of our institutions. The idea of "deep democracy" is by no means limited to behavior within the political institution, for all institutions are involved. We might note here our discussion in the above section of the pattern of social organization that includes patterns of social stratification and bureaucracy. Just as we had to take into account those near-universal patterns of behavior as we turned to the idea of deep interaction, so must we take them into account as we proceed with the ideas of deep dialogue and deep democracy. Our pendulum must swing far to the left if it is to gain the momentum needed to swing far to the right.

Deep Dialogue

Ralph Ellison's novel, *Invisible Man,* was about the invisibility of African Americans as unique human beings within a white society:

> I am an invisible man. No, I am not a spook like those who haunted Edgar Allan Poe; nor am I one of your Hollywood-movie ectoplasms. I am a man of substance, of flesh and bone, fiber and liquids—and I might even be said to possess a mind. I am invisible, understand, simply because people refuse to see me. Like the bodiless heads you see sometimes in circus sideshows, it is as though I have been surrounded by mirrors of hard, distorting glass. When they approach me they see only my surroundings, themselves, or figments of their imagination— indeed, everything and anything except me.
>
> Nor is my invisibility exactly a matter of a biochemical accident to my epidermis. That invisibility to which I refer occurs because of a peculiar disposition of the eyes of those with whom I come in contact. A matter of the construction of their inner eyes, those eyes with which they look through their physical eyes upon reality ... you're constantly being bumped against by those of poor vision ... out of resentment, you begin to bump people back. And, let me confess, you feel that way most of the time (Ellison 1947: 3-4).

The novel suggests not only the existence of racial prejudice, and not only the existence of other patterns of social stratification like sexism, ageism, religious prejudice, classism, and ethnocentrism. *Invisible Man* also suggests the relative invisibility of all human beings, as influenced by our stratified worldview or metaphysical stance, fully granting that individuals in some groups—as well as some individuals in any group—are more invisible than others. We would do well to return here to our very brief reference in the introduction to Part I of this book to "Bali Ha'i, a special island that does not yet exist, a utopia that we might dream about and hope that it can become reality. "Bali Ha'i" comes from the show *South Pacific,* which played on Broadway between 1949 and 1954 to enormous acclaim, and which has recently been revived on Broadway. Ensign Nellie Forbush encounters her own racial prejudice in this musical, given her Arkansas upbringing long before the civil rights movement. For Emile de Becque, the love of her life, comes with two mixed-race children.

Nellie's problem is illustrated by these lines from a song sung by Lieutenant Joe Cable:

> You've got to be taught before it's too late,
> Before you are six or seven or eight,
> To hate all the people your relatives hate
> (Quoted by Reed 2008: 16)

It is indeed a long time since James Michener wrote his novel, but present-day racism can still remind us of those nine black students who arrived at Central High School in Little Rock, Arkansas, on September 4, 1957, only to be greeted by a mob of hundreds of angry white people who started a riot that got the attention of the entire country. It is a long time since Governor Orval E. Faubus—a name that has been spelled as F-o-r-b-u-s-h as well—used the National Guard to block the integration of Central High School.

We might choose to link the happy ending of the musical with the successes of the civil rights movement and the ending of the 2008 American presidential election with the election of Barack Obama. Yet racism—along with sexism, ageism, classism, and ethnocentrism—still lives throughout the world, granting the very real progress toward the cultural value of equality that has been made. For racism is tied closely not only to our repressed cultural value of group superiority. It is also tied hand-in-glove to our equally repressed bureaucratic worldview. This is indeed an illustration of negative thinking. Yet such thinking, along with efforts to express emotions that we have continued to repress, is essential if further progress toward equality is to be made. Here, the concepts of the cortical-thalamic pause and deep interaction can prove to be most useful for helping us to achieve such progress. For they are not just vague or general ideas: They can become tools that we all can learn to use to attend to the momentary scenes in which we find ourselves, and to help us make others and ourselves visible, given that presently we are all largely invisible.

To help us in our efforts we require the efforts of social scientists throughout the world to integrate their knowledge of just how racism works. One illustration of that integration comes to us from the 1968 doctoral dissertation of Jack Levin, which goes by the jaw-breaking title, "The Influence of Social Frame of Reference for Goal Fulfillment on Social Aggression" (Levin 1968; see also Phillips 2009: 81–85). Although Levin did not explicitly contrast a bureaucratic worldview with an evolutionary worldview, he did much the same thing by contrasting what he called "two social frames of reference":

> These alternative frames of reference for goal fulfillment can be identi-fied as *relative evaluation* [roughly corresponding to a bureaucratic world-view] whereby the individual judges his personal performances relative to the productivity of other persons and groups, and *self evaluation*

[roughly corresponding to an evolutionary worldview] whereby the individual relies upon his other personal performances, past or present, as a standard of comparison (Levin 1968: 20, italics ours).

"Relative evaluation" is both an orientation to outward perception and thought as well as an orientation to emotional repression, thus illustrating central aspects of a bureaucratic worldview. It may be illustrated by the focus of African Americans on their failures to achieve equality relative to whites rather than a broader focus that also takes into account their own gains toward equality. By contrast, "self evaluation" is an orientation to inward perception and thought that involves less emotional repression. Although Levin did not see "self evaluation" as including a comparison of oneself with others, the individuals that he classified as self evaluators illustrated that orientation only to a limited degree. As a result, they combined inward with outward perception and thought. This combination along with less emotional repression illustrate major aspects of an evolutionary worldview. Relative evaluation may be illustrated by the focus of African Americans on the limitations of their achievements relative to gaining full equality. Levin's was a doctoral dissertation in sociology, yet he succeeded in taking very seriously the importance of personality structures, especially the individual's "frame of reference" or worldview. Thus, he was able to combine social structures with personality structures in his efforts to probe the roots of prejudice and discrimination, an approach that ranges widely over the extraordinary language of social science.

Levin mounted an experiment designed to contrast the degree of prejudice exhibited by subjects—students at Boston University—oriented to relative evaluation and students oriented to self evaluation. In order to do so, he created a microcosm of our stratified world with its large aspirations-fulfillment gap by deliberately blocking those subjects' ability to fulfill fundamental aspirations. Specifically, he led students to believe that they were taking an aptitude test for graduate school and then made it impossible for them to pass the test. The result was that the relative evaluators generally increased their degree of prejudice—his focus was on prejudice against Puerto Ricans—but the self-evaluators generally did not increase their own levels of prejudice despite their frustration over failing the mock aptitude test. This is of course no more than one small piece of evidence about the forces producing prejudice against a minority group. Nevertheless, it does succeed in illustrating the potential of social science research for probing the complex forces within the individual and society that produce prejudice and discrimination. And it also illustrates the importance of a broad approach to social science that takes into account both social and personality structures. In particular, it illustrates the importance of the contrast between a bureaucratic and an evolutionary worldview for understanding the genesis of prejudice and discrimination.

One way to move toward an evolutionary worldview is to change the way in which we relate to others so that we become more and more visible as unique individuals both to them and to ourselves. This is the idea behind our notion of "deep dialogue," a concept initially developed by Phillips in the edited volume, *Bureaucratic Culture and Escalating Problems: Advancing the Sociological Imagination*:

> To introduce the nature of deep dialogue by contrast with our ordinary conversations or professional communication, we might contrast "iron man" dialogue with "straw man" dialogue. Within "iron man" dialogue— a term that I used in my classes at Boston University—we listen so closely to a partner in conversation that we learn to extend the thrust of his or her ideas, even if only to provide an additional illustration, thus carrying them even further than the initial statement of them. By so doing, we make it easier to learn from them, seeing how they differ from our own hidden assumptions, metaphysical stance or worldview. We then attempt to either change those assumptions or reinforce them, depending on what we have learned from the exchange, and we then communicate the result of our analysis. This approach is quite the opposite of setting up another's argument as a "straw man," where we stereotype it negatively and weaken it so that we can easily refute it and thus have no need to examine our own assumptions and question them. Playing iron man illustrates the idea of deep dialogue which, I believe, is rare either in the academic world or in our personal lives. Straw man, by contrast, is our general pattern of discourse, where we remain unable to genuinely listen to another's ideas when they contradict some of our own hidden assumptions.
>
> This approach to deep dialogue suggests the reflexive approach that Mills and especially Gouldner called for, since one can learn to use dialogue as a basis for uncovering one's own hidden assumptions. Unless this is accomplished, one remains a victim of those assumptions, protecting them at all costs instead of learning the nature of one's own internal forces and how they shape our behavior. A reflexive orientation will point the Western individual toward more of an inward-outward orientation—fundamental to an evolutionary or interactive worldview— since the Western bureaucratic or stratified worldview points outward. And given the spread of the Western technological revolution throughout the world, that outward orientation is to be found among Easterners as well as Westerners, granting that Westerners generally share that orientation to a greater extent. Yet given the general prevalence of a bureaucratic or stratified worldview—as illustrated by the prevalence of bureaucratic organizations throughout contemporary society—taking

Mills's or Gouldner's advice is most difficult (Knottnerus and Phillips, eds. 2009: 190).

These two paragraphs provide us with a very general approach to the idea of deep dialogue. It certainly meshes with what we have emphasized in Chapters 2 and 5: a shift from outward perception and thought to inward-outward perception and thought. It is also based on a highly critical view of how we ordinarily relate to one another: failing to listen to others, stereotyping the ideas of others so that we can more easily parade our own ideas, and not learning from others as a result. Yet this is exactly what we should expect if we accept the idea that we have repressed the cultural value of group superiority, that our basic patterns of social relationships are stratified, and that our worldview is bureaucratic. Why should we pay serious attention to the ideas of others if we feel superior to them? What could they possibly have to say that would be of any value? Looking at our failures to communicate from the perspective of our aspirations-fulfillment gap, how can we reach out to others with both head and heart if our emotions are largely taken up in repressing that gap? And if our cultural values have been distorted in the direction of materialistic work-related ones, then what room is left for relationships that don't add to our pot of gold?

More specifically, we can proceed to define "deep dialogue" as a persisting pattern of deep interaction between individuals. Let us recall here that deep interaction, as discussed in the above section, focused on the interaction experienced by human beings and not just the very broad idea of interaction among phenomena. Further, the concept of deep interaction was defined as interaction among people that makes progress toward inward-outward perception and thought as well as toward emotional expression. Yet deep interaction, by contrast with deep dialogue, is a situational occurrence and not a pattern of behavior that persists over time, and that is the difference between these two ideas. Thus, deep dialogue emphasizes social structures by contrast with the situational emphasis of deep interaction. Yet the two ideas are the same in their achievement in moving toward both inward-outward perception and thought as well as toward emotional expression. And they are also the same in their focus on an evolutionary versus a bureaucratic worldview.

Deep Democracy

Just as our understanding of deep interaction was a basis for gaining understanding of deep dialogue, so can this latter understanding of deep dialogue become a basis for understanding the idea of "deep democracy." Let us recall our use of the concept of deep democracy at the end of the introduction to Part I. We did not actually define the term at that point.

Rather, we used it simply to suggest a number of fundamental goals that are widely shared throughout modern society, such as the following:

> To begin to spell out just what "deep democracy" means to us, we might parallel the speech that Martin Luther King gave at the Civil Rights March in Washington on August 28, 1963: "I have a dream that one day on the red hills of Georgia the sons of former slaves and the sons of former slave owners will be able to sit down together at the table of brotherhood." We have a dream that: There will be a future for our children, our grandchildren, our great-grandchildren, and their great-grandchildren.

Whatever this concept of deep democracy proves to be, it is by no means limited to the idea of political democracy, fully granting the importance of political democracy. For political democracy does not eliminate our patterns of racism, sexism, ageism, classism and ethnocentrism, although it certainly works against such patterns of social stratification. Neither does political democracy yield a world without wars that might well eliminate any future for the human race. The idea of deep democracy, following the above quotation, has to do not just with the political institution but rather with the full range of our institutions. Otherwise, it could not work to change our basic patterns of social stratification—illustrated by racism—as well as the persistence of wars and other acts of violence that threaten the continuation of our species.

Just as we defined deep dialogue in relation to deep interaction, so can we now define deep democracy in relation to deep dialogue: as a pattern of deep dialogue throughout the full range of a society's institutions that is the basis for the decisions that shape behavior throughout society. Such a pattern of behavior could go a long way toward the development of an electorate that gains the understanding that they require to make informed decisions in the face of the enormous complexity of modern society. Given this breadth of the idea of deep democracy as extending beyond the political institution, it becomes possible to understand its potential impact on patterns of social stratification throughout society as well as on patterns of violence such as warfare. Yet it remains for us to come down from the clouds of this general definition to its more specific implications.

Our focus on deep democracy's relationship to the full range of our institutions harks back to John Dewey's view of democracy, as discussed in Chapter 5:

> Government, business, art, religion, all social institutions have a meaning, a purpose. That purpose is to set free and to develop the capacities of human individuals without respect to race, sex, class or economic

status. And this is all one with saying that the test of their value is the extent to which they educate every individual into the full stature of his possibility. Democracy has many meanings, but if it has a moral meaning, it is found in resolving that the supreme test of all political institutions and industrial arrangements shall be the contribution they make to the all-around growth of every member of society (Dewey 1920/1948: 186).

Dewey centers here on the goal of individual development as the central task of every one of our institutions. Each institution—as discussed in Chapter 3—focuses on solving a given problem. Dewey is claiming here that, regardless of these specialized functions of institutions, there is an overarching problem that they should all address: "the all-around growth of every member of society." What Dewey is calling for is that institutions emphasize the fulfillment of people-oriented cultural values. These include not only individual personality, equality, freedom, and de-mocracy, but also understanding the world, solving problems, intimate and close relationships, and ultimate meaning.

Dewey's visionary approach to contemporary society joins the vi-sions of others. There is our own vision of deep democracy that we put forward in the introduction to Part I. There is Jane Addams's vision, as stated in her 1902 book, *Democracy and Social Ethics*: "The cure for the ills of Democracy is more Democracy.... A conception of Democracy not merely as a sentiment which desires the well-being of all men, nor yet as a creed which believes in the essential dignity and equality of all men, but as that which affords a rule of living as well as a test of faith" (Quoted in Knowles 2004: 3: 19). Also, we should not ignore—from Chapter 6—Rob-ert Fuller's efforts to move away from rankism or social stratification in our everyday lives, and thus move toward fulfilling the cultural values of individual personality and equality throughout all institutions. And let us also remember the people-oriented emphasis of E. F. Schumacher in that same chapter: "What is the meaning of democracy, freedom, human dignity, standard of living, self-realisation, fulfillment? Is it a matter of goods, or of people? Of course it is a matter of people." Equally relevant is Van Vogt's illustration of Venusians as having achieved an ideal civiliza-tion, presented in Chapter 5: "To understand the political situation here, you must reach out with your mind to the furthest limits of your ideas of ultimate democracy." In addition, we have Amy Chua's view of the failings of our present political democracy—as we described it in Chapter 4—in its development of economic stratification throughout the world: "[T]he United States has come to be seen as an oppressor of poor nations to the extent that its economic policies work to keep those nations at the lower end of the economic hierarchy among nations. For economic stratifica-tion among nations has continued in the contemporary world, and all the while a worldwide revolution of rising expectations continues to fan the flames of discontent."

As for coming down from the clouds of these general visions of democracy that proceed beyond what has already been achieved in the world, our own direction is toward what we have focused on throughout this book: progress in changing from our bureaucratic worldview to an evolutionary worldview. For it is our bureaucratic worldview that is much of the basis for our widening aspirations fulfillment gap, as illustrated by the concept of affluenza developed in Chapter 6. This movement toward an evolutionary worldview depends, we believe, on our learning to employ a strategy for problem-solving in everyday life that makes use of a broad scientific method, a method that invokes the extraordinary language of social science to confront the enormous complexity of human behavior. We see that strategy—which we have called the East-West strategy—as working initially to narrow our aspirations-fulfillment gap by bringing down our aspirations from their unrealistic height and giving more attention to our momentary situations. And we also see that strategy, given the momentum that we can achieve by learning to fulfill basic cultural values within the momentary scene, as working to move both our aspirations and their fulfillment in an evolutionary direction in the long run, with no limit to how far we might go.

This more specific vision of deep democracy still requires a great deal more concreteness. For example, we must come to grips with the concept of power, which is generally defined by political scientists and sociologists as the ability to control the behavior of others, against their will if necessary. This definition of power emphasizes the centrality of coercion or force yet ignores the potential of influence, which is not coercive. Let us recall here the enormous power of Franklin Delano Roosevelt's fireside chats on radio when he took office during the depth of the Great Depression in 1933. Those talks by themselves did not change the economic situation of the country. They were accompanied by a number of policies designed to revive the economy, some of which proved to be successful and some of which failed. But those talks—Roosevelt's "bully pulpit"—were most important in giving people hope in the possibility of their making it through very difficult times. And, of course, we have our contemporary situation of enormous and pressing problems in all of our institutions. Once again, the ability of a new president to influence us illustrates the importance of a definition of power that emphasizes the potential of influence and not just coercion.

This idea of influence, by contrast with coercion, has to do with the possibility that a leader can develop power. It is an evolutionary view of power, by contrast with a zero-sum view that sees power as a limited pie and focuses on the distribution of the slices of that pie. By contrast, a focus on influence sees that pie as potentially expanding.

And it is not limited to a single leader's influence, for all of us—potentially—can gain influence, including influence over ourselves and not just over others. In other words, there is such a thing as learning to solve problems that goes beyond our past ability to do so. Roosevelt's influence—and Barack Obama's influence—gave people hope and optimism, and that is basic to developing the motivation to learn how to improve their own personal situations even in very difficult times. Thus, influence can work to yield nothing less than the development or evolution of power, by contrast with a view of power as a fixed pie. And if power can indeed expand, then we can learn to move away from stratification and toward deep democracy. For those with the biggest slice of the pie of power and wealth can come to see the possibility of maintaining or even increasing their own slice while helping those below them to enlarge substantially their slices. There is a saying that a rising tide lifts all boats, and this is exactly what an expanding pie of power and wealth would achieve.

Granting the importance of influence in our view of power, we should include both force or coercion as well as authority in that definition if we want to be realistic about the nature of power at the present time. We would like to see a dramatic shift away from force, which we see as tied to our bureaucratic worldview. And we would also like to see a dramatic shift toward influence, which we see as linked to an evolutionary worldview. Yet it is important for us not to lose our sense of present reality, given our interest in an evolutionary way of life. Authority, such as the power of governmental officials to make decisions for the rest of us, is also a basic component of our present way of life. However, we would hope that a movement toward deep democracy would yield ever more input from "the people" to "the deciders" within government so that decisions based on authority increasingly reflect the will of the people.

We can achieve still more concreteness in our vision of deep democracy—moving further down language's ladder of abstraction—by taking up the example of Mohandas Gandhi's influence in helping free India from its position as a colony of Great Britain (Bondurant 1965; see also Phillips and Johnston 2007: 223-227). For example, there was Gandhi's salt campaign between 1930 and 1931, responding to the new British salt tax with its resulting hardships for the poor, for whom salt was a necessity. Gandhi along with others of the Indian National Congress mounted a civil disobedience campaign that began with a 200-mile march to the sea from Ahmedabad to Dandi, where volunteers would then violate the new tax by preparing salt from sea water. Volunteers learned to engage in constructive activities during their long march, helping villagers along the way. And they were forbidden to drink intoxicants and urged to overcome discrimination against Untouchables. When leaders of the salt campaign were arrested, shops closed throughout India, nonpayment of taxes was initiated, Indian officials resigned in very large numbers, and new leaders took the places of those who had been arrested.

The long struggle throughout India included Gandhi's fasting until near death in his successful efforts to stop violence from breaking out among his supporters. And the struggle also included sacrifices by others who were willing to endure the blows of police without striking back, sacrifices that reached the consciousness and conscience of the British public. Gandhi's techniques of civil disobedience followed these principles:

1. Refraining from any form of verbal or overt violence toward members of the rival group
2. Openly admitting to the rival group one's plans and intentions
3. Refraining from any action that will have the effect of humiliating the rival group
4. Making visible sacrifices for one's cause
5. Maintaining a consistent and persistent set of positive activities which are explicit (though partial) realizations of the group's objectives
6. Attempting to initiate direct personal interaction with members of the rival group, oriented toward engaging in friendly verbal discussions with them concerning the fundamental issues involved in the social struggle
7. Adopting a consistent attitude of trust toward the rival group and taking overt actions which demonstrate that one is, in fact, willing to act upon this attitude
8. Attempting to achieve a high degree of empathy with respect to the motives, affects, expectations, and attitudes of members of the rival group (Janis and Katz 1959: 86).

These principles that Gandhi followed enabled him to achieve sufficient influence over people throughout the Indian subcontinent to work decisively and persistently toward the achievement of independence. Here, then, is an illustration of the development or evolution of power, and not just on the part of Gandhi. For people throughout India learned that they could develop the power required to help achieve independence. Yet this was not a zero-sum game, where the British lost while India gained. For India remained part of the British commonwealth of nations and continued not only as a trading partner but also as an ally during World War II. And as a result of the above principles of civil disobedience, the British were not humiliated or subjected to violence, but rather were treated with respect to a great extent. And villagers who were not participating in the salt campaign were treated to aid by those involved in civil disobedience.

We can understand to a greater extent just how power was developed within India's struggle for independence by turning to the cultural values that were involved, values shared by the British people—who reacted against the coercion of the British police and who were sympathetic to the sacrifices by the Indians—no less than by the people of India. For Gandhi's principles of civil disobedience emphasized the fulfillment of such people-oriented cultural values as equality, individual personality, democracy, freedom, and the achievement of close personal relationships. As for the idea of deep democracy, it is the fulfillment of such people-oriented ideals throughout the institutions of a given society that points that society in the direction of deep democracy. For the sacrifices that people throughout India made for the cause of independence required them to confront as individuals their most basic assumptions, including the worth of their own lives relative to the achievement of independence.

Of course, deep democracy involves far more than a successful campaign of civil disobedience that follows people-oriented cultural values, and this illustration goes only so far in helping us to understand the nature of deep democracy and how it might be achieved. Granting that this campaign illustrates the development or evolution of power throughout a society, we believe that what is required for the development of deep democracy is nothing less than an evolutionary worldview and way of life. We have no more than begun to describe that worldview and way of life in the foregoing chapters. In the final part and chapter of this book we hope to come further down the ladder of linguistic abstraction in achieving understanding of an evolutionary worldview and way of life. Our focus there will be on the various institutions of society: scientific, educational, political, economic, religious, and family institutions. And we will continue to make use of the extraordinary language of social science to help us come down that ladder of abstraction.

PART IV

A Vision of the Future

WE BEGIN THIS CONCLUDING PART of the book by quoting from the penultimate chapter of Mills's *The Sociological Imagination,* "On Reason and Freedom," a title that takes us back to Enlightenment ideals for confronting the world's problems:

> I do not know the answer to the question of political irresponsibility in our time or to the cultural and political question of The Cheerful Robot [alienated man]. But is it not clear that no answers will be found unless these problems are at least confronted? Is it not obvious, that the ones to confront them above all others, are the social scientists of the rich societies? That many of them do not now do so is surely the greatest human default being committed by privileged men in our times (Mills 1959: 176).

Mills was appalled about the failure of his fellow social scientists to confront the mammoth problems of his day, including a cold war that might turn into a hot war at any moment, having just published *The Causes of World War III* (1958). Over the past half century the threats to the continuing existence of the human race have continued to increase, and we are equally appalled by that same failure that is being repeated in our own day. Social scientists continue to hide behind a cloak of value neutrality—as discussed in Chapter 3—continuing to fiddle while Rome burns. Yet the price of their irresponsibility—given escalating problems such as the possibility that small groups will use weapons of mass destruction on world populations—has increased enormously. That price far exceeds what was paid by the victims of the Holocaust, for what is at stake at this time in history is nothing less than the entire future of the human race.

Yet it is not just social scientists of the rich societies who are committing "the greatest human default ... in our times" with respect to their own situation. The rest of us are also responsible for our escalating problems, granting that most of us remain unaware of that responsibility. It was not just those Germans who were actively involved in the slaughter that Hitler perpetrated who made that slaughter possible: It was the rest of the world as well. For that slaughter was an extreme example of a pattern of social stratification, where those at the bottom not only are treated with disrespect but are actually eliminated. And that pattern of social organization—with its focus on conformity, emotional repression, and outward perception and thought—illustrates the bureaucratic worldview at work, a worldview that we all share to varying degrees, including us authors. Thus, insofar as we all fail to become, over time, deeply involved politically in world problems—given that the very future of the human race is at stake—we are all committing what we see at this time as nothing less than the greatest human default of personal responsibilities throughout history.

However, our aim in this book is not to throw guilt at the reader or at ourselves. Rather, our stance is scientific, following the pendulum metaphor for the scientific method applied to everyday life, and more generally following the East-West strategy. Our critical perspective must swing that pendulum as far to the left as we can manage, but only in order to gain momentum for a swing as far to the right as possible, where we constructively make progress on problems. In our view a deep critical perspective has been largely absent from the world of social science, as well as the world in general, largely because no realistic and broad vision of solutions to escalating problems has been developed. And that in turn has been based on a failure to shuttle far up language's ladder of abstraction to the level of metaphysical assumptions, such as those that define a bureaucratic worldview. We believe that our own efforts in this direction, which also have yielded the evolution of the individual and society as an alternative worldview, have cleared the way for the pendulum of the scientific method to swing very far in a critical direction.

Yet the ability to change what Thomas Kuhn has called a scientific paradigm—or the basic assumptions underlying a science—is quite difficult, given the invisibility of a paradigm and the longtime commitment of scientists to its assumptions. Thus, changing a cultural paradigm such as our bureaucratic worldview will prove to be far more difficult, since it shapes all of our thoughts, feelings, and actions. From this perspective, we can well understand the resistance of readers to the ideas we have advanced throughout the foregoing chapters. The six books on which this one builds most directly are, however, an unequal opponent when matched against the deep and invisible commitment to a bureaucratic worldview working in every aspect of our lives.

Nevertheless, we refuse to be pessimistic about the prospects for changing our worldview or, indeed, about the future of the human race. For none of us humans has gone very far in making use of the infinite potential of language. Further, none of us has as yet made use—in our everyday lives—of a scientific method that is broad enough to penetrate the complexity of human behavior and our escalating problems. And still further, none of us has employed the East-West strategy for problem solving with respect to both personal and world problems. We have continued to remain captured by an invisible bureaucratic worldview, despite all of our beliefs about our own freedom or autonomy. Yet, following Kuhn, once we bring that cultural paradigm to the surface and come to see how it contradicts our basic cultural values, and once we become aware of an alternative cultural paradigm that promises to resolve those contradictions, we can learn to move toward that alternative.

All of us can learn to do this, and not just social scientists. Although social scientists have a background in published knowledge, that knowledge is narrow, and the doctrine of value neutrality works to prevent them from grappling systematically with the big issues of the world along with their own personal problems. By contrast, the rest of us are far more oriented to putting to work the full range of ideas that we have so as to address our problems. That orientation to solving problems is at least as important as academic knowledge linked to a value-neutral stance. Thus, ordinary people can develop broad academic knowledge to help them solve problems, and academic social scientists can learn to broaden their knowledge and become committed to solving personal and world problems. Of course, this book does no more than open the door to any movement in these directions. What we all require—if indeed we are to learn to confront ever more effectively our escalating problems—is movement through that door as we proceed to change from a bureaucratic worldview and way of life to an evolutionary worldview and way of life. What we offer in this book in addition to a map is optimism about this possibility.

CHAPTER 8

Moving Toward an Evolutionary Worldview and Way of Life

THIS CHAPTER BY NO MEANS will be a summary of the fundamental ideas taken from earlier chapters, for we aim to press ahead on the implications of those ideas. In our first section, The East-West Strategy Revisited: From Social Science to Social Technology, we aim to move further into this problem-solving strategy and into how we can learn to employ it in one scene after another. Just as technologies like engineering and medicine developed on the basis of knowledge from physical science and biological science, so have personal and social technologies developed on the basis of knowledge from the social sciences. Yet existing personal and social technologies—like psychotherapy and education—have not been able to get very far in solving problems, given the failure of social scientists to integrate their knowledge, an integration that is essential for penetrating the complexity of human behavior and problems. And shaping that failure is an invisible worldview and way of life that works against scientific ideals for opening up to the full range of knowledge that is relevant to a given problem. It is also a worldview that works against the infinite potential of language for enabling us to learn how to address our problems. Given the invisibility of that worldview—which we have labeled "bureaucratic"— people generally continue to believe that our social technologies need no more than a bit of adjustment here and there rather than fundamental changes that open them up to a much wider range of knowledge. And we continue to see ourselves as no more than tiny cogs in the vast machine of society, failing to see our own infinite potential for evolving as individuals and helping to develop nothing less than an evolutionary society.

It is in that first section of the chapter, however, that we aim to clarify a direction that can help us learn to use the East-West strategy in our everyday lives. It is a strategy that opens up to the infinite potentials of language and the scientific method. Of course, we have already discussed that strategy in Chapter 7. But that has been no more than a scratching of the surface when compared to our total involvement in a bureaucratic approach to confronting problems. A metaphor can help us here to understand the East-West strategy more fully. Most of us are familiar with the contrast between seeing the glass half full and seeing the glass half empty as indicating an optimistic versus a pessimistic orientation to life. We discussed much the same contrast in Chapter 6 with our contrast between negative thinking and positive thinking. And our pendulum metaphor for the scientific method also gives us a similar contrast: a swing to the left looks to deep problems, much like seeing the glass half empty. And a swing to the right looks to solutions, like seeing the glass half full. This dichotomy between pessimism or realism on the one hand, and optimism on the other hand, is also linked to the dichotomy between the Eastern and the Western strategy. The Eastern strategy focuses on coming down from unrealistic aspirations, largely ignoring human possibilities. And the Western strategy centers on continually raising aspirations, largely ignoring the growing aspirations-fulfillment gap that results.

Yet we can learn to combine the best of the Eastern strategy with the best of the Western strategy, and thus learn to use what we have called an East-West strategy. To accomplish this, however, requires our learning to use the scientific method in everyday life, a method that applies the extraordinary language of social science to achieve understanding of problems and make progress in solving them. A most important problem in particular is that of communication with, and learning from, others. We take up this problem with the aid of an analysis of a film portraying stratification between two individuals who desperately seek love. Yet their aspirations remain unfulfilled due to their stratified relationship and the worldview that shapes that stratification. However, the East-West strategy promises to provide the basis for moving further and further away from stratification between two individuals who seek an intimate or close relationship on an egalitarian basis.

The second section of this chapter, The East-West Strategy and Institutional Change, centers on our six major institutions: science, the economy, education, the political system, the religious institution, and the family. Given the enormous complexity and diversity of each of these institutions—let alone when all of them are taken together—how can we hope to say anything about an institution that takes into account that complexity and diversity? Even almost all of those individuals who have been working as economists all their lives were not able to foresee the worldwide financial meltdown that occurred in the fall of 2008. Who, then, are we, with the gall to think that we have any answers to economic problems throughout the world? We are generalists—granting that we have put forward some concrete illustrations—and that orientation may well be useful, but our specialized knowledge of the academic literature on the economy is quite limited.

However, the above argument appears to be reasonable because it meshes hand-in-glove with our bureaucratic worldview and way of life. We need not choose one side of the dichotomy of specialist versus generalist. Just as we need not choose between seeing the glass half full and seeing it half empty, so is it the case that we need not choose between being generalists and being specialists. The saying, "jack of all trades, master of none," supports our bureaucratic worldview, yet we see it as grossly misleading. Specialists can learn—one step at a time—to become generalists as well. That will point them to climbing up language's ladder of abstraction—even to the level of their metaphysical assumptions—where they will be able to see much further than they can see at present. Thus, they can learn to open up to the wide range of knowledge that they require in order to understand what is actually going on within their specialized area. And generalists can climb down that ladder and learn to understand concrete phenomena that will test and broaden their general understanding.

More specifically, we aim to do no more than present a limited illustration for each of those institutions, seeking to demonstrate in a small way the potential of the East-West strategy. It is a strategy for learning to see the glass *both* half empty *and* half full: for realism combined with optimism. We hope that this will help motivate specialists working within all of these institutions to dip into that strategy, and thus to test its effectiveness. Generally, those illustrations will be drawn from our personal experiences—just as the first section of this chapter will make use of such experiences—since such illustrations will reflect what we know best. By so doing, we will be following the inward-outward orientation to perception and thought that is fundamental for an evolutionary worldview and way of life. This procedure will also require us to raise to the surface repressed emotions, thus following another basic aspect of an evolutionary worldview. This reflexive approach is basic to a broad approach to the scientific method, an approach that is in turn a key aspect of the East-West strategy. Thus, our purpose here is not to advertise ourselves. Rather, these examples with which we are familiar enable us to communicate in a concrete way so that readers will be able to relate those examples to their own personal experiences.

We end this book in a brief "Afterward." There we express some thoughts about both a key limitation of this work as well as a direction that can address that limitation. And we put forward an example of what might be done by others as well as by ourselves to move in that direction. As the reader might guess, it is an example of social technology. More specifically, it is social technology on an international scale.

The East-West Strategy Revisited: From Social Science to Social Technology

Just as Gautama Siddartha Sakyamuni, the Buddha—as discussed in Chapter 5—developed his Eastern strategy through a realistic view of old age, sickness, and death, so should we revisit our East-West strategy through a realistic view of what we have written in the preceding eight chapters. We begin with the idea that all of us, to varying degrees, are victims of a bureaucratic worldview and way of life. The problem for the Buddha was how to eliminate the needless suffering that results from a large aspirations-fulfillment gap, and his solution was to bring aspirations down toward our ability to fulfill them, and thus reduce substantially or even eliminate that gap. For us, this is the first step of our East-West strategy, and it is an essential one. It requires us to go beyond the Buddha's realistic view of old age, sickness, and death, granting that those phenomena should by no means be ignored. *In addition*, there are the phenomena of our bureaucratic worldview and way of life, including our bureaucratic personality and social structures. There are also the situational phenomena that we engage in within one scene after another: our outward perception and thought, our emotional repression, and our patterns of conformity.

To become aware of all these realities it becomes important—following Gouldner, as discussed in Chapter 1—to learn to remain more and more aware of all of these realities:

> At decisive points the ordinary language and conventional understandings fail and must be transcended. It is essentially the task of the social sciences, more generally, to create new and "extraordinary" languages, to help men learn to speak them, and to mediate between the deficient understandings of ordinary language and the different and liberating perspectives of the extraordinary languages of social theory (Gouldner 1972: 16).

Whatever else we have examined throughout this book, we have focused on presenting and illustrating our own take on the nature of the extraordinary language of social science, granting that this is no more than an initial effort and that our own take requires substantial improvement. For it is this language that can help us all, including us authors, to get a grip on the nature of reality, or what philosophers have called "metaphysics." It is also this language that can help us understand the enormous gap between our own assumptions about reality—or our metaphysical stance or worldview—and the nature of reality.

Thus, our own analysis with the aid of the extraordinary language has yielded our conclusions: We are victims of a bureaucratic metaphysical stance or worldview, and this worldview has in turn worked to shape our bureaucratic way of life. As a result, if we are indeed to follow the Eastern part of our East-West strategy, then we must learn to gain ever more awareness of how that worldview works to shape our every thought, feeling, and action. Just as the Indians in Buddha's day sought to avoid awareness of old age, sickness, and death, so do we at this time in history seek not only to repress emotionally that awareness. We also seek to repress awareness of our patterns of social stratification along with our cultural value of group superiority that violate our cultural value of equality. In addition to repressing awareness of our social and personality structures that conflict with our own values or ideals, we also repress our patterns of situational behavior that would yield similar conflicts if we were aware of them. These include our outward perception and thought, our patterns of emotional repression, and our conformity in one scene after another. We like to think that it is only others who engage in such repression of behavior—as well as in all of the behavior that causes our escalating problems—yet such thoughts merely conform to the outward perception and thought that is an essential part of our bureaucratic worldview. Following Walt Kelly's cartoon character, Pogo, "We have met the enemy, and he is us." Pogo joins not only Gouldner but also Socrates, who claimed that "the unexamined life is not worth living." And he also joins the biblical proverb from St. Luke: "Physician, heal thyself."

Following the Buddha's analysis—given that the first Noble Truth is the existence of *dukkha* resulting from the existence of problems that we have repressed and thus failed to solve—the second Noble Truth is the law of causality. If we remove the cause of *dukkha*, then *dukkha* will disappear. And for the Buddha as well as for us, much of the cause of *dukkha* is our wide aspirations-fulfillment gap, a gap that is rapidly widening in our own case and is thus working to threaten the very survival of the human race. Yet it is here that we differ from the Buddha with respect to his third Noble Truth, which involves the renunciation of aspirations, desire or "thirst" so that aspirations move close to our ability to fulfill them. In our own view, we must indeed lower our short-term aspirations so as to move away from *dukkha* and its accompanying emotional repression. Yet we can retain our long-term aspirations and even continue to raise them so long as we have ways to fulfill them. And it is a broad approach to the scientific method—used within our everyday lives—that can help us to lower our aspirations in the short run and then raise both our aspirations and our ability to fulfill them in the long run. The scientific method that we can learn to use is based on the extraordinary language of social science, a language that makes use of the infinite potential for learning or evolution that human language opens up to all of us.

More specifically, we can lower our aspirations in the short run by increasing our focus on whatever situation we are in. Let us recall here the slogan of Alcoholics Anonymous—"one day at a time"—that suggests such a situational focus. Following the argument of Swamiji Parthasarathy—as discussed in Chapter 7—it is "worries about the past and anxiety for the future" that tires the individual and creates stress, by contrast with an ability to discipline the mind and to stay focused on present objectives. We find much the same conclusion—that it is a failure to focus on our momentary situation that is much of the basis for our problems—in the ideas of Gurdjieff and Ouspensky, as discussed in Chapter 2: "We become too absorbed in things, too lost in things," by contrast with a focus on ourselves and our own personal situation. We see similar behavior in what has been labeled "attention deficit disorder" or ADD, also discussed in Chapter 2: "In the fast-paced, distraction-plagued arena of modern life, perhaps nothing has come under more assault than the simple faculty of attention." We would claim that ADD is by no means limited to a small proportion of children who have problems at school, but that we are all, to varying degrees, victims of attention deficit disorder, given the outward orientation of our bureaucratic worldview.

Following the Buddha's second Noble Truth, there are causes of this outward orientation that can be used to help us become more realistic. Those causes do involve our unrealistically high aspirations, which take us away from the momentary situation in a useless effort to consider multiple problems that can only lead to "worries about the past and anxiety about the future." But a more fundamental cause that lies behind our huge and growing aspirations-fulfillment gap, a cause that remains invisible, is our bureaucratic worldview. Building on the insights of Kuhn—as discussed in Chapter 5—once we have at least the beginnings of an alternative paradigm or worldview that promises to resolve the problems or contradictions within our bureaucratic worldview, we can face up to our situational problems instead of avoiding them with thoughts of the past or future. Further, we need not abandon high and increasing aspirations in the long run—as the Buddha implies and as the Springdalers have illustrated, as discussed in Chapter 3—but rather can move to an East-West strategy that retains those aspirations.

It is exactly here that we can bring to bear our evolutionary worldview with its accompanying extraordinary language, for it is this worldview and that language that holds out to us the promise of focusing on the problems within our momentary situation instead of avoiding them, and thus following the advice of Socrates, Gouldner, Pogo, and the New Testament. That language can alert us to a general direction within the situation: toward inward-outward perception and thought, the expression of emotions, and action along with interaction. And that language can also alert us to a more specific direction within the situation: toward negative thinking, use of the cortical-thalamic pause, and deep action, interaction, dialogue, and democracy. And if we are to build on Kuhn's understanding, we can also learn to see the conflict between our bureaucratic paradigm and the evolutionary paradigm not only in a general way but also within any given momentary scene. And, as a result, we can learn to move away from our present worldview and toward an alternative one, thus removing the most fundamental cause of our failure to pay attention to our own problems within any given situation. Further, guided by our extraordinary language, we can learn not only to lower our aspirations in the short run but also to raise them—along with our ability to fulfill them—in the long run. Thus, we can learn to continue to move along an evolutionary path for both the individual and society with no limit whatsoever.

We might come to understand our concepts of negative thinking, the cortical-thalamic pause, and deep action more clearly with the aid of an example. Let us assume that our choice has to do with some addictive action like smoking or not smoking a cigarette. Within our bureaucratic worldview we see no relationship between that choice and the future of the human race. But within an evolutionary worldview, the choice of smoking not only moves us closer to a variety of life-threatening diseases. It also illustrates our continuing conformity to a bureaucratic worldview, a metaphysical stance linked to increasing world problems that will, over time, yield the end of the human race. It is by no means the act of smoking that in itself is so dangerous for the fate of the human race. Rather, that act is one tiny part of an entire way of life—the bureaucratic way of life—that is taking us in a direction that leads us all over the cliff. And our movement in that direction is invisible no less than visible, as illustrated by its links to a widening aspirations-fulfillment gap that in turn works to escalate visible problems.

By contrast, an evolutionary worldview opens up the possibility that the choice of not smoking that cigarette enables the individual to take one tiny step along an evolutionary path that can lead, over time, to continuing progress on the range of escalating problems that threaten human society. And it is the extraordinary language of social science that can enable the individual to build links between his or her momentary choice in a given situation to the fate of human society. For example, smoking that cigarette might come to be seen as linked to any of the concepts associated with a bureaucratic worldview that are depicted in Figure 4-1, such as outward perception and thought, emotional repression, or conforming behavior. By contrast, the individual might come to see not smoking as linked to any one of the concepts tied to an evolutionary worldview depicted in Figure 5-1, such as inward-outward perception and thought, emotional expression, or action. By so doing, the individual can take a tiny step toward moving away from a bureaucratic way of life with its widening aspirations-fulfillment gap that intensifies our visible social problems.

In this book we have no more than begun to develop the detailed directions that we require to actually abandon our deeply structured bureaucratic way of life and move toward an evolutionary way of life. For that way of life encompasses the thousands of choices that we make every single day. Our overall emphasis has been on social science rather than on personal and social technologies that build on such scientific understanding. Those technologies are no less important for solving social problems than are the technologies of engineering and medicine for solving physical and biological problems.

Granting the overriding importance of personal and social technologies for moving away from our bureaucratic way of life, what is nevertheless equally crucial is our starting with an understanding of our personal and social problems that is based on integrated social science knowledge as conveyed by the extraordinary language. Imagine, for example, attempting to build a rocket that can land on the moon with limited understanding of the principles of physical science. Thus, we see our own efforts to integrate social science knowledge in this book as an absolutely essential step toward moving away from our bureaucratic way of life. Given our present commitment to that way of life, it is a most difficult step to take. Our daily experiences coupled with our entire background support a bureaucratic worldview. As a result, the many examples within this book are no match for the number of past and present experiences contradicting those examples that we all have. We are attempting here to be realistic, following the Eastern aspect of the East-West strategy.

Nevertheless, what we authors have on our side is nothing less than the incredible power of the tools of language—including the extraordinary language of social science—the scientific method, and integrated social science knowledge coupled with an applied strategy—the East-West strategy—derived from those tools. This may well be insufficient to compete effectively with the power of our bureaucratic way of life. Yet this is our own best effort to confront that power. We are hopeful that our own ability to understand the world situation at this time in history will increase as we continue to apply these ideas to our own behavior in everyday life. And we are convinced that, as world problems continue to increase, people will become ever more aware of their threatening nature and ever more open to seeking answers beyond those formulated by our specialized experts.

Given the above revisiting of the East-West strategy as applied to the choice of smoking or not smoking a cigarette, we can come to see *all* of our momentary choices—that appear to be quite trivial—as *also* invoking choices between worldviews, choices that affect the future of the human race. Just as all phenomena within our universe interact with one another at least to some extent, so is any problem that appears to be completely trivial—such as tying one's shoelace—in fact linked to the very problems that threaten the future of the human race. For it is a human being who aspires to tie a shoelace, and in the tying process he or she can approach the task from a bureaucratic or an evolutionary perspective or worldview. And that worldview is carried forward by the bureaucratic or evolutionary concepts that the individual is invoking, whether consciously or unconsciously.

In the former case—following Figure 1-2—she fails to see that action ("hand") linked to her basic emotions ("heart") or her fundamental ideas, such as her worldview ("head"), and thus she illustrates a bureaucratic worldview. In the latter case, following Figure 1-3, she takes a step toward learning to make those links, thus moving toward an evolutionary worldview. Within that step she must define this task as a problem, moving the pendulum of the scientific method to the left. And she makes use of concepts from the extraordinary language, such as learning an evolutionary worldview, to help her not only solve the shoelace problem but also make progress on changing her worldview. We might note that what is being accomplished is the linking of situational behavior—such as negative thinking or the cortical-thalamic pause—with structural behavior such as an individual's metaphysical stance or worldview. It is such links between situational and structural behavior that are the bases for changes in structures, to the extent that they are repeated in one scene after another. The key structural change we are focusing on is, of course, changing from a bureaucratic to an evolutionary worldview.

To restate these ideas, all of us have a choice to make—between a bureaucratic and an evolutionary worldview and way of life—within every momentary situation once we come to understand the nature of these two worldviews and their implications for our everyday behavior. Those implications are spelled out by the extraordinary language of social science, which enables us to tie together our momentary situational behavior—thoughts, feelings, and actions—to our personality and social structures. And it is the East-West strategy—which incorporates this extraordinary language within a broad approach to the scientific method—that we can learn to use in every choice we make at every moment, granting that we can learn to do this only one step at a time. Thus, we can learn to make a choice with respect to smoking a cigarette in one scene, and we can learn to tie our shoelaces in another scene, with an understanding that what we choose is linked both to our emotional expression and our evolutionary worldview.

We should be aware that, given the differences among individuals, a thought, feeling, or action that is evolutionary for one individual may point in a bureaucratic direction for another individual. For example, for one individual a slow tying of shoelaces might be accompanied by enjoyment of the fact that one has shoes or the fact that one has the coordination to tie them, thus yielding emotional expression. For another individual, a rapid tying of shoelaces might be accompanied by positive feelings that one has learned to act decisively within apparently trivial situations. Further, given the complexity of human behavior, the former act might yield emotional expression for a given individual within one setting, and the latter act might yield emotional expression for that same individual within another setting. As a result of these individual differences as well as situational differences, there can be no uniform types of behavior that we all of us should engage in for moving in an evolutionary direction. Even a choice of smoking a cigarette might well be evolutionary for a given individual in a given situation if, for example, it proves to be "the last straw that broke the camel's back," helping that individual to quit smoking.

Yet is it indeed useful to invent this new idea for confronting problems, namely, "the East-West strategy"? Why not simply refer to using the scientific method in everyday life? That would also incorporate the extraordinary language of social science, for that language would be needed to penetrate the complexity of human behavior. And by so doing, it would point us in the direction of changing from a bureaucratic to an evolutionary worldview and way of life. Let us recall, however, that the East-West strategy focuses not only on using the scientific method in everyday life, not only on using the extraordinary language of social science, and not only on a change from a bureaucratic to an evolutionary worldview and way of life. That strategy focuses, *in addition,* on the invisible problem of our escalating aspirations-fulfillment gap. That gap has been a problem that has plagued the human race—in our view—ever since we arrived on earth, as illustrated by the efforts of the Buddha 2,500 years ago. But at present, given the escalation of that gap linked to our continuing scientific and technological revolutions, the problem of the gap is threatening the very existence of the human race to an ever greater extent. Indeed, we believe that our escalating aspirations-fulfillment gap is the central problem facing the human race at this time in history. By failing to give this problem its due, any effort to use the scientific method in everyday life should—*given sufficient time*—discover this gap and develop procedures for addressing it. In our view, however, we may not have "sufficient time," given our escalating visible and invisible problems. We believe that the development of six books on which the present book is based—as cited in Chapter 5—that all focus a broad scientific approach on this problem of the aspirations-fulfillment gap can give us a running start for addressing this problem. And the East-West strategy, developed in the more recent books from that series of books and elaborated here, builds on all of that research.

However, let us bear in mind that the East-West strategy is no more than a beginning of efforts to develop effective social technologies. It was in Chapter 7—with our focus on the ideas of the East-West strategy, negative thinking, the cortical-thalamic pause, deep interaction, deep dialogue, and deep democracy—that we began to shift our emphasis from social science to social technology. For it was biophysical science *accompanied by biophysical science technologies*—and not biophysical science alone—that succeeded in shaping the world over these past centuries. And we believe that it will be social science *accompanied by social science technologies*—that we believe will succeed in confronting ever more effectively our present problems and shaping the world of the future.

Can we learn to develop the understanding of social science and social technology that we desperately require to make progress on our problems? Can we learn to become aware of the contradictions within our bureaucratic worldview and way of life instead of repressing them, like the Springdalers? Can we also become aware of a path leading away from those contradictions, a path leading toward an evolutionary worldview? And can we learn to apply social technologies to help us move along that path? Overall, can we learn to take personal responsibility for our own situation as well as the situation of the entire world instead of continuing to fiddle while Rome burns?

In the final section of this book, "The East-West Strategy and Institutional Change," we shall illustrate behavior within each of our institutions that is based on an affirmative answer to these questions. Our optimism here is based on our conviction that all of us humans have infinite potential for evolving intellectually, emotionally, and in the effectiveness of our actions. Not only has our interactive universe moved over some 14 billion years toward the evolution of phenomena with ever greater ability to interact, and not only are we humans the most interactive creatures in the known universe, but we believe that we humans, with the aid of language linked to the scientific method, can learn to interact ever more deeply with no limit whatsoever, just as we can learn to develop ever closer and more intimate relationships with one another. Despite the mammoth difficulties we face, we can learn to move away from our bureaucratic worldview and way of life and toward an evolutionary worldview and way of life.

The East-West Strategy and Institutional Change

We will assume for the examples to follow that individuals can indeed learn—just as Ashargin learned from Gosseyn, as described in Chapter 5—to continue to evolve with respect to "head," "heart," and "hand," with no limit whatsoever. We recognize that this is a huge assumption, yet we are convinced that it is supported by the evidence cited in this book along with the wide-ranging research on which this book is based. And it is also supported by our own personal experiences. Let us recall Ralph Waldo

Emerson's claim, quoted in the preface and in Chapter 4: "If a man write a better book, preach a better sermon, or make a better mouse-trap than his neighbor, tho' he build his house in the woods, the world will make a beaten path to his door" (Quoted in Knowles 2004: 307: 18). We would add that it would help greatly if the man was sufficiently committed to his work so as to persist in his efforts, if he took pains to communicate widely what he had achieved, and if he could convince others that they could come to do much the same by learning from his achievements.

We will, then, assume that—given our capacity to move toward an evolutionary way of life—some of us can learn to "write a better book, preach a better sermon, or make a better mousetrap" by using the East-West strategy in everyday life. And, as a result—given commitment, communication, and the potential of the rest of us—"the world will make a beaten path" to our doors. The East-West strategy may prove to be inadequate, and it is certainly limited in giving us all of the social technology that we require. In view of our escalating problems and increasing awareness of them, however, we believe that we humans will come up with other tools that are needed to make progress on those problems. However, our examples will focus on that strategy, building on the analysis in this book. In these few paragraphs we can hope to illustrate no more than a tiny portion of each of our major institutions, yet that may be sufficient to suggest the possibility of changes throughout each institution. Our focus will be on examples that we know best, namely, our own efforts and plans, granting that these may prove to be inadequate or most limited.

Science

Our focus here will be on the development of books written by individuals who are learning to use the East-West strategy in their everyday lives and, thus, learning to look both inward and outward, to express their emotions, and to achieve deep action and interaction along with deep dialogue. As a result, we see them as learning to integrate their understanding of phenomena to an increasing extent with the aid of negative as well as positive thinking, to make use of the cortical-thalamic pause to help them deal with their emotions, and to solve problems ever more effectively. This follows our assumption that individuals can continue to evolve. Under these circumstances each of them should be able to write what Emerson called "a better book,"

More specifically, we might indicate why such books would be "better" than those presently written, given this development of these individuals with respect to "head," "heart," and "hand." For one thing, these individuals would be able to develop cumulative knowledge of human behavior because they would be guided by a systematic extraordinary language that encompasses physical, biological, social, and personality structures, as well as what goes in within the momentary situation. This is a very far cry from present-day specialization throughout the social sciences with minimal integration. That present approach to knowledge is well illustrated by this recent statement by the executive officer of the American Sociological Association: "Within the ASA, sociological scholarship reflects the intellectual complexity of diversity, and the Association benefits from the dynamic energy displayed by our 44 sections" (Hillsman 2008: 2). This would make sense to us if indeed specialists in each one of those 44 sections addressed the complexity of human behavior and problems by opening up to the understanding within the other sections, but unfortunately that is very far from what actually occurs. Instead of being guided by a broad and systematic extraordinary language, the books written by specialists fail to follow the ideal of the scientific method to open up to all phenomena relevant to a given problem. As a result, these narrow books almost invariably fail to penetrate very far into the complexity of human behavior. And if we are to take this statement by the executive officer as illustrative of the sentiments throughout the discipline of sociology, then there is little or no awareness of sociology's failures.

On a positive note, what is crucial here is that those individuals who are genuinely developing or evolving would be able to continue to improve the books that they write, granting that social scientists generally would continue with the bureaucratic way of life that they share with everyone else. At the risk of an example that might appear to be self-serving, we might turn to this book and the six books on which it is based, with no implication that they will actually prove to attract the sales that would indicate that sociologists have in fact assessed them very favorably. There has been a progression of emphasis within the Sociological Imagination Group on the approach to the scientific method that has taken place over the eight years stretching from the publication of the first book, *Beyond Sociology's Tower of Babel: Reconstructing the Scientific Method* (Phillips 2001), to the present book. Initially, the emphasis was on "the web approach" to the scientific method, with a focus on linking the abstract concepts of social science. This changed to "the web and part/whole approach," shifting to a broader focus that took into account the importance of moving very far down language's ladder of abstraction. The next development was the abandonment of this new phrase in favor, simply, of "the scientific method," solidifying the idea that the approach followed the scientific ideals to be found throughout physical, biological, and social science. The present book represents yet another change in emphasis with its focus on all of us learning to use the scientific method within our everyday lives. Another change that this book illustrates is attention to social technologies—like the East-West strategy—along with the scientific method. That is a change that centers on progress in addressing the problem that has been at the heart of all of these books: our growing aspirations-fulfillment gap. And still another change is this book's more thorough and systematic treatment of the extraordinary language of social science. This includes a focus on the nature of the bureaucratic and evolutionary worldviews along with the nature of our cultural values.

The Economy

The sale of books represents no more than an infinitesimal proportion of the world's multitrillion-dollar economy. Nevertheless, it can provide an illustration of how the economic institution might move away from its present materialistic focus. Let us first step back some five centuries to the beginning of our continuing scientific and technological revolutions. Those revolutions, with their dependence on a scientific method that was captured by our bureaucratic worldview, centered on physical and biological science by contrast with social science. The result has been what we see today: the widespread disease of affluenza—as discussed in Chapter 6—with its focus on shopping until we drop. Once again, we are dealing here not just with an American problem but with an international problem.

If we look to the 15 cultural values discussed in Chapter 3, economies center on those that can best be fulfilled with the aid of physical and biological technologies rather than social technologies. Overall, we center on the cultural value of material comfort, and our stratified patterns of social organization have worked to fulfill cultural values that we love to repress: group superiority and conformity. There are also work-related values that are fulfilled to a degree, such as achievement and success, economic progress, and a narrow approach to science and secular rationality. As for people-oriented cultural values—including understanding the world as well as ultimate meaning—their fulfillment generally is left out in the cold, given the failure of social scientists to integrate their knowledge. Thus, social technologists like teachers, journalists, politicians, social workers, and psychotherapists have not been able to get very far in solving problems, granting their diligent efforts.

Indirectly, we can become aware of the world's materialistic focus by the nature of a given nation's gross domestic product or GDP, as discussed in Chapter 6 and as illustrated by this quote:

> GDP measures the size of the pie, not the quality of the ingredients— fresh apples or rotten ones are counted the same.... [T]he sale of an assault rifle and the sale of an antibiotic both contribute equally to the national tally (assuming the sales price is the same). GDP doesn't register, as Robert Kennedy put it, "the beauty of our poetry or the strength of our marriages, or the intelligence of our public debate." GDP measures everything, Kennedy concluded, "except that which makes life worthwhile (Uchitelle 2008: Wk3).

The efforts of the tiny country of Bhutan to focus on gross national happiness instead of the measurement that nations throughout the world have copied from the United States—gross domestic product—illustrates just how one-sided are the world's economies. As the quote suggests, what makes life worthwhile is excluded, namely, the fulfillment of our people-oriented cultural values.

We are convinced that "better books" in the social sciences not only can contribute in a very small way to a less one-sided or materialistic economy. They can also contribute in a very large way, granting that it will take time for their full impact on our people-oriented cultural values—including the values of group superiority and external conformity, which should be fulfilled to a lesser extent—to be felt. For those books will bring to the surface, to an ever-increasing extent, the contradictions within our bureaucratic worldview and way of life. They will also paint a picture of a path leading to an alternative worldview that promises to resolve those contradictions. The result should be an enormous expansion of our economy in the direction of fulfilling our people-oriented cultural values, just as the economy expanded over the past five centuries in the direction of the work-related cultural value of material comfort. Presently, efforts to counter unemployment center on jobs that repair a country's infrastructure or point to a green economy. Those jobs certainly are important, yet they continue our materialistic orientation. What we are suggesting is that new types of jobs can be created.

Let us recall what Emerson claimed: "If a man write a better book, preach a better sermon, or make a better mouse-trap than his neighbor, tho' he build his house in the woods, the world will make a beaten path to his door." That "better mousetrap" with respect to social science is nothing less than the individual human being who, as a result of his or her continuing development, can become far more "productive"—and not just in a materialistic way—of "whatever makes life worth while," including "the beauty of our poetry," "the strength of our marriages," and "the intelligence of our public debate." We might, for example, imagine the development of enormous demand for the understanding that could yield close and intimate relationships with others, for increasing our self-confidence and improving our self-image, for enabling us to express rather than repress our emotions, for communicating more effectively and thus learning to "preach a better sermon," for eliminating addictive rituals like drugs, alcohol, and overeating, and for reducing our fear and shame. In all of this, the East-West strategy might play a central role to the extent that it enables the social scientists who are writing better books—along with others who take those books to heart—to develop themselves as human beings, that is, to evolve. Of course, books alone would have a limited immediate impact on the economy, granted that they could have an impact in the long run. Given the existence of escalating problems that threaten the very existence of the human race, we require an immediate impact. Here, then, we must turn to the institution of education, looking not just to formal education but also to the mass media as well as the Internet for our ability to communicate both rapidly and very widely. Again, it is our learning to "preach a better sermon" that can prove to be most useful for expanding the world's economy.

Education

Let us recall the words of Schumacher that we quoted in Chapter 6:

> Education cannot help us as long as it accords no place to metaphysics. Whether the subjects taught are subjects of science or of the humanities, if the teaching does not lead to a clarification of metaphysics, that is to say, of our fundamental convictions, it cannot educate a man and, consequently, cannot be of real value to society.... What is at fault is not specialization, but the lack of depth with which the subjects are usually presented, and the absence of metaphysical awareness.... The sciences are being taught without any awareness of the presuppositions of science, of the meaning and significance of scientific laws, and of the place occupied by the natural sciences within the whole cosmos of human thought.... Economics is being taught without any awareness of the view of human nature that underlies present-day economic theory.... How could there be a rational teaching of politics without pressing all questions back to their metaphysical roots? (Schumacher 1973: 86–87).

The study of metaphysics presently is dead in the water throughout the educational institution, yet Schumacher joins us in emphasizing the overriding importance of learning the nature of our deepest beliefs and assumptions about ourselves and our world. Gilbert Gosseyn in Chapter 5 gives us telling metaphysical questions that we almost never consider: Who are we human beings? How have we become different from other forms of life as a result of the process of biological evolution? Just what is our intellectual capacity, and how can we learn to develop it? Where should we human beings be heading? How can we learn to confront effectively Enro the Red—Gosseyn's opponent—who stands for the patterns of social stratification throughout the world? Where should we humans be heading? Can we create a nonviolent society based on our potential to develop our emotions and ability to act effectively alongside of our intellect? What can we learn from Van Vogt's description of the null-A Venusian society and, more generally, from Korzybski's principles of general semantics, as stated in Chapter 5?

To answer these questions—and to respond as well to Schumacher's plea for attention to our metaphysical stance or worldview—we must climb far up language's ladder of abstraction and gain awareness of our fundamental yet invisible beliefs and assumptions about the nature of the world and ourselves, and of our past, our present, and our future. We must, more specifically, look to the nature of our "head," "heart," and "hand." It is exactly here that we require the extraordinary language of social science to respond to those questions, a language that can link our worldview to the full range of our personality and social structures along with concepts that focus on human behavior within the momentary scene. As a result, we can learn to bring to the surface and become aware of the contradictions within our bureaucratic worldview. And given our ability to conceive of an alternative evolutionary worldview with the aid of that language, we can learn to move in that direction. Far beyond the writing of books by a few individuals or even their ability to give us sermons on the mass media and the internet, the institution of education—from prekindergarten on up through postdoctoral studies and including the mass media—can yield movement from a bureaucratic to an evolutionary worldview.

As for how this enormous change in the institution of education can come about, that is no simple matter. Biophysical science can be separated from its technologies, just as biologists and physicists can be separated from physicians and engineers, and those technologies can still prove to be fairly effective. Yet social science—given its complexity—at the present time can be separated from social technology only at the expense of the effectiveness of those technologies. Those individuals who are writing better books and preaching better sermons will not be able to continue their own evolution without also developing the technologies enabling them to make progress on their own personal problems. Equally, their experience with these technologies—such as the East-West strategy for solving problems—will in turn point to the further development of their knowledge of social science. Thus, social science and social technology must develop hand in hand within the same individual if that individual is to continue evolving with no limit whatsoever.

Yet individuals who are evolving cannot limit their communications to others to pronouncements in the media, in the lecture hall, or on the Internet if indeed they hope to help others evolve. They must also learn to relate to others on a personal level, granting that this can be achieved only with a limited number of individuals. They must learn to rely not only on the messages that they send through the air but also on their interactions with others as they place their boots on the ground. They must learn to engage others in "deep dialogue." For in that way those "others" can learn to do the same thing with their own associates. The overall result, then, can be a widening network of individuals within all institutions, where genuine commitment to an evolutionary way of life is increasing. Ideally, the individuals involved should be influential within their institutions, with the result that their evolution will make them ever more influential.

Of course, this depends on the potential of the East-West strategy to enable the individual not only to become increasingly effective in making progress on personal and world problems. In addition, individuals must learn to communicate that progress to others.

We might add a thought here about the structure of the educational institution throughout the world, with its focus on the communication of knowledge developed within the many disciplines within the sciences, the humanities and the technologies. Generally, there appears to be far too much emphasis on discipline-based learning by contrast with problem-based learning. Within the discipline-based focus of social science, for example, students take courses in sociology, psychology, anthropology, history, political science, and economics, and they also take specialized courses within each of these disciplines. By so doing they obtain a smorgasbord of bits and pieces of knowledge with very little idea of how to integrate that knowledge for the purpose of solving any problem. Problem-based education would reverse this process. It would start with a problem—such as our escalating aspirations-fulfillment gap—and then bring to bear on that problem the full range of knowledge relevant to it.

Yet if problem-based learning is to be effective, social scientists must have developed a framework for integrating the knowledge within the social science disciplines, and they must also apply that framework so that integrated knowledge is already available. It is only then that students attempting problem-based learning will be able to bring to bear integrated social science knowledge on any given problem that they confront. We have aimed this book—based on the six books that have preceded it and with its development of the extraordinary language of social science—in the direction of providing that framework and presenting illustrations of integrated social science knowledge. The most important such illustration is our analysis of our growing aspirations-fulfillment gap. As a result, this book might prove to be useful within a class devoted to problem-based learning. A key advantage of such learning is that students can become more motivated to learn ideas that can prove to actually be useful in solving problems. And if education is conducted within a laboratory environment where students are free to come and go, they will interact with their instructor to a much greater extent than in a classroom.

Problem-based learning might well be extended to all fields of knowledge at all levels of education. For example, presently we have a sharp division between the applied or technological fields of knowledge—like engineering, medicine, education, business, journalism and mass communication, social work, library science, and law—and liberal arts and sciences fields like the physical, biological, and social sciences; philosophy; literature; language; art; music; and drama. Yet a problem-based emphasis within education would link those applied or technological fields with the fields emphasizing basic knowledge, such as the liberal arts and sciences. Medicine, for example, would then integrate the basic knowledge within biology and physiology to the clinical problems faced by students instead of separating basic and applied knowledge. Engineering would be linked with the physical sciences in a direct way. And social technologies—like education, business, law, journalism and mass communication, and social work—could be linked to social science. As for the humanities, they could also be linked to social science—just as we have made considerable use of philosophy, knowledge of linguistics, figurative language, and examples from literature and film—an interaction that we believe would help both fields immensely.

The Political Institution

Let us recall from Chapter 1 John Dewey's vision of democracy: "Democracy has many meanings, but if it has a moral meaning, it is found in resolving that the supreme test of all political institutions and industrial arrangements shall be the contribution they make to the all-around growth of every member of society." In our view, that "all-around growth of every member of society" has no limit whatsoever, given the potential of all of us to continue to evolve. This vision of democracy is central to what we mean by "deep democracy," as briefly discussed in Chapter 7. Building on Dewey, the focus of the scientific, economic, and educational institutions—granting that they have other values that they must fulfill—should be on nothing less than the evolution of all individuals involved with them. It is the political institution that is in the best position to allocate resources that can contribute to making this happen. But resources are by no means enough, for it is also boots on the ground that are required as well: Political leaders must develop deep dialogues with their key associates, as illustrated by such dialogues between the president of the United States and his cabinet members along with key members of his staff. And they in turn can do the same with their own staffs, and so on. In this way, political leaders—and leaders in all other institutions—moving along an evolutionary path can transfer their evolutionary worldview and practices to their close colleagues. Over time, evolutionary practices can spread to all institutions, especially given the communication of evolutionary ideas and illustrations throughout the mass media.

Indeed, given all of these changes in science, education, the economy, and the political institution—and given the information about the contradictions within our bureaucratic way of life coupled with information about an alternative way of life that might flood the mass media—there is every reason why there would be a shift throughout society from its bureaucratic organizations to evolutionary organizations, as hinted at in our discussion of the research of Constas and Udy in Chapter 7. They discovered that the rational or scientific aspects of bureaucratic organizations were opposed to both the bureaucracy's stratification as well as its narrow approach to knowledge. Following their lead, we may conceive of "scientific" or "evolutionary" organizations replacing bureaucratic organizations throughout all of our institutions. Just as modern bureaucratic organizations replaced preindustrial ones largely because of the former's use of scientific knowledge along with individuals with educated individuals, so might evolutionary organizations replace modern bureaucratic organizations because of their use of scientific knowledge that proves to be substantially more useful, and also because of the availability of individuals whose ability to use the East-West strategy yields productivity that continues to increase. Such a change would have a huge impact on all institutions, since their major tools for confronting problems at present are bureaucratic organizations.

There are other implications of a shift away from bureaucratic organizations and toward evolutionary organizations, for that would encourage decreasing prejudice and discrimination, such as racism, sexism, ageism, ethnocentrism, nationalism, and religious prejudice. We might recall here the Levin experiment, described in Chapter 7. Despite their frustration over failing the mock aptitude test, self-evaluators (closer to an evolutionary worldview) did not increase their level of prejudice against Puerto Ricans, by contrast with relative evaluators (closer to a bureaucratic worldview). For self-evaluators were on a stairway with respect to their own development and had nothing to gain by exhibiting ethnic prejudice. By contrast, relative evaluators were on a see-saw in their general approach to others, and they rose in their own estimation by putting down an ethnic group. If we generalize the results of this experiment, then we would expect movement away from a bureaucratic way of life with its see-saw orientation and toward an evolutionary way of life with its stairway orientation would also be movement away from prejudice and toward egalitarian interaction and relationships. And such relationships can yield enormous influence along with the solution of problems. And as we have seen in our discussion of Gandhi's struggle for India's independence from Great Britain—also discussed in Chapter 6—Gandhi's egalitarian relationship to British authorities was a crucial factor in India's success in obtaining independence.

Yet another illustration of a shift toward evolutionary organizations is a decline of what Robert Fuller has labeled "rankism"—as discussed in Chapter 6—which is not quite the same as patterns of stratification. Fuller elaborates on the nature of rankism, as quoted earlier:

> When rank has been earned and signifies excellence, then it's generally accepted, and rightfully so. But the power of rank can be and often is abused.... Power begets power, authority becomes entrenched, and

rank-holders become self-aggrandizing, capricious, and overbearing.... Rankism insults the dignity of subordinates by treating them as invisible nobodies.... Nobodies are insulted, disrespected, exploited, ignored.... It might be supposed that if one overcame tendencies to racism, sexism, ageism, and other narrowly defined forms of discrimination, one would be purged of rankism as well. But rankism is not just another ism. It subsumes the familiar dishonorable isms. It's the mother of them all.... [U]nlike racists and sexists, who are now on notice, rankists still go largely unchallenged....The consequences range from school shootings to ... genocide.... Hitler enjoyed the support of Germans humiliated by punitive reparations in the aftermath of World War I.... Similarly, President Milosevic of Yugoslavia traded on the wounded pride of the Serbs in the 1990s.... Attacking the familiar isms, one at a time, is like lopping heads off the Hydra of discrimination and oppression; going after rankism aims to drive a stake through the Hydra's heart (Fuller 2003: 5–7).

Rankism is illustrated by social stratification in modern society, but not in preindustrial society. For rankism has to do with a combination of stratification together with the cultural value of equality, which was not emphasized in preindustrial society. There, by contrast with modern society, people generally accepted their station in life and did not feel humiliated by the fact that they had little or no chance of moving up the ladder of social stratification. In modern society, hierarchy is accepted, but persisting hierarchy or social stratification conflicts with the very important cultural value of equality. As a result, we moderns tend to repress the existence of social stratification just as we repress the cultural value of group superiority.

Rankism differs from social stratification in that it abuses the dignity of subordinates—opposing such cultural values as individual personality and the freedom of the individual—whereas social stratification affects people-oriented cultural values only indirectly through its conflict with the cultural value of equality. Also, rankism can be expressed in any social situation, such as the interaction of strangers, and it can also be expressed in repetitive situations. Thus, patterns of sexism, ageism, racism, and ethnocentrism are indeed rankist in their abuse of the dignity and worth of the individual. But they can also be expressed in any situation where two or more individuals interact with one another. Thus, rankism is a far more general concept than the specific "dishonorable" isms. Rankism is like the open expression of prejudice by an individual toward another individual. It can include, for example, the prejudice against people who are overweight, who are short, who are members of another political party, who live in a given city or region of the country, who watch a great deal of television, who haven't gone to college, who are smokers, who have more than three children, and so on ad infinitum. There is no limit to what people might single out for prejudicial behavior.

In our view, rankism derives directly from our bureaucratic way of life, a way of life in which patterns of social stratification are fundamental elements. Thus, to the extent that we move away from such stratification and substitute evolutionary organizations for bureaucratic ones, not only will we move away from stratification, but we will also move away from the rankism that occurs throughout society. The Levin experiment probes further into the forces involved in the reduction of prejudice, as illustrated by a shift from our location on a see-saw to our location on a stairway. We might see that stairway as having an infinite number of steps that reach far out into the galaxy. And we might also see those steps as being as wide as the earth itself, so that there is room enough for everyone to climb without getting in one another's way. Still further, if someone else is able to climb faster or higher than ourselves, that need not threaten us to the degree that we have truly developed an evolutionary worldview. Indeed, awareness of the successes of others might help us in our own climb by teaching us how they have succeeded. And of course there would be no limit to how far we might proceed to climb.

There is no question but that political leaders must give priority to urgent problems, such as a worldwide financial meltdown and specific acts of terrorism. They must focus on putting out fires wherever they occur. At the same time, however, they can begin to alter past priorities. A green economy and attention to a failing infrastructure can certainly make progress in altering those priorities and work toward putting out such fires as unemployment, dependence on oil from the Middle East and global warming. Yet the allocation of resources that can speed evolution throughout science, the economy, and education has the potential to increase the "productivity" of the human beings throughout the world dramatically, something that putting out fires would fail to do. Here, "productivity" might be measured not just by a gross national happiness index—such as that developed by Bhutan—but also by a gross national evolution index, indexes that would supplement and not replace GDP. These would help us continue to expand our economic pie as measured by our GDP, but expand it in the direction of fulfilling our people-oriented cultural values (but not group superiority and conformity) to an increasing extent. And it would make it easier to close to an extent the increasing gap between the rich and the poor throughout the world, since economic equality could increase without the wealthy having to give up their wealth.

More specifically, political leaders—in addition to their own deep involvement in using the East-West strategy in their everyday lives to further their personal evolution and that of their close associates—could make substantially more funds available for research on the full range of concepts within the extraordinary language, and especially the concepts of bureaucratic and evolutionary worldviews. Also, they could use their access to the mass media—their "bully pulpit"—as an opportunity to "preach a better sermon." As for the institution of education, they could focus on providing the funds for experiments—such as working toward problem-based learning—on developing evolutionary instruction at all levels of education as well as throughout the mass media and the Internet. With respect to the economic institution, funds might be made available for experiments in transforming bureaucratic organizations within the political institution into evolutionary organizations, and thus providing a model that could be picked up throughout the economic institution. None of these experiments would involve more than modest expenditures, yet they could help stimulate a rapid change from a bureaucratic to an evolutionary society.

Religion

The academic disciplines within the humanities—like literature and philosophy—can provide students with a secular alternative to the focus within much of the religious institution on abortion, creationism, and the meaning of life. And the social sciences can join them to the extent that their approach to the scientific method is sufficiently broad. Presently, the academic world—including humanities departments in colleges and universities—is hampered by the reach and power of the doctrine of value neutrality, as discussed in Chapter 4. Yet we are convinced, on the basis of that analysis, of the "pernicious consequences" of that doctrine not only for the advancement of science but also for the educational institution at every level of instruction. This is why we have emphasized the importance of cultural and personal values within the extraordinary language of social science as well as outlined in Chapter 3 and continued in subsequent chapters. A focus on our values is, in our view, absolutely central to achieving an understanding of the human being as well as society. Yet it is not just the disciplines within the humanities that have had little to say about this subject relative to their long-standing traditions. It is even more so the social sciences and the biophysical sciences.

We need not continue to pursue a bureaucratic approach to specialization, keeping religion far away from the academic world, and also separating the humanities from social and biophysical science. For it is religion that has helped motivate us to consider the big questions at this time in history, such as the meaning of life. It is no accident that this has occurred at present, given escalating world problems with little understanding as to how to solve them. In our view what we require is deep dialogue about such fundamental questions within the religious institution—including our many religions—within the academic world, and also between those within the religious institution and those within the educational institution. Of course, efforts at such communication presently are ongoing to a limited degree. In our view those efforts can and should be greatly expanded. Further, we do believe that those present efforts will continue to be limited without the use by all parties concerned with the extraordinary language of social science, whether or not our own outline of that language comes to be accepted. Imagine, for example, trying to land an individual on the moon without making good use of the knowledge developed within physics and engineering. Similarly, imagine attempting such deep dialogue without building on the knowledge developed throughout the social sciences and social technologies over the past two centuries. However, we believe that such knowledge remains very largely unavailable to those within the religious and educational institutions without the extraordinary language to rescue it from its burial within our libraries.

For example, research on cultural values can include research on the values shared within all of the world's religions. By so doing, we will be able to learn the nature of the values that are shared by almost all of those religions. An effort to do to a limited extent—guided not by the extraordinary language but rather by the philosophy of pragmatism—is Abraham Kaplan's *The New World of Philosophy* (1961). There we examined both Kaplan's analysis of the nature of the philosophy of pragmatism as well as his understanding of Buddhism. Here is, then, an illustration of the joining of academic knowledge with religious knowledge. That book, based in part on his years of study while living in Asia, includes discussions of Hinduism, Confucianism, Taoism, and Zen. He includes an examination of what Asian religions share with Western ideas and philosophies, illustrated by pragmatism, analytic philosophy, existentialism, Freudianism, and communism. And he is able to emerge with a great deal that these Eastern religions have in common with Western ideas and philosophies. In our own view, the extraordinary language—coupled with new research on cultural values within religions as well as the academic world—would carry much further Kaplan's project. And that project points a direction away from the violent conflicts within and between religions.

The Family

Our focus here is by no means limited to the heterosexual family, granting the importance of that group throughout the world. This should not imply a focus on homosexual relationships or a plea for gay marriage, granting that such unions point in an egalitarian direction. Given that each institution is focused on solving certain problems within society as a whole, the family's problems have to do with the cultural values of the continuation of life as well as the achievement of intimate or close social relationships, as outlined in Chapter 3. There is also the problem that all institutions should confront, as suggested by John Dewey and quoted in Chapter 7: "the all-around growth of every member of society." Our focus here will be on the link between that all-around growth of the individual and close social relationships, a link that we give lip service to with the saying: You must learn to love yourself before you can learn to love anyone else. That saying goes along with our own emphasis on the importance of inward and outward perception and thought within an evolutionary worldview, by contrast with the focus on outward perception and thought within a bureaucratic worldview.

That our own development as individuals is slighted to an enormous extent in contemporary society is further illustrated by other basic aspects of our bureaucratic worldview: the individual's emotional repression rather than emotional expression, and the individual's patterns of conformity rather than patterns of interaction and deep interaction, as discussed in Chapter 7. Our own focus follows the saying that loving self is essential for learning to love others, but we do not merely give it lip service. To take that statement seriously involves nothing less than changing from our bureaucratic worldview—which points us far away from ourselves as individuals—to an evolutionary worldview. As we have discussed throughout these chapters, that change would require a fundamental change in our entire way of life.

Our argument here must appear to many to be an argument for selfishness and social irresponsibility with respect to friends and family, to the community, and to society as a whole. But that argument derives, we would argue, from the bureaucratic worldview of those who would mount such an argument. For their one-sided focus—indeed the focus that all of us share to varying degrees—points them toward an exclusive focus on social versus personality structures. Thus, our own emphasis on the importance of individual development *as well as* social development comes to be stereotyped as a focus on the individual *at the expense of* social relationships. In our view, individual development—intellectually, emotionally, and in our actions—follows not only John Dewey's vision of the primary responsibility of all of our institutions. It is also a basis for learning how we humans can relate to one another ever more fully, given our present failures to understand how to do so along with escalating problems throughout the world such as our increasing aspirations-fulfillment gap.

For further insight into our argument, we turn to Erich Fromm's concluding words in his *Man for Himself: An Inquiry into the Psychology of Ethics,* the book he wrote that followed his more well-known *Escape from Freedom* (1941, where he attempted to explain the rise of authoritarianism):

> *Our moral problem is man's indifference to himself.* It lies in the fact that we have lost the sense of the significance and uniqueness of the individual,

that we have made ourselves into instruments for purposes outside ourselves, that we experience and treat ourselves as commodities, and that our own powers have become alienated from ourselves. We have become things and our neighbors have become things...We are a herd believing that the road we follow must lead to a goal, since we see everybody else on the same road....

If I repeat now the question raised in the beginning of this book, whether we have reason to be proud and hopeful, the answer is again in the affirmative, but with the one qualification which follows from what we have discussed throughout: neither the good nor the evil outcome is preordained. The decision rests with man. It rests upon his ability to take himself, his life and happiness seriously: on his willingness to face his and his society's moral problem. It rests upon his courage to be himself and to be for himself....

I have written this book with the intention of reaffirming the validity of humanistic ethics, to show that our knowledge of human nature does not lead to ethical relativism but, on the contrary, to the conviction that the sources of norms for ethical conduct are to be found in man's nature itself (Fromm 1947: 249-251, back cover).

Fromm's focus on individual development points in the same direction as our own emphasis on the evolution of the individual and society throughout this book. We share with him the belief that in this direction lies the development of the ability to treat others not merely as things—just as we treat ourselves—but rather in a way that emphasizes "the significance and uniqueness of the individual." We also share with Fromm the belief that we need not continue emphasizing conforming behavior, where we follow the "herd." Perhaps most important, we share with him his optimism, his belief that "we have reason to be proud and hopeful."

It is over half a century since Fromm wrote those words, and—given increasing world problems—our need for optimism, pride, and hope is greater now than ever before. We are convinced that optimism is justified now more than in Fromm's time, even taking into account our more threatening problems. For now we have knowledge of human behavior that Fromm did not possess: what social scientists, philosophers, and many others have learned over these years. But it remains for us to learn how to make use of those bits and pieces of knowledge that presently are buried in our libraries. Our own effort in this book has been to provide a direction for doing so and, thus, to establish credibility for our own sense of optimism. Yet our efforts will come to naught unless we are joined by social scientists and others who are at least convinced that something is very rotten in Denmark and that they must take responsibility both for learning what is going on in the world and for doing something about it.

Afterward

Personal and Social Technologies

LOOKING BACK OVER THESE EIGHT CHAPTERS, it appears that we have indeed portrayed an image of a possible future for the individual as well as the world. And we have also sketched a general strategy for moving toward that future and illustrated how that strategy might be put to work. That East-West strategy for solving problems requires lowering our aspirations in the short run so as to narrow our aspirations-fulfillment gap. That is coupled with a very broad approach to the scientific method enabling us to continue to raise both aspirations and our ability to fulfill them in the long run with no limit as to how far we can go. It is a strategy that makes use of our most powerful tools, language and the scientific method, to go beyond what we have already achieved. It is a strategy that builds on the hard-won bits and pieces of social science knowledge, using the extraordinary language of social science to move toward unearthing them from their burial vaults in libraries and integrating them. It is a strategy that calls on us to learn to see the glass as *both* half empty *and* half full.

Yet our focus throughout the book has been on the latter part of the East-West strategy rather than on the former part: raising our aspirations and their fulfillment rather than lowering those aspirations so as to narrow the aspirations-fulfillment gap. Our approach has emphasized a Western strategy and not an East-West strategy, as illustrated by our analysis of institutions in Chapter 8. Within the institution of science we have called for "books written by individuals who are learning to use the East-West strategy in their everyday lives." In the economic institution we have looked to "an enormous expansion of our economy in the direction of fulfilling our people-oriented values" as well as "productivity that continues to increase." As for the institution of education, we have pointed toward "a problem-based emphasis" that "would link those applied or technological fields"—like engineering, medicine, education, business, journalism and mass communications, social work, library science, and law—"with the fields emphasizing basic knowledge, such as the liberal arts and sciences." Within the political institution we call for deep dialogue and deep democracy in that institution as a model for all institutions, involving a decline in what Robert W. Fuller has labeled as "rankism" in everyday life (in Chapter 6). Concerning the institution of religion, our focus has been on using the extraordinary language of social science to locate the values shared by all religions, with that as a basis for doing away with religious-based violence. And with respect to the family, our focus has been on "individual development as well as social development," thus calling for an emphasis on the evolution of the individual with respect to "head," "heart," and "hand" as a basis for increasing intimacy and closer relationships. We have emphasized seeing the glass as half full, and not seeing it as *both* half empty *and* half full.

Let us not forget that we foreshadowed these incredibly high aspirations in our introduction to Part I of this book. It was there—paralleling Martin Luther King's "I have a dream" speech at the Civil Rights March in Washington in 1963—that we put forward our own Bali Ha'i, our own special island, our own vision of the future. Among other things, we dreamed that "one day we will see peace on earth and fellowship among all human beings," that "one day we will be able to bring to the surface and reduce our stratified emotions like fear, shame, guilt, hate, envy, and greed, and we will learn to express ever more our evolutionary emotions like confidence, enthusiasm, happiness, joy, love, and empathy," and that "one day we all will learn to be poets, philosophers, and scientists."

Given our lack of emphasis throughout this book on the very concrete and increasingly threatening problems that we are confronted with at this time—but rather on our image of the future—we can easily understand a reaction among readers that we have described a utopia that can never become reality. How can our overall argument be credible if we ourselves have violated the very technologies that we have emphasized by focusing on a Western rather than an East-West strategy? How can we give others advice that we ourselves do not take? The Bible tells us, "Physician, heal thyself," yet we have proceeded to ignore that injunction. And if authors cannot themselves heed their own ideas, how can they expect others to follow their lead? Of course, what we have done is shared throughout the world, given our bureaucratic worldview. We have emphasized looking outward versus both inward and outward. We have repressed awareness of our one-sided behavior. And the result has been substantial conformity to that worldview with respect to our actions.

We stand guilty of failing to heal ourselves. Like Walt Kelly's Pogo, we have met the enemy, and he is us. *Yet it was a failure of social technology more than a failure of social science,* for we remain convinced that these pages do in fact put forward a direction for a breakthrough in social science. It is a breakthrough that was foreshadowed by the Enlightenment dream of a society based on reason, to which we have added the importance of the "heart" no less than the "head" and the "hand." It was also foreshadowed by the efforts of C. Wright Mills and Alvin W. Gouldner (discussed in Chapter 1), and of a great many others as well. And we have much to learn from our failure to apply the social technology that we have emphasized to ourselves. For one thing, it alerts us to the enormous power of our bureaucratic worldview to shape our very thoughts, feelings, and actions. Thomas Kuhn's *The Structure of Scientific Revolutions* (1962)—as discussed in Chapter 5—suggested the enormity of the problem of changing from one scientific paradigm to another. It appears to be far more difficult to change from one cultural paradigm to another.

However, there is a great deal that we can do now, given our awareness of our failure to emphasize personal and social technologies for evolution. Just as physical and biological technologies like engineering and medicine employed the scientific method to build on the achievements of physical and biological science, so can we now employ the East-West strategy to focus on personal and social technologies that build on our integration of social science knowledge within the foregoing pages. We shall begin with a section centering on the general strategy that we shall adopt. That strategy will link our own approach to the Western history of philosophy along with orientations from Eastern religions. It will invoke the importance of changing not only situational behavior but also personality and social structures. And it will be oriented to making use of the potentials of language, including the extraordinary language of social science. We shall then proceed to a section on specific tactics based on our strategy for individual evolution. That section will focus on concrete examples for different kinds of situations. As a result, we can succeed in opening the door to learning to use technologies for individual evolution. And we shall end with a section that points toward the optimism or idealism based on realism we require at this time in history.

Technology for Individual Evolution: Strategy

Our overall strategy is the East-West strategy—with its focus on language and the scientific method—discussed primarily in Chapters 5 and 8. It is a strategy based on accepting the idea that we are already deeply committed to employing a bureaucratic worldview and leading a bureaucratic way of life, granting that we would reject this idea because it conflicts with fundamental cultural values like equality and the ultimate worth of the individual. Yet the acceptance of our present commitment to that worldview, given the breadth and power of a worldview, makes it possible to apply a broad scientific method to all of our behavior. For the first and most important step of that method is awareness of and commitment to a problem. Since that worldview structures a large and increasing aspirations-fulfillment gap within the individual and society, that initial problem becomes one of narrowing the gap, following the Eastern element of the East-West strategy. Since we have sketched an alternative worldview or cultural paradigm that promises to resolve the problem of the large gap, we can learn to move toward that alternative one step at a time, applying the argument that Thomas Kuhn used for scientific revolutions to the problem of achieving a cultural revolution. That alternative paradigm is an evolutionary one, calling for using that broad scientific method to continue to raise both aspirations and achievements, keeping the gap between them quite limited.

That East-West strategy—by contrast with our emphasis in this book on a Western strategy—orients us to focus on what we can achieve in any given momentary situation. We can learn to look to our very small victories with respect to inward-outward perception and thought, emotional expression, and interaction. Yet at the same time we can come to link those victories with our images of the future, so long as we do not aspire to move beyond those small achievements until we are ready to do so. In this way we can learn to link an Eastern strategy with a Western strategy, for we will focus on the small successes that are within the reach of all of us while not abandoning our evolutionary vision. For that vision will be utopian only if we ignore what we do within any given momentary scene, and it will become a realistic guide for us once we learn to link it to what we do in everyday life. This is not a question of *first* using an Eastern strategy and *then* following it with a Western strategy. Rather, it is a strategy that makes *simultaneous* use of an Eastern and a Western orientation: It is an East-West strategy.

This approach is similar to that described by Ralph Waldo Emerson in his essay, *"Nature"* (1836/2000)—especially in the section on language—given his focus on using metaphors based on our everyday experiences to shuttle far up language's ladder of linguistic abstraction. We might use Emerson's words in that essay to help us understand just how we might proceed to use the East-West strategy—and neither the Eastern nor the Western approach—within our everyday lives, taking into account the role of the extraordinary language developed throughout Figures 2-1, 3-1, 4-1, and 5-1. And by so doing we might be able to clarify the nature of an evolutionary worldview and way of life. For we see that way of life not as "somewhere over the rainbow," as Dorothy sings in *The Wizard of Oz*, but rather as a concrete direction that anyone and everyone might adopt as they proceed with the mundane tasks we all have in our everyday lives. Emerson experienced many tragedies in his personal life, analogous to the problems linked to the disasters the human race has experienced throughout the twentieth century as well as the beginning of the twenty-first century. Yet his pendulum of the scientific method, which we believe that he was implicitly using, gained momentum from his personal problems, as illustrated by his view of the human being's infinite potential along with the infinite potential of language:

> Who looks upon a river in a meditative hour and is not reminded of the flux of all things? Throw a stone into the stream, and the circles that propagate themselves are the beautiful type of all influence.... It is easily seen that there is nothing lucky or capricious in these analogies, but that they are constant, and pervade nature. These are not the dreams of a few poets, here and there, but man is an analogist, and studies relations in all objects.... All the facts in natural history taken by themselves, have no value, but are barren, like a single sex. But marry it to human history, and it is full of life....
>
> The moment our discourse rises above the ground line of familiar facts and is inflamed with passion or exalted by thought, it clothes itself in images. A man conversing in earnest, if he watch his intellectual processes, will find that a material image more or less luminous arises in his mind, contemporaneous with every thought, which furnishes the vestment of the thought. Hence, good writing and brilliant discourse are perpetual allegories. This imagery is spontaneous. It is the blending of experience with the present action of the mind. It is creation (1836/2000: 14–16).

Emerson saw the possibility of individual evolution, just as we have indicated in our own "evolutionary manifesto" (in Chapter 1) that "one day we all will learn to be poets, philosophers, and scientists." For we can learn to tie our concrete experiences, like observing "the habit of a plant" or "the noise of an insect," to meaningful human ideas. For example, just as those experiences illustrate the interactions of plants and animals, so might we see them as steps on a long evolutionary journey toward the human being's interactive abilities based on language, abilities that are by far the greatest throughout the entire known universe. This metaphorical, figurative or poetic use of language is an approach within everyone's grasp, granting that our bureaucratic worldview teaches us to see it as the sole domain of poets, writers, dramatists, and filmmakers. Yet it is central to employing the East-West strategy from one moment to the next in one's everyday life. For it enables us to move very far up language's ladder of abstraction, even to the level of our worldview. And it also enables us to move very far down that ladder to our sensory experiences.

Social science had hardly begun to be developed in Emerson's day, and he was unable to link the broad scientific method discussed in these pages to his vision of the individual using linguistic analogies. Thus, he could not tie concrete personal experiences to the extraordinary language of social science. Yet at this time in history we are able to build on his understanding of the metaphorical potential of language as applied to that extraordinary language. For example, when we observe a plant or an insect and link that observation to our own interactive abilities, we are illustrating inward-outward perception and thought (by contrast with outward perception and thought), which is fundamental to an evolutionary worldview. When we see that this momentary analogy is actually taking us on an evolutionary path toward confronting personal and world problems—a path that anyone and everyone can take—we might well become "inflamed with passion" as a result of that accomplishment, thus moving toward emotional expression (by contrast with emotional repression). And when we see the widening circles that result from throwing a pebble into a stream as illustrating the breadth of human influence, we can be encouraged to shout out our discovery for the whole world to hear, thus illustrating deep social interaction (by contrast with conforming behavior).

Such movement from a bureaucratic toward an evolutionary worldview follows the East-West strategy as focused, for example, on the problem of our wide and widening aspirations-fulfillment gap. By paying attention to our momentary sensory experiences in everyday life, we are lowering our aspirations so as to focus on the specific problems that we are encountering in our concrete situation, such as conversing with a friend or crossing a street. Yet by learning—one step at a time—to see those experiences as illustrating the extraordinary language, we can also learn to raise both aspirations and achievements in an evolutionary direction. For example, we might employ a broad scientific method to help us not only to have a conversation but also to move toward deep interaction and deep dialogue (as discussed in Chapter 7). And we might also employ that same scientific method to help us not only cross the street but also to make full use of deep action in doing so. And we might learn to see our behavior as not only yielding situational changes pointing toward an evolutionary way of life. For we might also learn to see those situational changes as the beginning of structural changes, such as changes in our beliefs and assumptions, our values, our rituals, our self-image, and our worldview. It is in that way that we can build on Thomas Kuhn's insights in his *The Structure of Scientific Revolutions,* adding social technology to social science. For we can learn to fulfill the promise of our alternative cultural paradigm by changing not only our situational behavior but also our personality and social structures, thus moving toward fulfilling our biological potential as human beings.

Our East-West strategy is by no means a completely new idea, for its ancestry within the history of ideas dates back to the philosophy of pragmatism, as described by Abraham Kaplan in Chapter 5. Kaplan locates pragmatism within the Western history of philosophy in this passage:

> If we now ask, "What *is* the task for twentieth-century philosophy in the Western world?" ... [I]t is to assimilate the impact of science on human affairs.... The history of modern philosophy is, for pragmatism, a history of successive attempts to cope with this problem.... On one side we have science and technology, on the other side, religion, morals, politics, and art. The tradition of realism and empiricism—from John Locke and David Hume to Bertrand Russell—has turned largely in the direction of science, and has provided for human values no more solid foundation than a subjective emotional involvement. The idealist tradition—represented most influentially by Hegel and the conventional religionists—may do justice to human aspiration but cannot give any intelligible account of science and scientific method consistent with its own presuppositions. Other philosophies—like those of Descartes, Immanuel Kant, and contemporary neo-orthodoxy—try to resolve the dilemma simply by accepting it, thinking to settle the conflict between science and religion, between rational good sense and emotional sensibility, by assigning to each its own domain within which its sovereignty is to be undisputed.
>
> Pragmatism cannot rest content with either of the one-sided philosophies, which simply ignore the problem, nor yet with any dualistic philosophy, which mistakes a formulation of the problem for its solution. As against the scientific philosophies of our time, the pragmatist is determined to restore man to the position of centrality which is rightfully his.... As against the several idealisms, the pragmatist insists on the realities of conditions and consequences, causes and effects, in which ideals must be grounded if they are to have any impact on human life. And as against the philosophies which compartmentalize experience, the pragmatist argues that man cannot live divided against himself, affirming in the name of religion or morality what he must deny in the name of science. By circumscribing for each its own sphere of influence, we do not forestall conflict but only mark out the battle lines (1961: 16–17).

Kaplan describes here a philosophical framework for a scientific method broad enough to include idealism no less than realism. Pragmatism's realistic orientation is similar to our own Eastern orientation to lower aspirations so as to narrow our aspirations-fulfillment gap. And pragmatism's idealistic orientation is similar to our own Western orientation to continue to raise aspirations. Further, pragmatism is not a dualistic philosophy, as are the philosophies of Renee Descartes and Immanuel Kant, where idealism and realism are each assigned to its own domain. Rather, pragmatism seeks to integrate realism and idealism. This parallels our own efforts to link an Eastern with a Western orientation so as to emerge with an East-West strategy for solving problems. Thus, the East-West strategy draws from the traditions of realism and idealism within the history of Western philosophy, and it also draws from dualistic Western philosophy with its focus on the importance of both realism and idealism.

In addition to seeing the roots of the East-West strategy within the history of Western philosophy, we can also see its roots within the history of Eastern religion. We have emphasized the Eastern realism of Buddha as part of an East-West strategy, yet we would do well to add to that the Eastern realism of Confucius. But Eastern religion is by no means limited to realism, just as Western philosophy is not limited to idealism. For we also have the idealistic Eastern thought of Lao Tzu and Chuang Tzu as embodied in Taoism, just as we have the realistic Western thought of Aristotle, Locke, Hume, and Marx. Apparently, both Eastern and Western thought are too complex for any one-sided stereotype that views Eastern thought as realistic and Western thought as idealistic, granting that there is indeed that emphasis. There are also minor keys that accompany the major keys. And this combination of a major and a minor key also occurs within any given body of thought and within any individual. The realist is not without ideals, and the idealist is not without realism, just as our own idealistic emphasis in this book was not without a good deal of realism. Yet we believe, following our pragmatist orientation, that we idealists would do well to learn to be more realistic, and realists would do well to learn to be more idealistic. That, indeed, is what the East-West strategy points toward.

It is that strategy, with its use of the extraordinary language of social science, that points away from our focus on the dichotomous potential of language to the neglect of language's gradational and metaphorical potentials. For it is that dichotomous emphasis that has encouraged our simplistic split between realism and idealism, where we must choose between one or the other. This neglects a gradational orientation—as illustrated by the pendulum metaphor for the scientific method—where we can develop ever more idealism *and* ever more realism. It is that gradational orientation that can also help us to move far up language's ladder of abstraction so that we can uncover our fundamental assumptions or worldview, discover contradictions there, and move toward an alternative worldview. And that dichotomous orientation also neglects language's metaphorical potential, as is well illustrated by Ralph Waldo Emerson. For it is that potential that can help us to move from social science to personal and social technologies. We can learn to become poets in one scene after another, thus creating new personality and social structures as a result. Without such structural changes, we might continue to think about, talk about and write about moving from a bureaucratic to an evolutionary worldview and an evolutionary way of life. Yet we will be sharply limited in just how far we can follow that path, for the basic structures of our way of life will remain in place.

The foregoing strategy for individual evolution must be supplemented by illustrations of more specific or concrete tactics. Given the enormous complexity of human behavior and the difficulty of changing cultural paradigms, we all could make good use of hundreds of such examples. Yet we will have to make do with a limited number in the remainder of this Afterward. For this purpose we shall focus on examples taken from Phillips's personal experiences and written in the first person, with no implication that he has proceeded very far in these efforts. What he and the rest of us require are repeated behavior in one scene after another if we are to alter our personality and social structures. As the saying goes, one swallow does not make a summer.

Technology for Individual Evolution: Tactics

The key to learning to move from a bureaucratic to an evolutionary worldview and way of life is learning to use the extraordinary language of social science within one's everyday life. We have portrayed key concepts from that language—as we see it—in Figures 2-1, 3-1, 4-1, and 5-1, but additional concepts from that language can be found in the glossary. One key to our selection of concepts from the many hundreds that have been used throughout social science has been choosing those that can easily be linked systematically to one another. As a result, using any one of those concepts can invoke awareness of how the rest of them contribute to an understanding of any given phenomenon or situation. By contrast, the present situation of social science presents us with hundreds of concepts that bear little systematic relations to one another. This ability to integrate concepts is based on our ability to move far up language's ladder of abstraction so as to reach our metaphysical stance or worldview, and by shifting from a bureaucratic to an evolutionary worldview. Visually, we might contrast Figure 1-2 (The Bureaucratic Way of Life) with Figure 1-3 (The Evolutionary Way of Life), as discussed in Chapter 1.

Another criterion for selecting these concepts was their breadth of coverage of the phenomena of human behavior in all of their complexity. That breadth is based on our movement up language's ladder of abstraction from, say, concepts like "beliefs and assumptions" to the concept of "worldview." As a result, the extraordinary language can help us learn to see any one of our experiences as linked to more and more of our other experiences. By so doing, we can learn to move ever further in an interactive direction and fulfill ever more of our interactive potential. For example, this can help us to find common ground with others who apparently differ substantially from us and who might even be in a stratified or hierarchical relationship with us. And it can also help us to learn how we can narrow the gap between our aspirations and their fulfillment.

As for learning the extraordinary language and how to apply it, the following subsections go along with our division of the chapters of this book into "head," "heart," and "hand." Our focus will be on learning to link situational behavior—illustrated within each of figures 2-1, 3-1, 4-1, and 5-1—with the personality and social structures within those figures. Readers should recognize that it is indeed most difficult to change our structures, for that requires changing our behavior in scene after scene after scene. Yet such repeated changes in one scene after another can in fact alter structures, which are no more than repetitive behavior. Those structures must also include our worldview, for it is that structure that works to hold in place all of the other structures. Nevertheless, it is indeed possible to make such changes once we have in mind an alternative worldview that promises to be more effective in helping us solve our problems than our present worldview.

"Head": Inward-Outward Perception and Thought

In every situation we are in we can become aware of seeing our own bodies. By itself, that will succeed in changing nothing. But change will occur once we learn to tie such images, metaphorically, with concepts within the extraordinary language that point toward individual evolution. For example, as I [Phillips] sit at my desk typing these words I can become aware of my bent posture. And I can then link that posture to a self-image with limited self-confidence, and I can also link that posture to my bureaucratic worldview, where I function as no more than a tiny cog within the giant wheel of society. Yet given my understanding of the nature of an evolutionary worldview and an evolutionary self-image, I can learn to shift that self-image and that worldview. This change also has implications for "heart" and "hand." As for "heart," I can also become more aware of repressed emotions of guilt and shame that have been holding down my self-image. And with respect to "hand," I can sit up straight, accompanied by a more confident self-image along with progress toward an evolutionary worldview. Indeed, in any and every situation I can tie my perception of my body to my own evolution, thus confronting my problem—and everyone else's—of living within the prison of a bureaucratic worldview.

As I continue to type these words, I can also become aware of my looking outward at my computer screen for too many hours with little attention to myself. This is similar to my becoming aware of sometimes being glued to a seat watching television programs. We might recall here Ouspensky's statement that "we become too absorbed in things, too lost in things" from Chapter 2. And we might also recall the material on attention deficit disorder or ADD from that same chapter. My awareness of this problem is an instance of "negative thinking," as discussed in Chapter 7, namely, thinking that invokes problems that ordinarily would not be addressed. Yet I have a choice here. It is by no means essential for me to step away from the computer screen or the television set. For I can allow myself such behavior by following the Eastern aspect of an East-West strategy, lowering my Western orientation to continually raise my aspirations without regard to the aspirations-fulfillment gap that this revolution of rising expectations create. By doing so, I need not repress feelings of guilt or shame, for I can recognize my own limitations. But, alternatively, if I feel that I am ready to raise my aspirations to a limited extent, I can choose to move away from the computer screen or the television set. In that way I would be following the Western aspect of an East-West strategy, where I would be raising both aspirations and their fulfillment.

The above examples of looking at my posture and looking at my computer screen or television set illustrate inward as well as outward perception, with both illustrating a spatial—by contrast with a temporal—orientation. We experience such spatial perception in every situation that we encounter, and we can thus apply the same metaphorical approach—linking what we perceive to concepts within the extraordinary language—to every one of those situations. And by employing the East-West strategy, in every one of those situations we can choose to lower our aspirations so that they move closer to our ability to fulfill them, following the Eastern aspect of an East-West strategy. At the same time, we need not feel guilt or shame for doing so, since this strategy will take us, over time, toward raising both aspirations and their fulfillment. Or we can choose to raise our degree of fulfillment, just as I did when I turned off my television set or my computer screen, given that I felt that I was ready to do so without creating a large gap between my aspirations and their fulfillment.

In addition to this spatial orientation I can adopt a temporal orientation, with my perception of phenomena in a given scene as—metaphorically—taking me into the past or the future, but all within the framework of the East-West strategy along with making use of the extraordinary language of social science. For example, I can see my bent posture as illustrating a personal history of having had poor posture coupled with a large aspirations-fulfillment gap. Yet I can choose the Eastern aspect of the East-West strategy by accepting that posture and not feeling guilty about it, thus lowering my aspirations so that they are closer to my fulfillment. Alternatively, depending on how I feel at the moment, I can choose to sit up straight, thus raising my fulfillment and bringing it closer to my aspirations, thus following the Western part of the East-West strategy. In both cases I am learning to accept myself and, thus, improving my self-image and my conviction as to the worth of the East-West strategy as well as an evolutionary worldview.

In the same temporal way, I can see that television set from a historical perspective. I can choose to see it as illustrating the advance of the same one-sided physical-science technology that has yielded increasingly deadly weapons of mass destruction. Yet I can also accept that the existence of that technology, given its achievement of many worthwhile communications and its potential for increasing the kinds of communications that will advance an evolutionary way of life in the future. This follows the Eastern aspect of an East-West strategy, where aspirations move downward so as to be closer to fulfillment. Alternatively, depending on my situation at the moment, I can attempt to develop a program on television that does what I'm attempting to do in this book, thus attempting to raise both aspirations and their fulfillment and illustrating the Western aspect of an East-West strategy. In both of these ways I will be strengthening my commitment to an East-West strategy. And I will also be moving toward the development of an evolutionary worldview.

"Heart": Emotional Expression

Just as our sense of sight occurs within a split second, so does our sense of hearing operate in a moment, and such sense experiences that are repeated over and over again—such as listening to music—are no less useful than visual experiences as metaphors that can help us move toward an evolutionary way of life. For example, I recall listening to the Vienna Philharmonic Orchestra playing Strauss waltzes in a television performance on New Year's Day, 1999. I believe that such music—and music in general—illustrates emotional expression on the part of the composer, the conductor, the orchestra, and the audience. For if we assume that we are all being shaped by a bureaucratic worldview, then emotional repression is the name of the game, and music is one of our limited outlets for emotional expression.

Here, as in the above examples of my watching television or writing these words on my computer, I can choose to focus on the Eastern aspect of the East-West strategy or the Western aspect of that strategy, depending on what I feel comfortable with in the moment. From an Eastern perspective, I can lower my aspirations of changing the world very quickly by enjoying deep feelings of joy that those sounds convey to me. At the same time I can learn to accept—for the time being—a situation where almost all of us have quite limited outlets for emotional expression. And I can also accept—for the time being—the stratified relationship between the composer, conductor, and orchestra, on the one hand, and the audience, on the other hand. By so doing I'm learning to become more aware of the power of the bureaucratic worldview along with patterns of emotional repression and social stratification throughout society. And that awareness is essential for my evolution, since an awareness of and commitment to a problem is the first and most important step of a scientific method that is the basis for solving fundamental problems.

Yet I can also choose the Western aspect of the East-West strategy as I listen to those Strauss waltzes. For example, I can link my feelings of joy to my own quest for emotional expression, a quest that I've had throughout most of my life yet have never been able to fulfill to a substantial extent. In this case, however, I can link those feelings to emotional expression, to the cultural value of individual personality, and to an evolutionary worldview, and I can learn to do this in any other situation where I hear music. By so doing I will be able to raise both my aspiration for emotional expression and also the degree to which I'm able to fulfill that aspiration, thus moving in an evolutionary direction.

I might also approach my experiences with art in a similar way. My wife has an artist's eye for home decoration, arranging paintings, furniture, and objects in a most tasteful and pleasing way. Yet I had always paid little attention to my surroundings at home. However, at the time that I was listening to those Strauss waltzes I stood in our living room for perhaps half an hour and looked around at her achievements, and I was most impressed by the beauty of what I was seeing. Here, just as in the case of those waltzes, I could choose the Eastern aspect of the East-West strategy. I could become aware of my own insensitivity to art and architecture as part of my own pattern of emotional repression. Yet I could also accept—for the time being—that insensitivity as a product of my bureaucratic worldview and the stratification that exists between the artist and the general public. In that way I would be lowering my aspirations—for the time being—for emotional expression.

Yet I could also choose the Western aspect of the East-West strategy. Here, I had come to appreciate to a great extent my surroundings along with my wife's achievements. This was an illustration of emotional expression that can be linked to my efforts to move toward an evolutionary worldview, toward achieving ever more emotional expression in my everyday life, toward a more confident self-image, and toward the cultural value of the ultimate worth of every individual. Further, it was an experience that I could learn to repeat not only in my home or in museums and galleries, but also in the ordinary sights of natural and constructed beauty, just as Emerson described his own experiences. Of course, many people experience such beauty, but what I suggest here is the linkage of such experiences with a direction for individual evolution. In this way I and others can learn to raise both aspirations and their fulfillment, following the Western aspect of the East-West strategy.

"Hand": Deep Action and Deep Interaction

As I proceed to write these words I am aware of my "addiction" to writing books. Addiction is defined in the glossary as an individual's persisting pattern of action that subordinates individuality to dependence on external phenomena. Thus, it is a concept that covers much more ground than does the ideal of physiological addictions like drugs, drinking, and overeating. It is an example—within the extraordinary language—of an individual ritual oriented to a bureaucratic worldview, as discussed in Chapter 4. In my view, contemporary societies are addictive societies, just as Karen Horney argued—in Chapter 3—that contemporary societies encourage individuals to become neurotic.

Her analysis in *The Neurotic Personality of Our Time* (1937) included the existence of conflicting cultural values along with conflicts between cultural values and people's ability to fulfill them, an analysis supported by our own evidence on the existence of a bureaucratic worldview and way of life. The outward perception and thought, emotional repression, and conforming behavior that is structured by that way of life supports addictive behavior, whether it be physiological addiction or any other pattern of behavior that sharply limits the individual's possibilities by making him or her dependent on some external and narrow direction. Thus, as we see it, we are all addicted to one thing or another—just as we are all neurotic to some degree—in our addictive and neurotic contemporary societies.

I can find the roots of my own particular addiction to writing by returning to my own personal history. Prior to doing that, I might note that such a return to one's past is a most important tactic for achieving individual evolution not only in the area of "hand" but equally in the areas of "head" and "heart." As an illustration, we might recall from Chapter 5 Gosseyn's procedures for training Prince Ashargin—when he had somehow entered Ashargin's mind and body—in Van Vogt's *The Players of Null-A* (1948):

> Gosseyn imparts a basic approach to the Prince: "Prince, every time you take a positive action on the basis of a high-level consideration, you establish certainties of courage, self-assurance and skills." ... In the bedroom Gosseyn rigged up a wall recorder to repeat a three-minute relaxation pattern. Then he lay down. During the hour that followed he never quite went to sleep.... Lying there, he allowed his mind to idle around the harsher memories of Ashargin's prison years. Each time he came to an incident that had made a profound impression he talked silently to the younger Ashargin.... From his greater height of understanding, he assured the younger individual that the affective incident must be looked at from a different angle than that of a frightened

youth. Assured him that fear of pain and fear of death were emotions that could be overcome, and that in short the shock incident which had once affected him so profoundly no longer had any meaning for him. More than that, in future he would have better understanding of such moments, and he would never again be affected in an adverse fashion (1948: 115–116).

By returning to my own memories of my past, I would be doing much the same thing that Gosseyn was doing with Prince Ashargin: unearthing deep conflicts that presently work to prevent me from expressing my emotions and from developing a confident self-image. Instead, these conflicts push me toward conforming behavior, and toward reinforcing my bureaucratic worldview. At the same time, I could dredge up positive memories that could encourage my own continuing evolution. In any case, my memories would help me to improve my understanding of myself.

For example, I recall writing in a diary while in elementary school that I wanted "to do something to benefit the world, of great scope and of enormous size." There was the philosophy of idealism—by contrast with realism—with a capital "I." My subsequent life as a college professor served to strengthen that outlook on life. And my residence in the United States—with its Western rather than Eastern orientation—further strengthened that idealism rather than an East-West balance of idealism with realism. I might even add that my experiences as a male pointed me away from emotional development and toward intellectual development. Thus, it is an outlook that focuses on raising aspirations along with a widening aspirations-fulfillment gap. And, as a result, it is an outlook that encourages me to write books rather than to balance my ideas with deep action and interaction, as discussed in Chapter 8.

This initial understanding of my addiction to writing, based on this very brief analysis of my past, is strengthened by my understanding of this book as having emphasized a Western rather than an East-West strategy for problem-solving. It has emphasized social science rather than *both* social science *and* personal and social technologies. Yet with this understanding I am now in a better position to change my addictive behavior and learn more fully to use an East-West strategy in my own everyday life. And perhaps the reader can also learn from my own personal experiences. If so, then perhaps the reader will be willing to embark on the same personal experiment that I am pursuing: to move toward an evolutionary worldview and way of life.

Two More Things

In the foregoing illustrations of technologies for individual evolution, I emphasized the Eastern orientation to lowering aspirations so that they move toward their fulfillment. Yet I did not see clearly the importance of raising fulfillment simply by looking at the past—whether of society or of oneself—and giving due recognition to past achievements. This is a way of raising fulfillment by following an Eastern approach to being realistic about oneself and society, and by emphasizing the past and not just the future. For example, I can learn to feel good about just how far the United States has come in moving toward humanistic cultural values. I can also learn to feel good about what I have achieved personally in my efforts to move in that direction. In this way, I can learn to close the aspirations-fulfillment gap more rapidly, and thus move into a position to raise both aspirations and their fulfillment, following a Western orientation.

I believe that at this time in history—given the world's escalating problems and given the bureaucratic worldview that dominates our leaders along with everyone else—our only chance for the survival of the human race is the continuing evolution of "a few good men and women." For such individuals would be able to achieve nothing less than to increasingly *demonstrate* the possibility of continuing evolution *for any and all individuals.* And, as a result, that tiny group of individuals could continue to expand in number, and to expand exponentially. Books, media presentations, conferences, even communication with world leaders can indeed help, but *by themselves* they do not go very far to change anyone's bureaucratic metaphysical stance or worldview. Yet when such patterns of interaction are put forward by individuals who are succeeding in *demonstrating* the power of those ideas within what they are accomplishing in their own lives, there would be no limit to the influence of those ideas for changing the world. For the effectiveness of those demonstrations would continue to increase over time, following the infinite potential of every single human being. This will be my own future direction and that of my coauthor, and we welcome anyone wishing to join us in this evolutionary journey. We can be reached at bernieflps@aol.com.

Idealistic and Realistic Images of the Future

President George Bush senior, father of President George W. Bush—responding to the suggestion that he turn his attention from short-term campaign objectives to look at the longer term—responded: "Oh, the vision thing." Given our bureaucratic worldview, he is certainly not alone in failing to give serious attention to the future. It was Fred Polak, a Dutch sociologist—briefly cited in Chapter 1—who saw the image of the future as potentially the most powerful force for actually creating the future. Phillips and a colleague examined his approach in *The Invisible Crisis of Contemporary Society,* with the presentation of studies by Lawrence Busch that built on Polak's book (Phillips and Johnston 2007: 201, 212–218; Polak 1973).

It is our hope that the vision we have put forward in this book has the potential that Polak saw in images of the future. Given our current pressing problems, what we need most at this time in history is the optimism that is so closely linked to idealism. We saw that need demonstrated by millions of people during the American primary elections of 2008. We also saw that need expressed during the election that followed. We hope that our book will add credibility to the worldwide hope for the future that has accompanied those elections. At this time in history of fundamental and highly threatening worldwide problems, perhaps it is a sense of optimism that we all need more than anything else. Our aim has been to help provide an optimism or idealism that does not quickly fade but rather is long-lasting because it is based on realism.

Polak ended his own book, *The Image of the Future* (1973) with words that call for all of us to take responsibility for the future of society. We see our own image of the future as our Bali Ha'i, our special island, that also calls for such broad responsibility. In our view this vision is more than a dream: It is a direction that we can actually move toward one day at a time, one hour at a time, one situation at a time. Yet, as Polak suggests in the following passage—granting that our own special island might prove deficient—we all have a responsibility not only to create an image of the future that promises progress on our problems, but also to move toward our visions:

> Everyman, look to the harvest! It is the layman's responsibility to be aware of his own aspirations and those of the group to which he belongs. It is for him to choose the vision he will follow and to take responsibility for carrying it out.... No man or woman is exempt from taking up the challenge. Social scientist, intellectual, artist, leader, middleman of any breed, and the Common Man (and Woman) to whom, after all, this century belongs—each must ask himself, what is my vision of the future? And what am I doing about it? ... Man has the capacity to dream finer dreams than he has ever succeeded in dreaming. He has the capacity to build a finer society than he has ever succeeded in building.... Here lies the real challenge! There are among us even now dreamers and builders ready to repeat the age-old process of splitting the atom of time, to release the Western world from its too-long imprisonment in the present. Then man will once again be free to "seek the city which is to come" (1973: 305).

Glossary

Action   Behavior of the individual that emphasizes doing or movement more than thought or feelings, including behavior in isolation as well as social interaction

Addiction   An individual's persisting pattern of action that subordinates individuality to dependence on external phenomena

Affluenza   A focus on fulfilling the cultural value of material comfort as an addictive ritual

Alienation   An individual's persisting feelings of isolation from self, others, his or her own biological structure, and physical structures

Anomie   Substantial aspirations-fulfillment gaps that are widely shared throughout society

Anthropology   A science of human behavior that focuses on the range of human cultures and languages

Aspirations-fulfillment gap   The degree to which individuals fail to achieve their values

Assumptions   Beliefs that may be invisible to the individual or group

Beliefs   Persisting ideas or opinions of an individual or group

Biological structure   An organism or an element of an organism that interacts to a relatively great extent with its environment

Bureaucratic group   A set of individuals whose persisting hierarchy and division of labor limits its internal and external interactions and its ability to solve problems

Bureaucratic worldview   A metaphysical stance or basic assumption that erects barriers to interaction within the individual and society

Conforming behavior   An individual's thoughts, feelings, and/or actions in a situation that follow the requirements of group norms or values with little attention to one's own beliefs and values

Cortical-thalamic pause   One's momentary reflexive behavior involving perception and thought about one's emotions in order to balance those emotions with understanding

Cultural norms The beliefs, expectations and/or assumptions widely shared throughout society that exert pressure on the individual to conform to them

Cultural relativism The belief that all cultures are equally worthwhile regardless of the nature of their particular cultural values and norms

Cultural values The values, interests, ideals, or goals of individuals that are widely shared throughout society, illustrated by equality, freedom, individual personality, democracy, achievement and success, economic progress, material comfort, science and secular rationality, understanding the world, solving problems, intimate and close relationships, the continuation of life, and ultimate meaning, group superiority, and external conformity

Culture The values, norms, institutions, and worldview of a people or a society that yield a blueprint for living

Deep action An individual's action that makes progress toward inward-outward perception and thought as well as emotional expression

Deep democracy A pattern of deep dialogue throughout society's institutions that is the basis for the decisions that shape behavior throughout society

Deep dialogue A pattern of deep interaction focusing on communication

Deep interaction Momentary back-and-forth behavior among people that makes progress toward inward-outward perception and thought and/or emotional expression

East-West strategy An approach to confronting everyday or world problems using a broad scientific method that lowers aspirations until they are close to their fulfillment (East), and then continues indefinitely to raise both aspirations and their fulfillment (West).

Economic institution An institution in society centering on the problems of producing, distributing, and consuming whatever society has come to value

Economics A science of human behavior that focuses on the production, distribution, and consumption of whatever society has come to value

Educational institution An institution in society centering on the problem of communicating an understanding of the universe, including physical, biological, social, and personality structures

Emotional expression Showing one's feelings to oneself and others

Emotional repression hiding one's feelings from oneself and others

Epistemology Fundamental assumptions and beliefs that derive from a given metaphysical stance or basic assumptions about how to develop understanding of reality

Evolutionary group A set of individuals whose patterns of interaction and use of the scientific method enable them to continue to develop their "heads," "hearts," and "hands" with no limit whatsoever

Evolutionary worldview A metaphysical stance or basic assumptions emphasizing the increasing interaction and using the scientific method to develop the "head," "heart," and "hand" of the individual and society with no limit whatsoever

Extraordinary language of social science A system of concepts deriving from the history of research that is the basis for a scientific method broad enough to penetrate the complexity of human behavior

Falsification of memory A procedure of emotional repression in which the individual buries awareness of previous aspirations or values

Family An institution in society centering on the problems of achieving intimate or very close social relationships and/or the continuation of life from one generation to the next

Group A set of individuals who repeatedly interact directly or indirectly

History A science of human behavior focusing on the past of the human race

Individual A human being with the potential for continuing to develop "head," "heart," and "hand" with no limit whatsoever

Institution A system of cultural values and norms within a society focused on solving given problems

Inward-outward perception and thought An individual's sensations and ideas that are both reflexive and interactive

Interaction Back-and-forth actions among phenomena that affect their nature

Ladder of linguistic abstraction An image or metaphor for language's levels or degrees of generality and specificity, with metaphysical assumptions at the top and situational ideas at the bottom

Language A system of concepts, widely shared throughout society, for solving problems by means of its dichotomous, gradational, and metaphorical potentials for understanding and communicating experience

Metaphysics Fundamental assumptions and beliefs about the nature of reality that shape all human behavior

Negative thinking The individual's momentary ideas that are critical of existing phenomena

Outward perception and thought An individual's sensations and ideas that are interactive but not reflexive

Perception An individual's sensations—sight, hearing, touching, tasting and/or smelling—in a momentary situation that affect his or her behavior

Personality structure The individual's system of values, beliefs, assumptions, rituals, self-image, and worldview

Physical structure A persisting system of elements that interacts to a relatively small extent with its environment

Political institution An institution in society centering on the problems of developing, distributing, and using power

Political science A science of human behavior that focuses on the development, distribution, and use of power in society as a whole

Power The ability to affect the behavior of others through force, authority, and/or influence

Psychology A science of human behavior that focuses on the individual

Rankism hierarchical or prejudicial behavior in a situation, thus flouting people-oriented cultural values such as individual personality, equality, freedom, and democracy

Relative deprivation An individual's feelings within a momentary scene of an unjustified failure to fulfill values relative to others

Religious institution An institution in society centering on the problem of finding ultimate meaning or significance in life

Ritual An individual's persisting pattern of action that is meaningful and expressive to some degree

Scientific institution An institution in society centering on the problem of developing understanding of the universe, including physical, biological, social, and personality structures

Scientific method A procedure for solving problems that (1) defines problems so as to build on relevant previous knowledge; (2) develops ideas, hypotheses, or theories for making progress on those problems; (3) tests these ideas against experiences (such as available data, observations, or experiments); (4) assesses the researcher's impact on the research process; (5) uses procedures for analysis to develop conclusions about the applicability of those ideas, hypotheses, or theories; and (6) repeats this process as often as is required to make sufficient progress on the problem.

Self-image An individual's view of self

Situation A location in time and space

Social interaction Actions by individuals in a momentary situation that mutually affects them

Social organization Persisting and shared patterns of interaction within a group or society as a whole

Social relationship Persisting social interaction between individuals

Social ritual A ritual that is shared within a group or society as a whole

Social stratification A persisting hierarchy or pattern of inequality within a group, among groups, in society as a whole, or among societies, including classism, racism, sexism, ageism, ethnocentrism, and nationalism

Social structure The culture and social organization of society, or the norms, values, and social relationships within a group

Society A people with a culture and patterns of social organization

Sociology A science of human behavior that focuses on society as a whole

Structure A persisting system of elements

Technique of particularization A procedure of emotional repression in which the individual avoids thought at a high level of linguistic abstraction and focuses on a low level of abstraction

Technology A persisting pattern of action for solving problems

Unanticipated consequences Occurrences that deviate from the expected results of purposive actions, deriving from limited understanding of the situation

Value neutrality A doctrine that it is somehow possible to prevent one's values from affecting the conclusions one draws on the basis of experience; employed by many scientists to portray their conclusions as being free of any personal bias

Values Persisting motives, interests, ideals, or goals of an individual or group

Worldview The metaphysical stance, basic assumptions, or persisting image of reality of an individual or a society

References

Bardach, Janusz. *Man Is Wolf to Man: Surviving the Gulag.* Berkeley: University of California Press, 1998.

Baum, L. Frank. *The Wizard of Oz and the Land of Oz.* New York: Random House, 1960.

Bondurant, Joan V. *Conquest of Violence.* Berkeley: University of California Press, 1965.

Borgatta, Edgar F., and Rhonda J. V. Montgomery. *Encyclopedia of Sociology.* New York: Macmillan Reference USA, 2000.

Brown, Donald E. *Human Universals.* New York: McGraw-Hill, 1991.

Busch, Lawrence. "Macrosocial Change in Historical Perspective: An Analysis of Epochs." Unpublished doctoral dissertation. Ithaca, New York: Cornell University, 1974.

———. "A Tentative Guide to Constructing the Future: Self-Conscious Millenarianism," *Sociological Practice* 1 (Spring 1976): 27–39.

Chua, Amy. *World on Fire: How Exporting Free Market Democracy Breeds Ethnic Hatred and Global Instability.* New York: Doubleday, 2003.

Constas, Helen. "Max Weber's Two Conceptions of Bureaucracy," *American Journal of Sociology* 52 (January 1958): 400–409.

Dantzig, Tobias. *Number: The Language of Science.* New York: The Free Press, 1954.

de Graaf, John, David Wann, and Thomas H. Naylor. *Affluenza: The All-Consuming Epidemic,* 2d ed. San Francisco: Berrett-Koehler, 2005.

Dewey, John. *Reconstruction in Philosophy.* Boston: Beacon Press, 1920/1948.

Durkheim, Emile. *Suicide.* New York: Free Press, 1897/1951.

Easterly, William. *The White Man's Burden: Why the West's Efforts to Aid the Rest Have Done So Much Ill and So Little Good.* New York: Penguin Press, 2006.

Eisler, Riane. *The Chalice and the Blade: Our History, Our Future.* New York: Harper & Row, 1988.

Ellison, Ralph. *Invisible Man,* New York: Vintage, 1947.

Ely, Elissa. "Not Immune from the Inevitable," *The Boston Globe,* September 28, 2008, D9.

Emerson, Ralph Waldo. *The Essential Writings of Ralph Waldo Emerson.* New York: Modern Library, 1836/2000.

Ferguson, Niall. *The War of the World: Twentieth Century Conflict and the Descent of the West.* New York: Penguin Press, 2006.

Freud, Sigmund. *Civilization and Its Discontents.* New York: W. W. Norton, 1930/1989.

Fromm, Erich. *Escape from Freedom.* New York: Avon, 1941.

———. *Man for Himself: An Inquiry into the Psychology of Ethics.* New York: Fawcett, 1947.

Fuller, Robert W. *Somebodies and Nobodies: Overcoming the Abuse of Rank.* Gabriola Island, Canada: New Society Publishers, 2003.

Funakoshi, Gichin, and Genwa Nakasone. *The Twenty Guiding Principles of Karate.* Tokyo: Kodansha International Ltd., 2003.

Gawande, Atul. "The Power of Negative Thinking," *Sarasota Herald-Tribune,* May 4, 2007, A8.

Gouldner, Alvin W. *The Coming Crisis of Western Sociology.* New York: Basic Books, 1970.

———. "The Politics of the Mind: Reflections on Flack's Review of *The Coming Crisis of Western Sociology,*" *Social Policy* 5 (March/April 1972), 13–21, 54–58.

Hesse, Herman. *The Glass Bead Game (Magister Ludi).* New York: Bantam Books, 1943/1969.

Hillsman, Sally T. "The Strength of Disciplinary Diversity," *Footnotes* (November 2008): 2.

Huxley, Aldous. *Brave New World.* New York: Harper & Row, 1939.

Horney, Karen. *The Neurotic Personality of Our Time.* New York: Norton, 1937.

Hornig, Susanna. "Television's *NOVA* and the Construction of Scientific Truth," *Critical Studies in Mass Communication* (1990: 11–23).

Jackson, Maggie. "Attention Class," *Boston Sunday Globe,* June 29, 2008, D1-D2.

James, William. *Pragmatism: A New Name for Some Old Ways of Thinking.* New York: Dover, 1907/1995.

Janis, Irving L., and Daniel Katz. "The Reduction of Intergroup Hostility," *Journal of Conflict Resolution* 3 (March 1959), 85–100.

Jones, Alexander, ed. *The Jerusalem Bible: Reader's Edition.* Garden City, NY: Doubleday, 1966.

Kaplan, Abraham. *The New World of Philosophy.* New York: Random House, 1961.

Kelly, George A. *The Psychology of Personal Constructs,* 2 vols. New York: W. W. Norton, 1955.

Kincaid, Harold. *Philosophical Foundations of the Social Sciences.* New York: Cambridge University Press, 1996.

Kincaid, Harold, John Dupre, and Alison Wylie, eds. *Value-Free Science? Ideals and Illusions.* Oxford, UK: Oxford University Press, 2007.

Knottnerus, J. David, and Bernard Phillips, eds. *Bureaucratic Culture and Escalating Problems: Advancing the Sociological Imagination.* Boulder, CO: Paradigm Publishers, 2009.

Knowles, Elizabeth, ed. *The Oxford Dictionary of Quotations.* New York: Oxford University Press, 2004.

Korzybski, Alfred. *Science and Sanity.* Garden City, NY: Country Life Press, 1933.

Krugman, Paul R., and Maurice Obstfeld. *International Economics: Theory and Policy,* 6th ed. Boston: Addison-Wesley, 2003.

Kuhn, Thomas S. *The Structure of Scientific Revolutions.* Chicago: University of Chicago Press, 1962.

Lavine, T. Z. *From Socrates to Sartre: The Philosophic Quest.* New York: Bantam, 1984.

Lerner, Daniel. *The Passing of Traditional Society.* New York: Free Press, 1958.

Levin, Jack. "The Influence of Social Frame of Reference for Goal Fulfillment on Social Aggression." Ph.D. Dissertation, Boston University, 1968.

Lundberg, George A. *Can Science Save Us?* New York: David McKay, 1947/1961.

Mannheim, Karl. "On the Interpretation of *Weltanschauung*," *Essays on the Sociology of Knowledge.* New York: Oxford, 1952: 33-83.

Marx, Karl. *Early Writings.* Trans. and ed. by T. B. Bottomore. New York: McGraw-Hill, 1844/1964.

Merton, Robert K. "The Unanticipated Consequences of Purposive Social Action," *American Sociological Review* 1 (December 1936): 894-904.

———. "Social Structure and Anomie," in Merton, Robert K., *Social Theory and Social Structure.* New York: Free Press, 1949, 125-149.

Milgram, Stanley. *Obedience to Authority.* New York: Harper & Row, 1974.

Mills, C. Wright. "The Professional Ideology of Social Pathologists," *American Journal of Sociology* 49 (September 1943), 165-180.

———. *The Causes of World War Three.* New York: Simon & Schuster, 1958.

———. *The Sociological Imagination.* New York: Oxford University Press, 1959.

———. *Sociology and Pragmatism: The Higher Learning in America.* New York: Oxford University Press, 2000.

Murray, Donald M. "In Life as in War, Overcoming Fear One Small Step at a Time," *The Boston Globe,* October 30, 2001, 11B.

Nietzsche, Friedrich. *The Gay Science.* Trans. by Walter Kaufmann. New York: Random House, 1887/1974.

Orwell, George. *Nineteen Eighty-Four.* New York: Harcourt Brace Jovanovich, 1949.

Ouspensky, P. D. *The Fourth Way: A Record of Talks and Answers to Questions Based on the Teaching of G. I. Gurdjieff.* New York: Vintage, 1957/1971.

Pappas, Theodore, ed. *Britannica Concise Encyclopedia.* Chicago: Encyclopedia Britannica, 2002.

Peirce, Charles S. "The Fixation of Belief," in Peirce, Charles S., *Philosophical Writings of Peirce.* New York: Dover, 1877/1955: 5-22.

———. "The Scientific Attitude and Fallibilism," in Peirce, Charles S., *Philosophical Writings of Peirce.* New York: Dover, 1896/1955: 42-59.

———. "The Approach to Metaphysics," in Peirce, Charles S., *Philosophical Writings of Peirce.* New York: Dover, 1898/1955: 310-314.

Phillips, Bernard. *Social Research: Strategy and Tactics.* New York: Macmillan, 1966, 1971, 1976.

———. *Sociological Research Methods: An Introduction.* Homewood, IL: Dorsey Press, 1985.

———. *Beyond Sociology's Tower of Babel: Reconstructing the Scientific Method.* New York: Aldine de Gruyter, 2001.

———. *Armageddon or Evolution: The Scientific Method and Escalating World Problems.* Boulder, CO: Paradigm, 2009.

Phillips, Bernard, ed. *Understanding Terrorism: Building on the Sociological Imagination.* Boulder, CO: Paradigm, 2007.

Phillips, Bernard, and Louis C. Johnston. *The Invisible Crisis of Contemporary Society: Reconstructing Sociology's Fundamental Assumptions.* Boulder, CO: Paradigm, 2007.

Phillips, Bernard, Harold Kincaid, and Thomas J. Scheff, eds. *Toward a Sociological Imagination: Bridging Specialized Fields.* Lanham, MD: University Press of America, 2002.

Polak, Fred L. *The Image of the Future.* San Francisco: Jossey-Bass, 1973.

Postman, Neil. *Amusing Ourselves to Death: Public Discourse in the Age of Show Business.* New York: Penguin, 1985.

Postrel, Virginia. "The Poverty Puzzle," *The New York Times Book Review,* March 19, 2006, 12.

Raushenbush, Hilmar S. *Man's Past: Man's Future.* New York: Delacorte, 1969.

Reed, Roy. "Nellie Forbush's Hometown," *Lincoln Center Theater Review* (Spring 2008): 15-17.

Scheff, Thomas J. *Bloody Revenge: Emotions, Nationalism, and War.* Boulder, CO: Westview, 1994.

Schumacher, E. F. *Small Is Beautiful: Economics as if People Mattered.* New York: Harper & Row, 1973.

Simmel, Georg. "Metropolis and Mental Life," in *Georg Simmel on Individuality and Social Forms,* ed. by Donald N. Levine. Chicago: University of Chicago Press, 1903/1971: 324-339.

Uchitelle, Louis. "GDP Does Not Equal Happiness," *The New York Times,* August 31, 2008: Wk 3.

Udy, Stanley H., Jr. "'Bureaucracy' and 'Rationality' in Weber's Organization Theory," *American Sociological Review* 24 (1959): 591-595.

Van Vogt, A. E. *The World of Null-A.* New York: Berkley Publishing, 1945/1970.

———. *The Players of Null-A.* New York: Berkley Publishing, 1948.

Vance, Jack. *The Languages of Pao.* New York: Daw Books, 1958.

Vidich, Arthur, and Joseph Bensman. *Small Town in Mass Society: Class, Power, and Religion in a Rural Community.* Garden City, NY: Doubleday, 1960.

Vygotsky, Lev. *Thought and Language.* Cambridge, MA: M.I.T. Press, 1962.

Wallis, Claudia. "Swami, How They Love Ya," *Time,* October 29, 2007, 102-103.

Weber, Max. *The Protestant Ethic and the Spirit of Capitalism.* New York: Scribner's, 1905/1958.

———. *Economy and Society.* New York: Free Press, 1964.

Weiner, Eric. "Where Happiness Makes Sense," *Sarasota Herald-Tribune,* November 17, 2006, 21A.

Whitman, Walt. "Song of Myself," in *Leaves of Grass.* New York: Random House, 1892/2004: 23-24.

Whorf, Benjamin. *Language, Thought, and Reality.* Cambridge, MA: M.I.T. Press, 1963.

Williams, Robin M., Jr. "Major Value Orientations in America," in *American Society,* 3d ed. New York: Knopf, 1970: 452-500.

Index

263

About the Authors

Bernard Phillips, a student of C. Wright Mills at Columbia, received a Ph.D. at Cornell and taught at the University of North Carolina and the University of Illinois before teaching at Boston University. He cofounded ASA's Section on Sociological Practice, founded the Sociological Imagination Group, and founded a series of monographs with Paradigm Publishers, "Advancing the Sociological Imagination," which he coedits with J. David Knottnerus. He can be reached at bernieflps@aol.com.

David Christner has worked closely with Bernard Phillips for a decade in an effort to help fulfill the aims of the Sociological Imagination Group. He is the founder of World Health Advanced Technology, which focuses on the development and testing of enercel, a substance used for achieving biofunctional health.